Negus

Troubled
and Troublesome

Troubled and Troublesome

Coping With Severely Disordered Children

*

Masud Hoghughi

BURNETT BOOKS
in association with ANDRE DEUTSCH

First published 1978 by
Burnett Books Limited
in association with
André Deutsch Limited
105 Great Russell Street London WC1

Printed in Great Britain by
Ebenezer Baylis and Son Ltd
The Trinity Press
Worcester, and London

ISBN 0 233 97040 1

For Pat, Farid and Fariba

Contents

Preface

Neither plenitude nor vacancy. Only a flicker
Over the strained time-ridden faces
Distracted from distraction by distraction
                    T. S. Eliot: *Burnt Norton*

Eliot may have as well been speaking for and about extreme
children, who strain and stretch to distraction everyone who
tries to cope with them. Because they do not just go away or
receive miraculous cures overnight for the troubles they experience and present, they lurch from one receptacle to another
until they reach a place whence they may not part. The havoc
they wreak along the way, but particularly in their destinations,
is out of proportion to their small numbers.

This book emerged from the desire to understand these
children and know better why they have such a cataclysmic
effect on so many people, so that we too, at Aycliffe, may not
become intolerant and, in seeking to survive their impact,
reject them yet again.

When I first mooted the idea of a secure assessment facility,
many experienced colleagues questioned its wisdom and
warned me against its troublesome consequences. When I
talked of admitting girls to the same unit they felt they had at
last good reason to question my sanity. After all, everyone
knew how explosive the mixing of disordered boys and girls
was even in open conditions, but under security. . . ? We
invited distinguished practitioners to talk to us about the
problems we were likely to face and they told us many stories
about events under security, particularly with girls, that made
us queasy. At the time, we also scoured the literature to see
what other people's experience of managing disordered children had been, and were not reassured.

9

But most worrying, other than the homespun and the received wisdom, there was little to hear and even less to read that was detailed and articulated enough to guide us in what we should do, or more importantly, what we should not.

In the event, we opened our facility with boys and after a while admitted girls. It says much for the open-mindedness of the DHSS and my own Board of Managers, who placed their care and concern for troubled youngsters before their legitimate misgivings about a new venture of this sort, that they approved the project. Since then, the Managers and Trustees of Aycliffe School and officers of Durham County Council have taken a special and personal interest in our work with these children. I am grateful for their continued support. I should state, though, that the ideas expressed in this book are strictly mine and do not necessarily reflect their views.

The practices described in this book have emerged over a period of time in intensive discussions with my colleagues at a variety of levels. All of them, particularly the staff of Royston and the senior staff team, deserve the credit for any good that may have been done with the children.

As always, I have been particularly grateful for the very efficient help given by the Librarians of the School of Education, Newcastle University and of the Cambridge Institute of Criminology.

My colleague, Susan Nethercott, helped provide much of the original empirical data on which an earlier version of this study was based. I have derived much benefit from my long discussions with her regarding the study. Many individuals and groups have contributed to my thinking about the problems of these children. Among them my Irish and Scandinavian friends merit greater appreciation than my acknowledgement here can give them.

Farrell Burnett's encouragement and concern ensured that my spirits did not flag and the book was completed on time. No purple passage can sufficiently extol how indispensable Doreen Kipling's help and caring has been. And, I am sure my wife would not wish me to reproduce here her versions of what she has contributed to this book!

This work, though modest and limited, brings together much of what we have learnt in dealing with severely disordered children. As a result, I now believe that there would be fewer of these children if they were not subjected to so much mismanagement. If the tone of this book is critical, it is because I believe that courtly speech serves neither the interests of the children nor that of the wider society. Our services to both would only improve if we are prepared to be more questioning of our own and others' assumptions and practices. It is to this end that I hope the book may stimulate a more rational and just approach to extreme children.

MASUD HOGHUGHI
May, 1978

PART I

*

Extreme Children

CHAPTER I

*

Introduction

DIFFICULT and disordered children have always been a source of worry and anguish to those who have to deal with them. Over the years numerous facilities have been set up within the penal, medical/psychiatric, educational and social services to meet the problems they present. Many eventually find the sort of treatment they need at a particular stage of their development and this, combined with normal maturation and chance events, ensures that their condition does not get any worse, or even improves.

Some, however, present problems of such extent and intensity that they exhaust the tolerance and coping ability of those around them. They go from one facility to another, cross boundaries between different services, without seeming to profit from their experiences, and create deep feelings of helplessness and anger among those who have to deal with them. They go from bad to worse. Eventually they end up in some sort of intensive residential facility, be it a hospital, a penal establishment or a community home. Such children exist in all western countries and no one nation seems to have found adequate ways of coping with them. Different countries show varying levels of concern with the problem, reflecting varying interest in children and the issues of social welfare, justice and control which they so frequently crystallise.

This book is about such children – those who have reached the end of the jagged line of intervention and have to be placed in a specialised, restrictive facility because they have pushed people responsible for them to the end of their tether.

For a variety of reasons which will be discussed in the course of this book, the number of such children appears to be increasing. Whether and however such appearances tally with reality, those who are responsible for dealing with disordered children, such as police, magistrates, teachers, psychiatrists, and field and residential social workers, believe that the quality of disorder presented by them is also getting more serious. Such feelings, though often dismissed by a variety of people on arcane methodological grounds, should nevertheless be taken seriously, as they play an important part in determining how the children and their problems are perceived and what sort of decisions are made about what should be done with them.

The feelings of helplessness and inadequacy among those working with such children is exacerbated by the fact that they do not have access to any systematic body of information about other people's experiences, or even elementary knowledge of what works and what does not so they can decide on their own actions. More specifically, this lack of information relates to *what* sorts of behaviour should be expected of these youngsters, *why* they behave in this particular way and *how* they can be managed. Parents, teachers, field and residential social workers, who are in the front line of tackling the often gruelling and destructive conflicts presented by these children, are often the worst equipped to seek or provide empirical information about how to cope with them. They are too caught up in simply surviving the dramatic impact of the children to take stock of their own actions and place them on a systematic basis so as, at the least, not to make the same mistakes repeatedly. In any case they do not have the time, the orientation or the necessary resources, including skills, to transform their experiences into usable information. As a result of this, when asked about their children, their comments are limited to generalities, deeply imbued with emotional reactions to the difficulties of the children and the hopelessness of trying to cope with them in a satisfactory fashion.

If parents and practitioners are too preoccupied with coping to do research on their own work, then it would be reasonable to assume that policy makers and administrators, who have the time, the distance and adequate research resources, are concerned enough to highlight the problems these children present and the effects of the processes they undergo, if for no other reason than to get some information about the legitimacy of spending the large sums of money involved. However, the history of provision for disordered children in the United Kingdom has been as influenced by piecemeal innovation and temporary fashions as it has been immune to any systematic research into its whys and wherefores or any search for evidence about its efficacy and usefulness. In the United States, there has certainly been no shortage of research. But in the context of even deeper susceptibility to ideologies and shifting fashions, American responses to these children have been even more multifariously confused than their European counterparts.

Much more often than not, policy makers and administrators make social innovations without much apparent thought (if published material, including government circulars, is anything to go by) about the evidence for their innovations and how they are to be implemented in order to achieve particular results. They seem to assume that practitioners whose job it is to put innovations into effect, have the skills to translate policy into practice and will produce the required result. Practitioners, on the other hand, assume that no innovation will be made unless the policy makers have reason to believe that its enactment would be within the power and available skills of the practitioners. Should they claim inability to put the new ideas into effect they would undermine their own professional credibility and this may lead to the redundancy of the service they render.

The result of this is that policy makers and practitioners get locked into a mutually reinforcing cycle of ignorance. Instead of each helping the other to achieve a truthful appraisal of what is happening and how it may be improved, they engage in ritualised encounters (such as White Papers, Memoranda of Evidence, conferences, 'Training and Development' activities, etc.) where pretended aspirations are presented as reality and a restatement of problems in new terminology is confused with solutions. This is so particularly where the issues involved are controversial but do not involve a large number of people. If too many people were affected by such practice, they would protest, make the matter public and, in a democratic country, make life difficult for both policy makers and practitioners. The less vocal the people affected (such as children), the more this mode of operation becomes prevalent and as time passes, the original acts become compounded by new ones. This process is further facilitated if the 'client' group carries some form of social stigma and ambivalence, as do disordered and delinquent children.

This situation has been particularly true of the idea and practice of placing severely disordered and delinquent youngsters into residential facilities and a burgeoning network of secure accommodation. Although the first purpose-built secure units for the treatment of such youngsters date from the early sixties, hardly any information has been published on them, either by the practitioners or by the government departments which have been responsible for them.

Perhaps the most tragic outcome both for the community and the children who reach the end of the line is, that for all that society knows, whatever mistakes were made in the very first secure unit are being still perpetuated. As a result of this non-empirical approach, children are being dealt with in ways which are more dependent on received wisdom than on fact, with questionable justification and even more questionable outcome.

As may have become clear through the foregoing introductory remarks, a major contention of this book is that certain children are, and others are allowed to become, severely disordered because of the inadequacy of the interventions in the course of their development. A major reason for this inadequacy of intervention is that children are dealt with in a haphazard fashion under crisis situations rather than in a cool headed manner before crises have occurred. But, this latter approach presumes a kind of empirical rationality which is as yet absent from this field.

Dealing *rationally* with any problem has three components: the nature, the extent and the identifying characteristics of the problem must be adequately *described* so that subsequent identifications become easier and more homogeneous; the problem must be *understood*. A natural corollary of understanding is the ability to *explain*. Explanations seek to establish general relationships between phenomena so that one problem can be clarified in terms of something else which has already been adequately understood and accounted for; the most important element as far as social services and helping agencies are concerned, however, is the element of management or (in politically more emotive terms) *control*. Describing and explaining the problem are both ancillary to the main problem a social agency has of controlling or managing the problem presented to it. From the viewpoint of this argument, therefore, and contrary to the classic paradigm of the natural sciences, the adequacy of any description, explanation and form of social intervention is exemplified by the extent to which it enables the control of that problem to be achieved. Accordingly, this book aims to describe the severely disordered children, attempts to explain why they become so and finally to provide some tentative guidelines as to how they could and should be managed. Thus it may provide a basis against which other attempts at more sophisticated description, explanation and management of such children can be made.

The findings are based on a study of one secure facility, nominally intended for assessment, but acting more immediately and urgently as a refuge for children who present such severe problems that the local authorities responsible for them do not know what else to do with them. The secure provision discussed is not typical of others in the United Kingdom or elsewhere. Nevertheless the children who come to it are the extreme end of the population of disordered children and are likely to be sufficiently typical of all extreme children to make a study of them of wider applicability. A suicidal child is the same whether in the UK, US, Sweden, Japan or elsewhere, although each country is likely to treat them differently. The problems of management they present, though reflecting the attitudes and competence of those who manage them, are also likely to be of more universal concern.

But no child emerges from a vacuum. These children seem to have undergone a complex process of being classified as particularly problematic by a whole variety of social agencies. It is the interaction of these children with people and institutions which produces the final level of difficulty which is then defined as a crisis and which warrants their admission to a specialised secure facility. An attempt will be made in the course of this book to highlight steps in this process of identification and some of the issues which underlie it.

From the moment of admission, these children do not only have to work through their own crises and anxieties but have also to cope with the pressures of an equally troubled peer group, as well as the constraints of a secure environment and the staff's perceptions of their task with these children. The development of the children's problems are continued through and complicated by this further stage. Because the placement of such children in highly specialised settings is dictated by the extreme level of their disturbance – and this is likely to remain constant from one era to another – it is important to understand the dynamics of the interaction of the children with such an environment and the difficulties they raise. This may then make it possible to find ways of making life in such an environment less damaging and more rewarding for everyone.

A major factor in not only preventing such problems but also in alleviating them when they have occurred, is through intensive staff training and support. The training of social workers, both field and residential, is too large and contentious an issue to be covered in this book. As will become clear, however, the training of the professionals involved does not appear to have made much of an impact on either the quality of the identification of the children or the process of social intervention which allow them to reach the end of the line. Nor do the traditional, orthodox approaches to training do much to prepare workers to cope with behavioural crises either in the field or residential settings. Part of this book will be taken up, therefore, with discussing the problems that staff face in dealing with such children and the handling techniques they employ. This is not because these techniques are regarded as universal prescriptions for coping with such crises, but because they at least provide a baseline against which the capability of any group of people in dealing with such children can be evaluated, and for setting a level from which more sophisticated and rigorous handling techniques can be evolved.

Finally, the book addresses itself to a consideration of wider issues in relation to severely disordered children. Assessment is as fashionable a concept as it is confused. As an attempt to specify the child's problems, it falls within a large area long dominated by clinical and ideological classificatory systems, particularly psychiatric. It is suggested that psychiatric approaches to non-organic disorders of adolescents are fraught with problems which render them confusing and counterproductive. An alternative approach is proposed which, though not without difficulties, is likely to be more useful to those who actually have to work with the children.

An important element of this is the process of social identification of extreme deviants and the way society evaluates its own duties and rights in relation to such children. Despite national and cultural differences in attitudes to rights and duties, countries as widely divergent as the United Kingdom, France, Finland and the United States find it necessary to lock up many of their disordered children.

The use of detention and its euphemistic equivalents raises complex and fundamental issues of the rights of children and the judicial aspects of the whole process. These have been far from clear and even further from being publicly articulated. The book concludes with a brief look at some of the issues.

Although the empirical data contained in this book derive from the work of the Regional Assessment Centre at Aycliffe, the book is not about Aycliffe School. The school simply happens to be the facility in which these children were assessed and studied. It will be left to further research to confirm how far extreme children in other facilities are like those described in this book. The study could have been carried out in any other similar facility which catered for mixed groups and collected the relevant information. The empirical findings of this study have been used as a basis for making points which are of wider relevance to understanding and managing disordered children.

A word of explanation about some of the terminology in this book may be appropriate. The terms 'children', 'young people', 'youngsters', etc. are used interchangeably. They refer, as is now common practice, to persons of either sex up to the age of 18.

The title of this book was chosen to reflect the impact of these children. They are, undoubtedly, very troublesome and cause a great deal of aggravation among the people who have to deal with them. But equally, to anyone who bothers to look even fractionally beneath their troublesomeness, it becomes evident that most are deeply troubled. I have chosen the label 'severely disordered' rather than 'disturbed' which is the more conventional adjective used to describe them. This is because 'disturbed' has particular connotations of mental imbalance which, as will be seen, are not necessarily applicable to all these children. Although 'disordered' may also be seen as having this sort of implication, it is less psychiatrically tinted and more factually correct in indicating a lack of structure in the lives and behaviour of these children. I have also used the adjective 'extreme' interchangeably with 'severaly disordered' as being possibly the least theoretically presumptive of labels available for such children.

It should be evident to any reader that every idea or statement in this book is capable of considerable elaboration. Such elaboration would certainly lead to modification of some of the statements made. Limitations of space do not allow for exhaustive discussion of any one of the issues but I hope to at least provide a systematic basis for other attempts at elaboration.

CHAPTER 2

*

The Context of the Study

IN empirical studies it is not customary to give details of the context in which the study is carried out. And yet, such details are essential, particularly in studies of problem people, if sense is to be made of how they arrive at the place to be studied and how much their behaviour, in all its variety, is the result of particular features of the environment in which they find themselves.

This study is based on children admitted to Aycliffe School, which is one of the six regional facilities (formerly Classifying Approved Schools) dealing with the most severely disordered and delinquent children in England. The establishments serve the following areas: Aycliffe, the northern quarter; Red Bank, the northwest; Tennal, the Midlands; Kingswood, the southwest; Stamford House, London; and Royal Philanthropic, the southeast. Aycliffe was the first of these to be designated for the 'classification' of delinquent boys in 1942. It is the only one of the regional centres to have a secure facility for the assessment of severely disordered boys *and* girls. Other establishments have been known to start mixed facilities but have given up the attempt after a short while, for reasons which will become clear in the course of this book. As with all the other centres (except Stamford House) Aycliffe also has its own 'Training School'. It is important to note this, because assessment and treatment as specialisms in an integrated setting provide each other with beneficial feedback, perspectives and guidelines to development which each is denied when working in isolation.

Over the years, the School has transformed the label of

'classifying' with its zoological overtones to assessment and the notion of training to one of treatment. These are the subject of extensive documentation elsewhere (Hoghughi, 1973, 1975, 1977). The regional centre receives, for assessment, children who are pre-selected for their extreme behaviour. As will be argued later (Chapter 7), social workers' decision-making is profoundly influenced by crisis orientation and evaluation of risk. They appear only to take 'extreme' measures when the situation has reached critical proportions. The centre, in the child care system, is an 'extreme' provision and therefore children only come to it if no other facilities are relevant to their problems and needs. The factors which ensure this are its cost, which is higher than average; the waiting list, which means that no child can be admitted immediately other than under emergency conditions; and, in the case of some local authorities, the distance. Additionally, there is a tendency on the part of most local authorities to use local resources rather than one which is explicitly a regional one.

The centre accommodates sixty children in four houses, only one of which is secure. Admissions for assessment are subjectively evaluated by the senior staff in terms of the youngster's problems and likely needs and allocated accordingly to one of the four houses, the secure one being called Royston.

This house operates as an integral part of the centre. It is, however, known within the region as the only integrated *secure* facility for children who come into the care of local authorities and is approved for such purpose by the Department of Health and Social Security. No applications for direct admission to it are accepted. Nevertheless, the knowledge of the existence of the house leads to requests by the local authorities and central government for admission of particularly disturbed and dangerous children who, the authorities believe, can only be contained in it. Senior staff of the centre, while maintaining their discretion regarding the placement of the child, take full account of the possible impact of a child's behaviour on himself and the public and, whenever appropriate, place him in the secure house. These include all the children convicted of grave crimes who must be kept under conditions of security until assessment has been completed and the Home Secretary has decided what should be done with them.

Additionally, there are some children who are admitted and placed elsewhere in the centre, but who find difficulty in coping with the total openness and relative freedom of the establishment and who engage in persistent absconding and other seriously disruptive or irresponsible behaviour which warrants placing them in secure conditions, even if temporarily.

All girls are placed in Royston in view of their need for greater protection and supervision and they remain there until they leave the school. After assessment, they are placed in considerably freer conditions, when appropriate, spending large portions of their time outside the house.

In the case of boys, if by the time of their assessment meeting there is good evidence that their behaviour has stabilised, they are transferred to an open house. Thus, even children convicted of gravest crimes have been placed under open conditions. This is generally successful and children are rarely returned to secure conditions. While transfers are inevitable because of waiting lists and frequent requests for emergency admissions, it is important to note that such transfers always take place after the most careful and hard-headed evaluation of the child; it is acknowledged that risks can never be eliminated and that such risks should be evaluated in a wider context of costs and benefits both to the child and the community.

The secure house came into being in an attempt to cope with an apparently mounting problem of absconding in a regional 'classifying' school which found it undesirable and impracticable to use traditional 'detention' rooms. These were essentially single 'cells', punitive in practice if not in intent and totally unsuitable for the increasingly disturbed population of youngsters sent for assessment. Because of financial constraints and the projected plans to hand over approved schools to local authorities, it was not possible to build a new facility and, therefore, an already existing house was converted for this purpose.

The shell of the house had to be left untouched. This placed major limitations on the type of environment which could be created. Within those limits the aim was to create a facility to contain severely disordered boys who presented absconding risks and were liable to have outbursts of aggression against themselves, others, or property.

At the time of planning it was not possible to obtain the necessary finances for the possible use of the house for girls. It was, however, thought very likely that girls would be admitted before long. The conversion was, therefore, so designed as not to exclude the management of mixed groups.

The house comprises six single bedrooms (including two 'separation rooms') and two four-bed dormitories; a large lounge; a large games-and-classroom, washrooms, etc., together with office and night supervisor's room, all within the secure perimeter. Outside this perimeter there are store-rooms, a small laundry, one interview room or classroom and bedrooms for staff. The house is intended for twelve children but more often accommodates between thirteen and fourteen. The number of girls is limited to a maximum of six at any given time.

As a rule, all the children take their meals in a general dining room with youngsters from the other houses and participate in recreational activities such as swimming, cross country runs, etc., *outside* the school. Although there are occasional problems with the management of individual children in these circumstances, the benefits accruing to the children and the release of tension built up between them and a secure environment is felt to be well worth the cost. Many of the children, particularly the most disordered, are taken out under individual supervision to ensure that the close confines of the house do not become oppressive and lead to even more unacceptable behaviour.

From the inception of the idea of the facility, a very high level of building specifications was laid down. The house is carpeted throughout as an aid to reducing noise and to creating a softer atmosphere. Extensive use is made of wallpaper. The decorative schemes are particularly carefully chosen to reduce tension. Furniture is either purpose made for security and aesthetic appeal or bought from manufacturers with the same primary criteria in mind. One important consideration is that items of furniture should not be usable as weapons, though this particular aspect has been relaxed in view of the emerging atmosphere of the house.

Within the wider financial constraints of the school, this facility is the best equipped, and any of its important needs are fulfilled without hesitation. There is a wide range of games and materials, colour television, good quality stereo radio and record playing equipment, domestic cooking appliances and facilities for hairdressing, make up, etc.

The perimeter security is limited to the windows and the doors. This security is generally regarded as being of considerably less importance than the atmosphere which enables the staff to reduce tension and the impulse to become violent or to run away. The importance of this latter aspect is emphasised by the fact that the children spend a significant portion of their daily time *outside* conditions of security.

The single most important element in the management of disordered youngsters is the number and quality of staff engaged with them, with particular emphasis on the word 'engaged'. If there are too few staff they will be so taken up with routines and basic body minding that they will not be able to either notice or take steps to pre-empt the frequent build-ups to explosive outbursts of the children. If they are not of a high calibre, their sensitivity will be generally impaired and they will not be able to use the wide range of coping skills necessary with children of the type admitted to Royston. From the start, therefore, the house has had higher staffing levels than the rest of the centre and where possible staff have been specially selected for it.

Currently its team includes fourteen members of staff of whom one is the House Warden/Team Leader, and the rest are teachers and houseparents, divided equally between sexes. Vacancies in the staff team are filled quickly from elsewhere within the school. This is facilitated by the fact that no member of staff is appointed to one particular part of the school, thereby enabling the school to deploy its staff where they are most needed.

In an 'assessment centre', the major task is the assessment of children and preparation of assessment reports. This, however, cannot be done unless the 'care' requirements of the children have already been met. Care requirements involve aspects of physical well-being of the child, his emotional stability and an acceptable level of social functioning. None of these can be achieved unless the child is in a physically and emotionally stable state, so that before anything else is attempted, the child can be protected against damaging experiences emanating from himself or others. Thus, in reality, the job requirement of the staff is a high order of 'management', of which the smaller part is the preparation of an assessment report.

The staff are deployed both functionally and in terms of the amount of time they spend on the house so that each 'shift' provides an adequate combination of care, management and assessment skills as well as appropriate ratios of both sexes.

Because of the number of children, an attempt is made to ensure that at no time are there less than three members of staff on duty. However, due to vagaries of rotas and unforeseen circumstances this is sometimes reduced to two or increased to five. Although frequently the staff are hard pressed and could do with greater help, it is felt that the physical limitations of the house would make it difficult to involve a larger number of staff with the groups of children unless the children were to be taken out of the house. In any case, the total staff establishment is finite and extra help cannot be given without unacceptable sacrifice elsewhere.

An important cornerstone of the management of the house is a detailed, rigorous programme which ensures that the children are being appropriately occupied and stimulated. Such a programme is essential, not only to ensure that the staff are deployed in areas where they are of greatest benefit to the children, but also that the assessment programme is completed in time. The children are appropriately occupied not only to highlight their problems and potentials as an aid to assessment, but also to prevent boredom and the consequent disturbances.

The Study

There is a large volume of research literature on disordered and delinquent youngsters. Almost all of it, however, is concerned with either boys or girls alone in a variety of settings which makes comparison between them difficult. But such a comparison is important not only because of major differences between youngsters of the two sexes in a whole range of problem areas – offending, depression, parasuicide – but also because of the reputation of disordered girls as being dramatically more difficult than boys and the increasing tendency to treat them together.

Because the centre receives a mixed population who are accommodated in the same unit, it was felt to be particularly worthwhile to compare the two sexes to test the prevalent notions about the differences between them. A major focus of this study is, therefore, the comparison of boys and girls and the problems of managing mixed groups. Because generally fewer girls than boys are referred for assessment in the first place and turn out to be more difficult to place than the boys, fewer go through the centre than boys, roughly of the order 1:20.

Samples

The house was opened in May 1973. The first girl was admitted in June 1974 and the study data was collected between that date and 31st December 1976. During this period sixty-one girls were placed there. Of these, one girl was admitted twice and in view of her changed circumstances was regarded as an extra admission. The group, therefore, consisted of sixty-two girls (Sample A).

This group has been compared with a sample of boys placed in the same house during the same period (Sample B), where each boy's name is the first to appear in the house register after the admission of the girl. There is otherwise no matching between these two samples.

In view of the special nature of the boys admitted to the house and the fact that they are known to be different from the rest of the boys referred to the centre and would, therefore, provide an unsatisfactory sample against which to assess girls, the third sample comprises boys admitted during the same period as the above two samples but who were placed in one of the other three open houses (Sample C). This sample was matched for age with the girls in the study group. Such a design makes it possible to detect important differences between girls on the one hand and boys of different levels of difficulty on the other. Drawing conclusions about the characteristics of such an extreme population becomes, therefore, empirically feasible and acceptable.

It should be noted that even Sample C are at the extreme end of the 'normal' population of difficult youngsters. It so happens, however, that within the assessment population of the centre, they constitute the *normal* three-quarters majority. This point should be borne in mind when interpreting the results. The fact that the three samples may not be different from each other does not mean that they are not substantially different from other children who present such problems as to warrant sending them to the centre. For that sort of comparison an epidemiological or cohort research design such as that employed by Rutter *et al* (1970) and (West 1969 *et seq*) would be required.

Sources of Information

The two sources of information for the study are Data Cards and Assessment Reports. For several years a punched data card has been used to collect systematic information on all the children admitted. The card has proved a particularly fruitful source of information for purposes of research and for providing up-to-date pictures of the children in all their diversity. A fuller introduction to this data card and the definitions used for completing the cards has been provided elsewhere (Hoghughi and Porteous, 1976).

In interpreting the information on these cards it should be borne in mind that not all the figures add up to 100% because of the multiplicity of circumstances which a card can present. So far no satisfactory way has been found of codifying information in a manageable form which yet takes account of the complexity of these circumstances.

Assessment Reports have evolved continuously since the opening of the school and are subject to regular reviews and modifications. The format of the present report which is standard for all children was established in 1974. The staff are instructed in both the theory and practice of assessment and are coached in report writing according to pro-formae and notes which constitute a handbook. Thus an attempt is made to ensure the uniformity of assessment reports both in structure and parameters of the content. These are modified according to the particular configuration of the child's characteristics. Despite this, and because of the different backgrounds and orientations of the staff, uniformity is neither possible, nor is it believed in the last analysis, desirable.

Upon the admission of a child, a member of a house team is designated as the report writer for that child. From then on it is his task to ensure that all the information that will subsequently appear in the report becomes available. This includes all relevant background material which has been updated and cross checked for accuracy, general information about the functioning of the child, which includes reports from psychologists, social workers, physicians and other specialists, as well as the observational data which result from the comments of individual members of the house team and others on their daily contact with the child. Thus, although reports are presented by one individual member of staff, they are the results of contributions by a wide range of people. This prevents the report from being the sum of personal attitudes and biases of one particular member of staff concerning a child (see the Appendix with sample report).

Information on the discharge and placement of children is presented elsewhere (Hoghughi, 1973). These discharges range from, at the one extreme, placement of the child back with his family and local school (26% at present) to, at the other extreme, certification under the Mental Health Act 1959, and placement in special hospitals. The large majority of the children (though not of girls) are placed in Community Homes with Education on the Premises, i.e. former approved schools.

Analysis

Although the data contained on the cards and in the reports are susceptible to a wide range of statistical analyses, for the purpose of this report simple descriptive statistics (N and %) and tests of significance (t – tests, x^2 and simple cluster analysis) have been adopted. In interpreting this body of data, limitations of such analyses resulting from variations of estimates of percentages should be borne in mind. Also, many of the differences which do not appear significant at present may become so with larger samples. Levels of significance range from $p = 0.10 - 0.001$. P-levels have not been included in the tables but reference is made to significant differences in the text. Comments on the results are given in the context of wider experience with these children.

CHAPTER 3

★

Who Are the Extreme Children?

SINCE 1974 when local government reorganisation took place, two types of authorities, County Councils and Metropolitan District Councils, have social services responsibilities. The boundaries have been so drawn that the County Councils have populations roughly equal, as do the Metropolitan District Councils. These new local authorities cut across the old boundaries of County Councils and Borough Councils, each of whom also had social services functions. These old authorities had different levels of provision for children which were subsequently incorporated into the new structure. Therefore, the new authorities have different ranges of capability for coping with their own disordered children. Even allowing for this, however, there are major variations in the pattern of referrals of severely disordered children which cannot be accounted for in terms of simple provision of facilities. This illustrates the points discussed later (in Chapter 7) about the variability and ambiguity of criteria employed by different local authorities in their identification and processing of disordered children. Certain local authorities produce more disordered children, not only because of environmental circumstances such as unemployment, poverty, incidence of family pathology, etc., but also because their service is such that more children are likely to reach crisis points which require crisis intervention.

Rigorous criteria are employed for accepting children as emergencies, allowing them to bypass the waiting list and be admitted as soon as is humanly possible. These criteria relate to the gravity of the circumstances and involve those acts which

B
33

either have or are likely to place at severe risk the child or the community. Apart from serious crimes such as murder, arson and rape, emergencies comprise severe acting out behaviour by a youngster, in the home or another institution, which cannot be contained by any of the other resources to which a social worker can gain access.

Taking the numbers of boys and girls admitted during the period of the study, the proportion of emergency admissions of girls to boys is of the order of 60:1. This is a colossal difference and becomes even more significant when it is borne in mind that fewer girls are placed in the care of local authorities for presenting serious problems than are boys, either by virtue of offending or other aberrations. The ratio is a rough numerical index of the burden of problems presented by extreme girls and boys.

TABLE I: PREVIOUS PLACEMENT

| | Girls | | Extreme Boys | | Other Boys | |
| | A | | B | | C | |
	N	%	N	%	N	%
CHEs (former approved schools)	8	13	7	11	11	18
Local assessment centres	23	37	12	19	13	21
Family group homes	8	13	12	19	9	14
Hospitals	3	5	1	2	1	2
Special schools	—		4	6	—	
Detention centres	—		7	11	6	10
Remand centres	1	2	7	11	2	3
Hostels	6	10	—		—	
Home	13	21	12	19	20	32

The results show that the pattern of admissions is differentially related to the immediately prior placement. More boys have a history of having spent some time in a CHE (former approved school) but girls predominate among admissions from local assessment centres and, increasingly, hospitals.

This is an important fact in understanding the process of the social identification of the extreme children, as local assessment centres, hospitals and other facilities are used predominantly as emergency and specialised placements for those children who have been presenting serious problems which cannot be contained elsewhere. And yet, when the children present problems with which they cannot cope, the children are referred to an end of the line facility. Invariably, in the case of girls, admissions from hospitals have been from the acute wards where the girls have been taken after self-destructive acts, have been placed on tranquillising medication, but have presented problems which have been beyond tolerance of the hospital staff. This factor, combined with the unease of psychiatrists to place children on compulsory orders under the Mental Health Act or to subject them to debilitating doses of medication, leads them to diagnose the girls' problems as severe behaviour or personality disorder and thereby inappropriate for psychiatric intervention. These diagnoses then legitimise the psychiatrists' statements that the girl is inappropriately placed in a hospital and lead to their demand that she should be removed by the social workers back into their own care.

TABLE 2: REASON FOR REFERRAL

	A		B		C	
	N	%	N	%	N	%
Assessment only	26	42	10	16	54	87
Absconding from previous placement	16	26	21	34	5	8
Extremely bad behaviour in previous placement	13	21	25	40	3	5
Suicide attempts at previous placement	6	10	3	5	—	
Section 53 or unsuitable remand placement	1	2	3	5	—	

The difference in referrals from detention and remand centres (both penal establishments) reflect the relative infrequency with which girls are placed in such facilities. Since March 1977 in the case of girls, and August 1977 in the case of boys, no girl aged under fifteen, or boy under fourteen, may be normally placed in a prison department establishment.

It should be noted that the above categories are not mutually exclusive. *All* children are referred for assessment but the reasons for referring them are widely varied.

The two extreme groups are much more like each other than they are like 'ordinary' boys. Considerably more ordinary boys are referred for assessment than are those who are placed in security. Most of these ordinary boys have exhausted whatever facilities to which the local authority has prior access and it has been recognised that attempts should be made not only to stabilise them but also to obtain a cool, critical look at their problems and treatment requirements.

In the extreme groups, as is to be expected, absconding is a more important problem than it is with ordinary boys. Boys also appear to have presented their former placements with more intolerable behaviour than have the girls – though the incidence of such behaviour among both is very high. On the other hand, girls present a significantly bigger problem of attempted suicide, which seems to be rising rapidly. Generally more boys commit grave crimes and are placed in remand centres than do girls, which accounts for the difference in the number of their placements in security over the study period.

The above result substantiates the suggestion hinted at earlier, that by the time of referral the children have brought the referral agencies to the end of their tolerance. It indicates only superficially the depth and the extent of the children's problems which are manifested and assessed at greater length in the course of their stay at the centre.

The average age of the extreme boys (14·2 years; s.d. 20·6 months) is slightly lower than that of the girls (14·8 years; s.d. 14·4 months) and the ordinary boys (14·7 years; s.d. 15·2 months). The most noticeable difference in the two groups is the variation of the ages within each group; severely dis-ordered boys show a wider age range (more younger boys are among them) than do the girls at a significant level.

TABLE 3: HOME ENVIRONMENT

	A N	A %	B N	B %	C N	C %
Rural	—	—	7	11	4	6
Owned	2	3	2	3	8	13
Council	50	81	51	82	42	68
Rented	4	6	4	6	4	6
Large Estate	24	39	24	39	25	40
Delinquent Area	34	55	34	55	35	56
Post War	10	16	13	21	7	11
Overcrowded	8	13	9	14	5	8
Less than 3 bedrooms	8	13	8	13	7	11

There are more boys than girls who come from rural areas. Fewer of the extreme children come from families who own their home and the figures show that more of them live in council houses. Slightly more also live in overcrowded con-ditions. Although these differences are not very striking, the general impression is that both groups of extreme children come from slightly worse physical environments than those of the boys in the open houses. It is worth noting that almost half the children in each sample come from areas where delinquency is not a major problem. Although previous research (e.g. Morris, 1957) has suggested that there is a definite geography of social disorder, a closer look at the extreme groups suggests that they are more evenly distributed over the geographical area than are ordinary delinquents.

Fewer girls than boys come from homes which are considered to be poor. The girls also contain a greater proportion of children from materially good homes.

TABLE 4: INSIDE HOME

	A		B		C	
	N	%	N	%	N	%
Poor	13	21	14	23	17	27
Reasonable	35	56	39	63	34	55
Good	14	23	9	14	11	18

TABLE 5: FINANCES

	A		B		C	
	N	%	N	%	N	%
Poor	24	39	22	35	19	31
Reasonable	29	47	36	58	36	58
Good	9	14	4	6	7	11

Contrary to the expectations from the above findings, more of the extreme children come from financially poor homes. Unlike the normal run of 'socialised' delinquents, analysis of individual cases shows that few of the extreme group's problems are directly associated with material or financial poverty of the home. Thus, it is unlikely that material improvement will significantly reduce their chances of presenting serious problems. This is the first indication of the qualitative difference between the 'normal' run of young offenders and their disordered peers.

Considerable significance is attached both in theory and research to parent-child relationships in the aetiology of adolescent disorder, particularly delinquency (e.g. Bowlby, 1951; Andry, 1960; Rutter, 1971). This is, however, a fluid area both theoretically and empirically (e.g. Clarke & Clarke, 1976) and something of a nightmare for the researcher who has to codify the information which is not always as 'hard' as it might look.

TABLE 6: FAMILY SITUATION

		A N	A %	B N	B %	C N	C %
Mother	Dead	3	5	2	3	3	5
	Separated	7	11	8	13	5	8
	Divorced	13	21	10	16	13	21
	Cohabit	7	11	8	13	10	16
	Away	5	8	5	8	7	11
Father	Dead	6	10	5	8	5	8
	Separated	8	13	10	16	7	11
	Divorced	11	18	11	18	11	18
	Cohabit	5	8	2	3	5	8
	Away	6	10	6	10	12	19
Parents together		25	40	27	43	21	34
Stepmother		5	8	3	5	3	5
Stepfather		8	13	11	18	5	8
Stable set up		18	29	18	29	19	31

On the basis of information available on the family, it is not possible to discern many consistent or significant differences between the samples. No one sample shows a preponderance of disturbance of bond with parents apart from the higher number of extreme boys who have stepfathers, compared with other boys who in turn have many more fathers 'away' than do the rest. In general, it is worth noting that fewer than half the children are from intact homes. The findings also marginally confirm the general trend of previous research findings, that disturbance of the relationship with the father is commoner than that with mother among disordered adolescents.

This 'bare bones' picture of the home, however, says nothing about the amount of stress that has led to or resulted from the disturbance of parent–child relationships. Death of a parent has its own serious effects on ordinary children (see Brown, 1961; Greer, 1972). With extreme children, the consequences of such an event are likely to be even more cataclysmic, because they are so much more at the mercy of environmental stress than normal children and, because of the disorganised nature of their families, less likely to receive support at times of distress. Unresolved grief reactions and various defence mechanisms in relation to a dead parent are frequently observed in such children long after the event.

The reactions of the children to the break up of the family are even more complex. Almost from birth, they are caught up in the conflict which eventually leads to their parents' separation. The development of emotional bonds with the parents is disturbed by the conflict of loyalties. This is exacerbated by the fact that for reasons of both lack of space and attitudes to child rearing, they are not even shielded from the worst of parental violence. The result of this and the interaction of troubled parents with their children is that the seeds of deep mutual ambivalence are sown at an early age and emerge with increasing force when the children begin to present problems.

Other studies of these same extreme groups (Gibson, 1977; Solberg, 1975) have shown that even in homes which remain intact there is a considerable amount of conflict and aggression between the parents and the children. Analysis of individual cases shows that fights between the girls and their parents, particularly mothers, are more frequent than is the case with boys. Boys, on the other hand, are subjected to more frequent physical punishment by their parents, particularly fathers, than are the girls. These differences are interesting because they suggest that extreme girls are basically more aggressive; or they become so because they model themselves on more aggressive mothers; or they displace the beatings to which they are subjected; or they engage in behaviours which more frequently 'warrant' a beating in their particular milieu.

These explanations and others like them are of interest in attempting to account for the preponderance of non-accidental injuries caused by mothers to daughters as well as the increasing crimes of violence by girls. Gibson (*op. cit.*) has shown that children who have committed offences against the person come from families which are intact but in which there is a good deal of aggressive conflict between the parents. This is further illustrated by the following table.

TABLE 7: MARITAL PROBLEMS

	A		B		C	
	N	%	N	%	N	%
Long standing	35	55	42	68	31	50
Recent	4	6	2	3	4	6
Severe	22	35	26	42	23	37
Separations	16	26	20	32	78	13

The separations are temporary as opposed to those in the previous table which were permanent up to the time of assessment. Taken together with evidence of marital disharmony, they indicate the degree of instability to which the extreme children, who may in any case be genetically or constitutionally at risk, have to adapt. It is hardly surprising that some of the most destructive behaviour of the extreme children is manifested within their own homes. This point is further reinforced when the sources of stress within the family are considered.

The figures show a striking difference in sibling relationships between the extreme children and others. They are less likely to emulate older brothers or sisters and more likely to be in frequent physical conflict with them. They are also often 'misfits' in their own families. Although there may be an element of scapegoating in this, analysis of the individual cases shows that these children present more problems to their families than do their siblings.

Almost one third of all the children have siblings who are also in care. The incidence of mental or physical illness among the girls' mothers is greater than among the boys' mothers. There is a significantly higher incidence of the girls' conflict with and rejection by their mothers than is the case with the boys. Within the extreme group, the girls' mothers are generally more uncooperative than the boys' mothers in attempts made by agencies to rehabilitate the girls.

TABLE 8: FAMILY PROBLEMS

	A N	A %	B N	B %	C N	C %
Siblings:						
Handicapped	4	6	2	3	1	2
In care	31	50	30	48	30	48
Conflict	17	27	15	24	—	—
Modelling on elder siblings' behaviour	14	23	14	23	28	45
Mother:						
Drinking	9	14	7	11	8	13
Disabled/physically ill	10	16	8	13	5	8
Mental illness	15	24	9	14	11	18
Rejecting	19	31	9	14	10	16
Uncooperative	16	26	6	10	16	26
Employed full time	6	10	8	13	6	10
Father:						
Drinking	23	37	23	37	19	31
Disabled/physically ill	8	13	10	16	6	10
Mental illness	4	6	3	5	2	3
Rejecting	18	29	17	27	14	23
Uncooperative	4	6	12	19	12	19
Violent	18	29	24	38	12	19
Occasional unemployment	9	14	13	21	8	13
Persistent unemployment	16	26	23	37	9	14

The incidence of persistent or occasional unemployment and violence among the extreme boys' fathers is much greater than that among the fathers of the other two groups and they are also more likely to be uncooperative than the girls' fathers.

In general terms the picture suggests that more of the girls have 'problem' mothers and more of the extreme boys have 'problem' fathers. The result is far from conclusive, though a picture of sex linked association between the disorders of parents and children may be emerging (cf. Rutter, 1971).

There is a considerable literature on the roles of parents in the socialisation of their children (e.g. Newson & Newson, 1970; West, 1973; Bloch, 1974; Cooper, 1974). However, little is known about the intimate, inner dynamics of the family and the minutae of parent-child interaction to make any detailed causal picture feasible. The present results suggest that, in the family setting, if mothers present problems, then their daughters are more likely in the long run to suffer than their sons. Alternatively, if daughters present problems, their mothers are more likely to react adversely than would their fathers. The close ties between mother and daughter appear as necessary and prevalent as they are vulnerable to damage. These ties are, of course, affected by the father, by other siblings and other aspects of the family condition. It would seem appropriate to attach a similar importance to the relationship between fathers and sons, but both pictures are so complex as to defy generalisation.

TABLE 9: FAMILY OFFENDING

		A		B		C	
		N	%	N	%	N	%
Mother	Prison	6	10	1	2	—	—
	Frequent offender	5	8	—	—	3	5
	Petty offender	3	5	1	2	1	2
Father	Prison	13	21	10	16	8	13
	Frequent offender	5	8	4	6	5	8
	Petty offender	1	2	8	13	8	13
Offence against child		2	3	2	3	—	—
Siblings	Prison	2	3	2	3	3	5
	Borstal	6	10	7	11	6	10
	Community School	15	24	15	24	12	19
	Probation/Supervision	16	26	16	26	12	19

The number of mothers who have received prison sentences

or who are known offenders is higher in the girls' group. This is consistent with the previous findings which show that more of the girls have 'problem' mothers.

More of the girls' fathers have also been serious enough offenders to receive a prison sentence. The same difference holds between the boys' groups, though less markedly. The proportion of petty offenders among the boys' fathers is much higher than that among the girls'. The offences against the child referred to here are sexual assaults and are known to have been committed against only the severely disordered children.

There is only a small difference in the offending histories of the siblings of the three groups, slightly more of the extreme group have siblings who have also been in community homes, on probation, or under supervision.

In general terms, therefore, the extreme children are more likely to come from homes where there is a higher incidence of law breaking. This may imply criminal attitudes among the parents or permissive attitudes to their own children's mis-behaviour and increased opportunities for the children to emulate their parents' behaviour. These findings are in accord with one of the more consistent findings in criminology (e.g. West, 1973). The interpretation of the results may range from one suggesting a genetic basis to criminality (e.g. Shah & Roth, 1974) to one arguing for the prevalence of social and political determinants of crime (Taylor et al, 1975).

The prevalence and long history of family problems may account for the fact that less than half the extreme children have spent the whole of their lives with their parents.

TABLE 10: CHILD WITH PARENTS

	A		B		C	
	N	%	N	%	N	%
All life	28	45	33	53	31	50
Most of life	20	32	20	32	22	35
Very little	11	18	9	15	8	13
Nil	3	5	—	—	1	2

Although the differences here are not very striking, it is of interest that the girls on the whole seem to have spent the most time away from their parents. Other than in individual cases, it is not possible to surmise the cause and effect relationships of the parent–child separations with subsequent disorders of the children. In the case of the severely disordered children, separations appear to as much follow as precede their problem behaviour and their effects exert a complex, deleterious influence on the self-image and control of the children well into their future (cf. Rutter, 1971, 1972).

TABLE 11: FEELINGS TOWARDS FAMILY

	A		B		C	
	N	%	N	%	N	%
Very strong positive	10	16	4	6	3	5
Very strong negative	19	31	9	15	6	10

The girls are significantly more likely to express strong feelings about their families than the boys in either group. Within each group the strong feelings expressed are more likely to be negative than positive. They are, however, subject to rapid changes, depending on the parents' latest show of affection. The changeability of emotional expressions is as much a hallmark of this population as it is the wide range of its extremes, particularly among the girls. By comparison most boys seem flat.

TABLE 12: RUNNING AWAY

	A		B		C	
	N	%	N	%	N	%
Home	21	34	23	37	17	27
Community Homes	15	24	29	47	12	19
Remand	20	32	11	18	4	6
Other	22	35	26	42	10	16

The main differences here are between the extreme children and the ordinary boys. The extreme children are more likely to have run away from home, residential schools, remand placements or other institutions. The only difference within the extreme groups is that more girls have absconded from remand places whereas more boys have absconded from community homes. This latter difference is dramatic and reflects one of the major selection criteria for placement in security, namely persistent absconding from other facilities.

Absconding has always been one of the major headaches of residential establishments, particularly those dealing with delinquent children (Clarke & Martin, 1971). Alongside violence and persistent serious offending, it is one of the most frequent and important grounds for labelling a child 'severely disordered'. It is also responsible for much of the frustration, anger and exhaustion, particularly of magistrates and the police, with delinquent and disordered youngsters. It is accepted even by liberal groups as a legitimate reason for locking up a youngster if reasonable alternatives cannot be found (Howard League, 1977).

For many of the extreme children, running away appears to indicate their inability to adapt to the behavioural boundaries set for them in various environments. Running away seems to have become one of the generalised responses to any pressure they cannot tolerate. Even so, the amount of running away from home of all the children is surprising and illustrates, yet again, the deep ambivalence of most of the children to their families.

TABLE 13: PERSONAL HISTORY

	A		B		C	
	N	%	N	%	N	%
Premature	2	3	2	3	1	2
Birth complication	5	8	1	2	6	10
Early hospital	12	19	6	10	7	11
Normal milestones	38	61	46	74	34	55

TABLE 13: CONTINUED

	A		B		C	
	N	%	N	%	N	%
Wandering	10	16	8	13	4	6
Illegitimate	10	16	8	13	3	5
Fostered	5	8	6	10	2	3
Adopted	2	3	1	1	1	1
Children's Home	19	31	12	19	15	24
Care Order	55	89	58	93	57	92

The differences here appear somewhat complicated. There are more of the extreme children who are illegitimate, who are reported to have wandered from home at an early age, and who have been fostered. This accords with previous findings that they come from slightly worse physical home environments and are more likely to have a 'problem' parent.

Within the extreme groups the boys are less likely to have suffered from birth complications, needed hospital treatment early in infancy, or been in a children's home. More of them were deemed to have reached developmental milestones within the normally accepted limits. Twice as many girls as boys have suffered from such early physical problems as to warrant hospital treatment. These problems range from encephalitis and fits to glandular fever and inability to take food and are reflected in their subsequently poorer physical condition.

TABLE 14: LEISURE

	A		B		C	
	N	%	N	%	N	%
Youth Club	5	8	7	11	11	18
Established hobbies	6	10	2	3	4	6
Regular boy/girl friend	4	6	6	10	9	14

There is a difference between the girls and the ordinary boys. The boys are more likely to go to Youth Clubs than the girls and are also more likely to have regular girl friends than the girls are to have boy friends. The slight differences between the extreme and ordinary boys may be accounted for not so much by their ages as the greater discrepancy in their levels of socialisation. The more difficult boys are more immature and socially isolated and hence less likely to have acquired regular interests or girl friends.

In general, these children are not very 'clubbable'. They lead lives which are impoverished in social relationships and leisure activities. This does not appear to be so related to paucity of opportunity as to reflect their personalities and modes of adaptation. They are generally extremely difficult to motivate to persist with any pursuit such as youth club attendance.

TABLE 15: OFFENDING HISTORY

	A		B		C	
	N	%	N	%	N	%
Offender	40	64	50	81	58	94
'Recommittal'	12	19	21	34	24	39
Onset within 2 years	17	27	15	24	19	31
3 or less court appearances	26	42	22	35	22	35
Burglary	19	31	39	63	48	77
Theft	30	48	40	64	47	76
Taking and driving	1	2	19	31	13	21
Sexual	2	3	3	5	—	—
Arson	6	10	17	27	6	10
Damage	2	3	15	24	12	19
Breach of peace	—	—	—	—	—	—
Shoplifting	12	19	8	13	2	3
Others	17	27	6	10	6	10
Always solo	5	8	5	8	3	5
Joint and solo	17	27	30	48	39	63

TABLE 15: CONTINUED

	A		B		C	
	N	%	N	%	N	%
Always joint	18	29	15	24	16	36
Up to 5 offences	17	27	12	19	15	24
6 to 10 ,,	12	19	13	21	22	35
11 to 20 ,,	6	10	14	23	14	23
21 to 50 ,,	5	8	10	16	6	10
Over 50 ,,	—	—	1	2	1	2

The main differences here are between the boys and the girls. More of the girls are non-offenders, and fewer of them have been 'recommitted' (i.e. sent to another community home with education). Although there is no difference in the numbers in each group who have started to offend recently or who have less than three court appearances, there are striking differences in the types of offences committed by the boys and girls.

More boys commit burglary, theft, taking and driving, arson and damage whereas more girls commit shoplifting and 'other' offences. This latter category includes the least frequent offences, ranging from 'cruelty to animals' to 'murder' and 'manslaughter'.

The preponderance of arsonists in the extreme group is dramatic and reflects both the rise in the offences of arson and the deliberate policy of placing these children, who are in any case often under special Orders (Section 53 of the 1933 Children and Young Persons Act), under closer supervision.

The figures also show something of the extent of proven offending of difficult youngsters, particularly where it concerns girls. The girls are less likely to be involved in joint offences; this is compatible with the differences in the types of offences committed by the girls and boys. There are also differences in the extent of the children's offending. The girls and the less discordered boys are more likely to have been involved in less than ten offences whereas the extreme boys are just as likely to have long offending histories as short ones.

With the possible exception of suicidal and self-destructive behaviour, offending by a youngster is most likely to bring him to the attention of social agencies and warrant their intervention. However, a vast proportion of offending goes undetected (McClintock & Avison, 1968; Ryall, 1971; Belson, 1975) and what is detected and followed up is dealt with in a whole variety of ways (Priestley *et al*, 1977). Despite public belief to the contrary, most children do not persist in offending beyond a caution or the first court appearance. There is a process of gradual filtering of these children as more and more of them are dealt with by a range of facilities. Of those who remain in the care of social services departments and are not dealt with in the penal service (i.e. detention centres and borstals), only those who present extreme offending and other problems are referred for assessment.

This is supported by the large proportion of 'recommittals' in the population. Other studies (Hoghughi & Heptinstall, 1972) have shown that only about 15% of the former approved school population had been through the system more than once. By contrast about one quarter of the girls and over one third of the boys in the present study are 'recommittals' and have thus shown their unsusceptibility to at least one instance of serious institutional intervention. If for no other reason than this, as well as the general characteristics of such children, they present more serious problems of management than their peers.

The differences between extreme girls and boys in offending have been traditionally attributed to the lesser tendency of girls to manifest their (and their families') disorder in delinquent behaviour. Although the number of girls engaged in persistent delinquency remains substantially lower than the boys (Criminal Statistics, 1976; Priestley *et al*, *ibid.*), this has been challenged as reflecting more the social processing of deviant girls than their propensity to offend (Campbell, 1977). In the extreme population, however, it remains true that most girls are referred for other reasons (e.g. severely disordered behaviour) than for offending.

TABLE 16: PREVIOUS DISPOSAL

	A		B		C	
	N	%	N	%	N	%
Fine	12	19	16	26	32	52
Attendance Centre	—	—	2	3	2	3
Supervision	16	26	22	35	22	35
Intermediate Treatment	—	—	—	—	2	3
Remand	9	14	12	19	11	18
Detention Centre	—	—	6	10	6	10
Community Home	12	19	31	34	24	39
Educational/Medical Treatment	6	10	11	18	5	8

In keeping with the greater numbers of boy offenders, more boys than girls have been put under supervision, on remand, or admitted to community homes previously. The less difficult boys have been fined more often, whereas more of the extreme group are deemed to have been in need of special medical or educational treatment in specialised facilities such as schools for the maladjusted.

TABLE 17: SPECIAL AGENCIES INVOLVED

	A		B		C	
	N	%	N	%	N	%
NSPCC etc.	6	10	4	6	—	—
CGC/SPS	16	26	26	42	2	3
Other	4	6	8	13	2	3

The figures show that only children from the severely disordered group have been involved with voluntary organisations concerned with prevention of cruelty to children. This suggests that they may have been subject to parental abuse or suffered other kinds of disadvantage which would warrant this form of intervention. Concern with severe child abuse is a relatively recent phenomenon. This may be why information on this aspect of the youngsters' histories is scant, other than in serious cases. This is despite the fact that many of the children are known subsequently to have been subjected to disproportionate physical chastisement as a method of control, though erratically, often when it was too late and shorn of those elements which would make punishment effective. The extreme group are also more likely to have attended Child Guidance Clinics or been involved with the Schools Psychological Service, compared with the less difficult intake.

TABLE 18: SPECIAL SCHOOLING

| | A | | B | | C | |
	N	%	N	%	%	%
Maladjusted	3	5	5	8	1	2
Day ESN	2	3	6	10	4	6
Residential	8	13	15	24	5	8
Behaviour problems	34	55	38	61	24	39
Expelled/suspended	6	10	16	26	10	16
Teacher assault	6	10	2	3	—	—

A substantial proportion of seriously disordered boys have a history of residential schooling, which has been ineffective in coping with their problems and from which they have been excluded or withdrawn. It is noteworthy that only a negligible minority of the extreme and none of the 'ordinary' (though it ought to be remembered, difficult) group are reported to have assaulted teachers. The girls seem more prone to this form of aggression than do the boys.

These findings are surprising in view of the much publicised 'violence' of school children. They suggest that either such violence is really much less than it is suggested or that being

violent to teachers is not associated with other extreme behaviours which lead to the children becoming identified in this
way. The majority of all extreme children have exhibited
behaviour problems at school and consequently less of them
have good school records. More boys than girls have been
expelled or suspended from school with may suggest that the
boys' behaviour was more disruptive or dangerous than the
girls'. Alternatively, perhaps the measures taken to deal with
the problems presented by girls are different. The fact that
more girls than boys have assaulted teachers may support this.

Although there are no differences in the overall numbers who
have truanted there are differences in the extent of the problem.
The numbers of persistent truants in each group are fairly
similar but the extreme children are more likely to be described

TABLE 19: TRUANCY

	A		B		C	
	N	%	N	%	N	%
Persistent	21	34	24	39	21	34
Frequent	26	42	18	29	12	19
Occasional	8	13	16	26	22	35
Long standing	35	56	31	53	29	47
Recent	19	31	25	40	26	42

as 'frequent' rather than 'occasional' truants. More boys than
girls are reported to have recently started to stay away from
school.

The results show that truancy is one of the major problems
presented by all difficult children; crises often seem to result
from it. Taken together, about 90% of the children are truants
from school with over a third of them persistent and about half
with long standing histories. Truancy is a multi-faceted
phenomenon (Tyreman, 1968; Turner, 1974), often reflecting
the condition of the school as of the child (Power et al, 1972).
In the case of the extreme children the results suggest their
inability to cope with structure as well as a tendency to run

away from stressful situations to what they deem to be less demanding and more exciting alternatives. In the extreme group, as many have truanted alone as with others.

During the period of assessment, all children are seen, often more than once, by the team of psychologists who are by training and expertise primarily interested in clinical, social and forensic aspects of the children's functioning.

Their reports comment in turn on intelligence and attainments; significant aspects of social background; patterns of personality and an account of the socialisation of the child and the reasons for his/her particular pattern of adaptation. They use a wide ranging vocabulary which does not lend itself to categorical analysis. For the sake of completing the picture, however, a summary is presented.

The IQs of the three groups, obtained from the WISC (or WAIS in some cases) are shown below:

TABLE 20: INTELLIGENCE QUOTIENTS

	A	B	C
Average full scale	85·2	87·0	90·8
s.d.	12·0	13·5	10·5
Verbal IQ	84·8	88·4	90·8
s.d.	10·9	13·3	10·5
Performance IQ	89·2	92·2	93·3
s.d.	14·0	13·3	10·9

Although the girls' scores are lower than the scores of both groups of boys, their IQs are only significantly lower than that of ordinary boys. The differences in levels of intellectual functioning are consistent over both verbal and performance parts of the intelligence tests. As no up to date intelligence test data for disordered and delinquent girls exist (cf. Cowie *et al*, 1968) it cannot be said whether the relative intellectual dullness of the girls is true only of the extreme end or true of such girls in general.

TABLE 21 : LEVEL OF FUNCTIONING

	A		B		C	
	N	%	N	%	N	%
Very limited ability	8	13	14	23	3	5
Below average	20	32	15	24	14	23
Low average	17	27	16	26	18	29
Average	17	27	15	24	23	37
High average	0	0	0	0	2	3
Above average	0	0	2	3	2	3
Considered to be potentially better than their present level of functioning	9	15	17	27	19	31

In addition to giving IQs, the psychologists also comment on the child's level of functioning in the standard terminology indicated above. They also state if a child's intellectual potential may be better than that indicated by the test results, taking into account both history and present condition.

There are significantly more extreme children in the lowest ability ranges than there are ordinary boys. This is particularly true of the boy's group which contains the largest number of functionally subnormal adolescents. Analysis of individual histories shows that (1) many of these children have been placed in more demanding situations than they could have been reasonably expected to cope with; (2) conversely, some have been treated as subnormal dependents without any ability to contribute to the direction of their own lives; and (3) their limited ability makes it difficult to engage in the kind of 'relationship therapy' so beloved of social workers, which relies on giving insights as a basis for self-control and adaptation.

TABLE 22: ATTAINMENT

	A		B		C	
	N	%	N	%	N	%
Retarded	40	64	36	58	34	55
Average	16	26	17	27	23	37
Superior	6	10	9	14	5	8

The majority of all children admitted are backward in basic attainments with fewer of the extreme group being regarded as 'average' at school. Such massive retardation does not only reflect the level of scholastic adjustment of the children which is bad enough and does not ideally equip them for future adaptation in an industrial society. It can also be seen as an important corollary of the children's self-image as failures who are unlikely to do well at anything. Although it is unnecessarily melodramatic to suggest that the children who have not been given their educational due (despite the vast panoply of special educational resources) seek to settle the score by their predatory and anti-social behaviour, their anger and resentment at their own incompetence is hardly ever disguised. It is one of the more pathetic experiences when these children try to get another child or an adult to write a letter for them or read the paper to them, without letting on that they are incapable of doing so themselves.

There are myriad ways of construing, measuring and describing personality. Most constructions and measurements, however, say more about their own origins than about the personality they purport to describe. In the present context, the psychologists use a battery of diverse personality measures, augmented by observational data and intensive interviews. They use a wide descriptive vocabulary aimed at communicating in as much of a commonsense language as possible their technical findings. Of these, the characteristics which significantly differentiate the groups are as follows:

TABLE 23: PERSONALITY DESCRIPTION

	A		B		C	
	N	%	N	%	N	%
Anti-authority	10	16	16	26	9	15
Aggressive	14	23	8	13	6	10
Very anxious	10	16	13	21	5	8
Group dependent	9	15	6	10	13	21
Impulsive	7	11	12	19	12	19
Lacking self control	12	19	5	8	6	10
Extrovert	7	11	11	18	12	19
Sensitive	10	16	15	24	10	16
Insecure	38	61	33	53	28	45
Emotionally unstable	20	32	17	27	5	8
'Delinquent' self-image	5	8	16	26	17	27
Stubborn	9	15	3	5	1	2

According to the above results, seriously disordered boys are more anti-authority, as well as anxious and sensitive. The only area in which less difficult boys predominate is in their greater group dependence. As will become clear in the next chapter, the extreme group have enormous difficulty in social functioning, particularly in groups.

Otherwise, the girls emerge as substantially the more abnormal group in comparison with both extreme and ordinary boys. Fewer girls are seen clinically as impulsive and extroverted with a delinquent self-image but more are emotionally and socially immature, aggressive, deficient in self-control, stubborn and emotionally unstable.

When commenting on the problems which the children had to come to terms with, the psychologists appeared to isolate two problem areas for both groups of boys, i.e. 'truancy' and 'difficulties with making meaningful or lasting relationships' with other people. This was not so with the girls. There were many more problem areas mentioned ranging from 'home circumstances' to 'obsessions' but also including both truancy and personal relationships.

It is interesting to note that the severely disordered group contained two boys who were considered 'effeminate', had problems of sexual identity, and were ridiculed and disliked by the other children because of this, yet there is no mention of any specific problems relating to two girls who were considered 'tomboys'. Both these girls are reported to have expressed the desire to 'have been born a boy', wore trousers, had their hair closely cropped and yet were popular with the other children, their tomboy qualities appearing to render them even more endearing. In general, it is interesting to note that although many of the girls have had previous sexual experience that created difficulties which led to their referral, most of these difficulties pale into insignificance in the context of the girls' many other problems.

TABLE 24: MALADJUSTMENT

	A		B		C	
	N	%	N	%	N	%
Severe	13	21	18	29	3	5
Moderate	16	26	24	39	23	37
Aggressive	16	26	13	21	7	11
Emotional	20	32	18	29	12	19
Behavioural	21	34	34	55	18	29

The results show the extreme children to be much more severely maladjusted than ordinary boys. The girls' maladjustment is shown mostly through aggressive, explosive outbursts and disordered emotional relationships. The boys' difficulties, on the other hand, are shown mainly through odd and sometimes bizarre acts. In this sense, the boys present a more pathological picture than do the girls.

The above descriptions do not, of course, even give a hint of the complexity of the personality and clinical state of the extreme children, because they simply indicate the areas of significant difference among the samples. In general terms, the clinical state of the children is as complex, confused and confusing as possible. This is partly because, as will become clearer in Chapter 8, approaches to the classification of children's disorders are severely theory bound and, in general, say more about the clinician's frame of reference than about the client/patient.

Analysis of individual cases indicates that whereas few of the children suffer from *formal* clinical pathology (i.e. textbook syndromes), almost all deviate significantly from the norm on a number of personality traits such as anxiety, impulse control, empathy, sensitivity, stability, etc. In addition almost all have either fluid and ill-formed or largely negative views of themselves and their chances of being able to lead a moderately fulfilling life. For many of the boys, a criminal and 'tough' self-image seems to have already become established by their early teens, which they test out and find confirmation for in their dealings with authority.

Apart from their general characteristics, most of the severely disordered boys and girls show specific clinical problems for which they are deemed to require specialist psychological treatment. The fact that such treatment is not available in most of the establishments to which the majority of the disordered children are sent points to one reason why at present most of these children's conditions go from bad to worse.

Not all the children are interviewed by one of the consultant psychiatrists who visit. Over the years a constant proportion of about 15% of the intake have been found to warrant psychiatric examination after psychological screening, though this figure appears to have risen sharply in the past two or three years. The proportion of children in the present study seen by the psychiatrists is indicative of the amount and kind of problems such children present. Half the girls and slightly fewer of the extreme boys (42%) present such problems on arrival as to warrant psychiatric examination compared with 11% of the ordinary boys group. Also, the extreme children, particularly girls, are usually seen more than once for both 'differential diagnosis' and treatment.

The psychiatric report itself is divided into description of clinical state and recommendations.

TABLE 25: CLINICAL STATE

	A		B		C	
	N	%	N	%	N	%
No psychiatric disorder	10	16	9	15	1	2
Depressive	6	10	5	8	3	5
Personality disorders (various)	12	19	5	8	3	5
Organic	2	3	2	3	0	0
Others	1	2	5	8	0	0

About one third of the severely disordered group are seen as not suffering from any *formal* psychiatric disorder. The emphasis on 'formal' is important because (a) it does not preclude the existence of dysfunction, but (b) that psychiatric intervention is not considered appropriate. In the extreme group, significantly more girls suffer from psychiatric disorder than do boys.

Depressive states are, surprisingly, not significantly more common among girls than boys, given that girls are prone to more frequent and dramatic self-destructive gestures.

Equally surprising is the significant preponderance of girls in the category of 'personality disorder'. This is an exact sounding 'diagnostic' label (cf. Chapter 8) for those youngsters whose troublesomeness does not fit easily into any other explanatory category and has, in the past, been largely used with boys. One implication of this diagnostic category is that the fundamental source of difficulty, viz. the personality disorder, is not susceptible to treatment.

Attention should also be drawn to the 'organic' and 'other' disorders which in a larger sample would be significantly more common among the extreme children, particularly boys, than the others. 'Organic' problems refer mainly to disorders of the brain and the nervous systems whereas 'others' encompasses dysfunctions ranging, in this context, from hypoglycaemia through Fröhlich syndrome to pre-psychotic states.

In presenting these results, the detailed recommendations pertaining to each child have been discarded in favour of more common categories. Often more than one recommendation is made for a child, which accounts for the higher figures in the following table than in the previous one.

TABLE 26: TYPE OF RECOMMENDATION

	A		B		C	
	N	%	N	%	N	%
Further psychiatric treatment	19	31	13	21	5	8
No further psychiatric oversight	12	19	13	21	2	3
Medication	13	21	6	10	1	2
Further medical tests	4	6	2	3	0	0
Follow up EEGs	7	11	2	3	3	5

Extreme children, particularly girls, are significantly more likely than others to require further psychiatric treatment and medication. The overall impression of the extreme children in relation to psychiatrists is that they present problems which do not easily fit into psychiatric symptomatology and classification. By and large, therefore, most psychiatric intervention is limited to a general diagnosis and prescription of psychotropic drugs as an aid to management.

The most obvious implication of the above findings is the limited diagnostic utility of psychiatry in relation to severely disordered adolescents. Children reach the end of the line frequently after psychiatric diagnosis, drug therapy and out-patient counselling which have all failed to produce the desired result. Thus they carry *psychiatric* labels which psychiatrists cannot remove by offering appropriate treatment. And yet, psychiatric assessment cannot be dispensed with not only because it may uncover a formal disorder which is susceptible to physical treatment but also because of the present social importance attached to availing disordered children of psychiatric competence.

Medical reports are compiled in a standard form from previous medical records and notes made by the centre's own Medical Officer and nursing staff.

TABLE 27: PREVIOUS INJURIES

	A		B		C	
	N	%	N	%	N	%
Only minor injury	21	34	26	42	22	35
1 serious	6	10	5	8	7	11
More than 1 serious	4	6	4	6	4	6

Although there is no significant difference between the groups, it is noteworthy that about 15% of the population have suffered at least one serious accident.

TABLE 28: NUMBER OF OPERATIONS

	A		B		C	
	N	%	N	%	N	%
1	10	16	10	16	12	19
2	4	6	2	3	2	3
3	2	3	0	0	1	2
4 or more	0	0	0	0	1	2

Almost a quarter of all the children have undergone at least one surgical operation, a significantly higher proportion than is expected for the normal population. These range from operations on undescended testicles to colostomies. The groups are not significantly different.

TABLE 29: NUMBER OF SERIOUS ILLNESSES

	A		B		C	
	N	%	N	%	N	%
1	15	24	14	23	10	16
2 or more	2	3	1	2	2	3

There is no significant difference between the groups, though it may be worthy of note that five of the named serious illnesses relating to the extreme groups were meningitis.

All children are examined by the nursing sister on admission and their condition is noted.

TABLE 30: CONDITION OF ARRIVAL

	A		B		C	
	N	%	N	%	N	%
Dirty	2	3	6	10	5	8
Extensive tattoos	0	0	3	5	1	2
Little tattoos	29	47	18	29	24	39
Infested hair	17	27	16	26	19	31

There are no significant differences between the groups, though it is surprising that more girls were tattooed than were boys of either group. In almost all cases the girls' tattoos were self inflicted, unlike those of the boys' extensive tattoos which were mainly professional. There is some research (e.g. Lepine, 1969; Measey, 1972) which shows the relationship between tattoos and both psychiatric disorder and criminally deviant behaviour. While the connection is frequently observed, it is no more adequately explained, even by the children themselves, than many other correlates of deviant behaviour.

Children who engage in tattooing themselves seem to have a high pain threshold and relatively little sensitivity to physical pain. This is also borne out by their frequent involvement in accidents and incidents which should be physically painful but from which they emerge with no apparent hurt. Whether such insensitivity to pain is constitutional or the result of conditioning it ensures that severely disordered youngsters are not deterred from physically painful encounters. Whether this is related to the greater physical aggressiveness of these youngsters (West & Farrington, 1977) is yet to be established.

But tattooing and generally deficient care of the body also reflects the low self-esteem in which most of the children, particularly severely disordered girls, hold themselves (Cowie *et al*, 1968). This is further shown by their infested hair which also reflects the level of care given to them by *others*.

Of all the new admissions, only children in the extreme groups (15% of the girls, 10% of the boys) are on psychotropic medication. Most are on high dosages of tranquillisers, sometimes of veterinary strength, found necessary to bring their behaviour under control. All medication is reviewed by the Medical Officer on their admission. Much more frequently than not, the medication is regarded as unnecessary in the new setting and, therefore, phased out.

TABLE 31: CLINICAL ASPECTS

	A N	A %	B N	B %	C N	C %
Physical defect	—	—	1	2	1	2
Brain damage (suspected)	7	11	3	5	2	3
Epileptic	1	2	5	8	—	—
Enuretic persistent	4	6	4	6	—	—
„ occasional	11	18	10	16	9	14
Encopretic	2	3	2	3	—	—

The severely disordered children bear a greater burden of medical problems than do the less difficult. There is a greater incidence of suspected brain damage amongst girls, though more of the boys are diagnosed as epileptic. Persistent enuresis and encopresis are also more common among them. Venereal diseases are not frequently encountered among the extreme children. This is surprising in view of the fact that many of the girls have had a history of promiscuous behaviour, often leading to care proceedings. Some, indeed, seem to have made a fairly comfortable income from prostitution.

On admission, the children undergo a routine medical examination. All subsequent visits to the nurse, doctor or hospital are also recorded together with any medication or treatment which may be prescribed.

TABLE 32: NUMBER OF TIMES SEEN BY
NURSE/DOCTOR/HOSPITAL IN ADDITION TO ROUTINE MEDICAL

	A		B		C	
	N	%	N	%	N	%
1	21	34	7	11	13	21
2	8	13	7	11	2	3
3	2	3	1	2	0	0
4	2	3	1	2	0	0
5 or more	4	6	1	2	0	0
Total of children	37		17		15	
Total of visits	71		33		15	

The girls visit the nurse, doctor or hospital, and receive significantly more medication than the boys of either group. The
same difference holds between the two groups of boys. Most
of these are accounted for by the self-destructive acts of the
extreme children which warrant medical intervention.

It is perhaps worth noting that all the medication, except for
four cases, prescribed for ordinary boys, was for external use
to treat complaints like athlete's foot, scabies, dermatitis, etc.

TABLE 33: NUMBER OF DIFFERENT MEDICATIONS

	A		B		C	
	N	%	N	%	N	%
1	16	26	7	11	12	19
2	7	11	9	15	2	3
3	6	10	1	2	0	0
4	2	3	0	0	0	0
5 or more	2	3	0	0	0	0
Total of children	33		17		14	
Total of medications	66		28		16	

The other four cases consisted of prescriptions for cough

medicine, penicillin for sore throat and valium which was administered to a boy at the hospital prior to the manipulation of his broken fingers.

In contrast, a much larger proportion of the girls' medication was of the psychotropic and analgesic kind followed by treatment for gynaecological conditions. It is not possible to establish whether this significant difference is due to cultural patterns of dealing differentially with male and female problems or whether a genuine difference in expressing 'medical' problems exists. It is suspected that elements of both exist in dealings with severely disordered girls.

The overall impression of the medical condition of these children is that they have a multitude of medical problems. Although there is no evidence of major neo- or post-natal difficulty, most have had a dismal subsequent history marked by frequent illness, accidents both inside and outside the home, some serious, and surgical operations. They are mostly of either slight physique and look under-nourished or obese. Whether they are constitutionally less well endowed than their normal peers, as has been suggested in a number of epidemiological studies (e.g. Newcastle 1000 Family Survey) or whether poor parental and social care is responsible for their state is not possible to determine from these results.

It may, however, not be too far fetched to suggest that their poor physical and medical condition contributes to the poor adjustment of children who may not feel well, but cannot articulate the fact. Combined with their apparently lower susceptibility to pain, it may then make it easier to understand why they get into so many physically painful and sometimes dangerous scrapes. The above results taken together with other aspects of the youngster's physical appearance such as greasy skin, scars, bad teeth, etc., suggest that many are likely to have been and to continue to be at a disadvantage from their unattractiveness. This sets up a vicious circle of reactions to reactions which can only exacerbate their problems.

CHAPTER 4

*

Disordered Children in Groups

RESIDENTIAL facilities for children are designed for group living, not because this is thought to be particularly beneficial to them, but because financial and resource restrictions make it inevitable. Bearing this in mind, it is surprising how little thought goes into the design of such facilities from the viewpoint of group dynamics, and how little the disordered behaviour of individual children is seen in the context of their groups.

As was shown at the beginning of the last chapter, most disordered children have a history of residential placement and frequently it is their disordered behaviour in groups which has led to their exclusion from just such settings. It is, therefore, essential from an assessment point of view not only to observe and evaluate their functioning in groups but also to note how much of their behaviour is a reaction to specific group variables. Also, children are much more susceptible to behavioural cues from their peers than adults and, therefore, this element should be considered in any attempt to understand and predict their behaviour.

It is, however, important to bear in mind that none of the above elements remain constant. In an assessment setting, particularly, the group composition changes constantly and with each change the child is presented with a new situation to which he has to adapt. This, though a matter of degree, has to be accepted as inevitable reality. Instead of allowing it to become a damaging limitation, it can be turned to advantage. Given that a group is a collection of individuals, and individual for-

67

tunes, tempers and reactions change, the group provides a singularly rich arena in which to understand the child, his total social competence and the kinds of problems he is likely to present in a social environment.

In studies of disordered children, information about group behaviour is prominent by its absence. This accounts, in part, for the very poor understanding of these children's problems. Because this descriptive basis is missing, it has not been possible to proceed either to explaining the problems or, even more crucially, to developing or teaching appropriate coping and treatment skills.

From the moment of a child's admission a 'Comments File' is kept in which staff record their observations relating to the child. These observations are collected both on a random basis as well as through time and behaviour sampling in specifically programmed situations. The comments are then collated by the member of staff responsible for the child's assessment report. Thus the observation section of the report gives a relatively comprehensive account of the child's behaviour during the assessment period according to the standard format of observations.

It would neither be sensible nor possible to observe the totality of a child's behaviour. Points of reference are, therefore, required to structure such observations. These can either emanate from a theoretical or clinical framework, such as watching out for a particular form of neurological disorder, or in order to test a particular hypothesis, such as one girl only 'blows' when women tell her to do something. Alternatively, they can be so designed as to give some indication of the child's reactions to a variety of situations which enable wider inferences about his problems to be drawn, for example he has little sensitivity to distress in others. The assessment report provides systematic information under a number of headings (see sample report in the Appendix). Its basis and structure has been presented elsewhere (Hoghughi, 1974).

For the purpose of this study, observations of behaviour in groups have been reduced to twenty-five questions relating to aspects of children's behaviour in groups. The answers to the questions were taken from the actual statements in the reports and not from implication, in order to minimise interpretive bias.

ANALYSIS OF THE OBSERVATIONS ON BEHAVIOUR

a. *General*
1. How did the child impress on arrival?
2. How did the child settle into the house?
3. Did the child exhibit any unusual mannerisms?
4. How communicative was the child?
5. How well could the child tolerate frustration?
6. How did the child behave when frustrated?
7. Did the child have any 'observable' fantasy life?
8. Did the child express any thoughts about his/her future?
9. What was the child's general demeanour?
10. How did the child appear to feel about his offences?

b. *Peers*
11. How did the child figure in group situations?
12. Was the child liked by the other children in the house?
13. Did the child attempt to manipulate the other children?
14. How good was the child at judging other people's reactions?
15. Was the child ever in conflict with other children?
16. Did the child show any sexual interest in any of the other children?

c. *Staff*
17. How did the child react to the staff?
18. Did the child form any relationships with any members of staff?
19. Did the child attempt to manipulate members of staff?
20. Was the child liked by members of staff?

d. *Management*
21. How did the child react when asked to do things?
22. How did the child respond to the threat of sanction?

23. How did the child respond to the structured environment of the house?
24. How did the child react to praise and encouragement?
25. How powerful was peer group pressure in affecting the child's behaviour?

The results of the analysis are given in the following tables.

General Behaviour

Girls are more suspicious and withdrawn on admission than the boys. The extreme boys are more upset than either of the other two groups and ordinary boys more placid but less cheerful than the others. These differences are all statistically significant.

TABLE 34: STATE ON ADMISSION

	A		B		C	
	N	%	N	%	N	%
Upset	4	6	14	23	4	6
Suspicious	10	16	4	6	1	2
Cheerful/boisterous	9	15	9	15	2	3
Placid	22	35	26	42	42	68
Withdrawn	17	27	9	15	13	21

As was seen from information in the previous chapter, most children are admitted from other specialised settings, following some crisis or other. Many of the children, particularly girls, are under medication to ensure that they do not present any important handling problems during transfer.

It is recognised that the manner of the child's admission and his first encounter with the staff have a prolonged and central bearing on his subsequent behaviour. The admission procedure is, therefore, deliberately designed to be low key and non-threatening. Admissions are always taken by members of senior staff who explain in the presence of the social worker the purpose of the child's admission to him and what he may expect to find in the new setting. Whenever possible, local authorities are asked to bring the child accompanied by a parent.

Perhaps this is what accounts for the placidity of the majority of the children on admission. It might also be thought that the majority have been through so many hoops that another change of environment does not have much of an impact on them, as perhaps it should. Enough of them, however, create enough tension at the time of arrival as to ensure that the admission process remains a central area of concern. It has its funny sides, like when a small boy threatens senior staff with a beating if they should dare keep him, and its grotesque aspects, as when a tiny boy of nine being admitted is so heavily drugged ('because he was so violent') that he has to be carried bodily in an accompanying housemother's arms.

TABLE 35: ADAPTATION TO HOUSE

	A		B		C	
	N	%	N	%	N	%
Settled quickly	28	45	24	39	14	23
Did not settle easily	12	19	15	24	15	24
Not mentioned	22	35	23	37	33	53

The extreme group appear more likely to settle quickly than ordinary boys. This may reflect the special effort made by the team to settle a child quickly. As will become clear later, the staff are particularly conscious of the threat and stress that a secure facility is likely to cause in children. The care taken over the original process of admission is, therefore, redoubled by the staff. This is an important element in preventing subsequent trouble. But it does not always work – there are still instances where the child becomes terrified, weepy or very aggressive and requires special efforts at settling.

The extreme groups exhibited many more unusual or eccentric mannerisms (21% of both boys and girls) than the group of ordinary boys (5%). These range from twitches and eructations to peculiar gaits. The present findings may provide a partial explanation of why the extreme children are regarded as 'mad', 'lunatic' and 'cracked' by the rest of the children they come across.

TABLE 36: LEVEL OF COMMUNICATION

| | A | | B | | C | |
	N	%	N	%	N	%
Talkative	22	35	24	39	16	26
Quiet/withdrawn	16	26	25	40	25	40
Mood swings	16	26	5	8	2	3
Not mentioned	8	13	8	13	19	31

Girls are significantly more prone to mood swings and are less likely to be quiet or withdrawn than the boys in either of the other two groups. This is the opposite of their reaction at the time of arrival. This confirms one of the major characteristics of girls which is by itself the cause of more staff and group tension than any other: these mood changes are frequently unrelated to any observable events. When manifested by one girl, the mood change sweeps through other girls like an epidemic and may result in a group outburst. Such group behaviour is hardly ever witnessed among boys, however disturbed the boys may be.

Even staff with considerable experience or those who have come to know a girl become almost visibly worried as they detect the emanations of a gathering black mood in a girl, followed by a storm of variable violence. The main reason for this worry is that they cannot explain why the moods should come and go so frequently with so little precipitation or warning. Analysis of individual cases has failed to indicate a pattern of reasons or circumstances for such outbursts. Most of the usual hypotheses – pre- or peri-menstrual tension, worry about something, etc. – have not been found to be particularly illuminating or relevant. The phenomenon of mood changes in girls, both singly and in groups, remains one of the more puzzling differences between severely disordered boys and girls.

TABLE 37: FRUSTRATION TOLERANCE

	A		B		C	
	N	%	N	%	N	%
Easily frustrated	26	42	20	32	19	31
Average tolerance	15	24	17	27	25	40
Very tolerant	21	34	25	40	18	29

More girls are easily frustrated than boys. Although the difference in numbers is not significant, the girls are markedly worse in the rate and frequency with which they become fed up with whatever is in hand. Again it is not clear whether this difference, like the previous one, is due to biological factors, result of conditioned impatience (through modelling on their mothers or otherwise), or a particular pattern of adaptation shaped by their experience.

TABLE 38: BEHAVIOUR WHEN FRUSTRATED

	A		B		C	
	N	%	N	%	N	%
Explosive/aggressive	30	48	17	27	14	23
Tearful	3	5	13	21	8	13
Good control	27	44	28	45	35	56
Not mentioned	2	3	4	6	5	8

The girls are much more explosive and aggressive when frustrated than the severely disturbed boys who are, surprisingly, more tearful than the others. About half the children remain reasonably in control of their tempers even when thwarted.

This is fortunate, because without it, the life of staff and other children would become even more stressful than it usually is. The finding gives substance to the conviction among practitioners that girls are much more violent and difficult to control when aroused than are boys. The girls' outbursts are often cataclysmic in their ferocity and have to be seen (and heard) to be believed. They follow no particular sequence but involve elements of shouting, hitting, swearing, crying, throwing things and running at high speed from one place to another.

The force of these explosions terrify the other children. It has even been known for big burly boys to scamper away and cower in corners until a smallish girl's temper has subsided. There is no way the other children can be shielded from the damaging psychological impact of such scenes which show why so many otherwise competent peole have come to an early breaking point with the girls. The only observable effect of these explosions on most of the girls themselves seems to be some slight weariness, when everyone else around them is drained of energy.

TABLE 39: EXPRESSED FANTASY LIFE

	A		B		C	
	N	%	N	%	N	%
Overt fantasies	9	15	19	31	4	6
Daydreams	5	8	0	0	0	0
Not noticeable	48	77	43	69	58	94

Seriously disordered boys are significantly more expressive of their fantasies than either of the other two groups. These fantasies range from heroic deeds in the past to stashed away riches of the present. It is not clear from this finding whether there is a genuine difference in levels of fantasy or these boys are less inhibited in expressing theirs. Other evidence could be adduced to support both hypotheses.

Only a small minority of any of the groups spontaneously express hopes and goals for the future. Most of them, even when asked, find it difficult to think of what they would like to (or is likely to) happen to them in the future. This may be for cognitive reasons or related to their perception of time. It appears more likely, however, that their whole socialisation history, the shattering of their former hopes and the inconstancy of the people they have dealt with, have led them to adopt a strictly here-and-now mode of adaptation which guards them against further disappointment.

TABLE 40: COUNTENANCE, GENERAL DEMEANOUR

	A		B		C	
	N	%	N	%	N	%
Smiles easily	21	34	24	39	13	21
Mixed	17	27	8	13	10	16
Sullen/surly	11	18	14	23	9	15
Not mentioned	13	21	16	26	30	48

The disordered children are the more easy smilers. They also contain the girls who have, as is by now to be expected, more of a mixed (or mixed-up) demeanour than the boys who are somewhat more surly.

All the children are admitted following some form of behaviour which has been deemed unacceptable. They know this and can, therefore, be expected to react to it. As the results show, however, most of the children are non-committal and largely indifferent to what they have done and its consequences. Perhaps they do not want to betray any personal reactions, but this is not wholly credible in view of the multitude of other feelings they freely express. A significant proportion of extreme children are quite boastful about their escapades and only a tiny minority of boys express any contrition. Perhaps more important than the children's reactions is the reaction of retributiveness which their indifference seems to provoke from official agencies (cf. Piliavin and Briar, 1964).

75

TABLE 41: ATTITUDE TO THEIR MISDEMEANOURS

	A		B		C	
	N	%	N	%	N	%
Boastful	10	16	10	16	7	11
Deliberately avoid mention	2	3	0	0	2	3
Contrite	0	0	1	2	4	6
Non-committal	50	81	51	82	49	79

Attitude and Behaviour to Peers

Much research has shown that for most young people, particularly those in institutions, peer groups are of much greater importance than the adults who apparently hold the key to their public welfare (Polsky, 1962; Buehler *et al*, 1966). In order to understand a child it helps, therefore, to know how he makes out in a group. This is particularly important in predicting his treatment needs in another (likely) group setting. Also, unless an oppositional relationship exists between the children and staff which would render any information from the former suspect, children are often remarkably astute judges of each other and a crucial source of insight towards a more perceptive assessment. What information is gained from peer groups is, therefore, given considerable prominence.

TABLE 42: GROUP DEPENDENCE

	A		B		C	
	N	%	N	%	N	%
Leader	15	24	6	10	19	31
Easily led	15	24	11	18	10	16
'Loner'	16	26	29	47	18	29
Well-integrated	16	26	16	26	15	24

In mixed groups, more girls impress as forceful members and assume a leadership role, usually of a subversive, plotting kind.

Other girls tend to follow them more frequently than do the boys who, in this context, mainly run errands for the girls. Almost half of the seriously disordered boys are insular and have great difficulty in integrating with the group. This appears to be due more to their oddity and social incompetence than to their wish to remain outside a particular group. It is almost always a boy and never a girl, however disturbed, who is the butt of the group.

Another important aspect of group dependence is that it indicates the degree to which group pressure can be used as a means of controlling its members' behaviour. A group-dependent child is much more likely to respond to group pressure than one who is not. In this context significantly more extreme boys are insular and 'untouchable' by the group than are girls or less difficult boys. This is yet another indication of the 'oddness' of these boys even in relation to their disordered peers.

TABLE 43: POPULARITY

	A		B		C	
	N	%	N	%	N	%
Liked	14	23	22	35	29	47
Disliked	16	26	15	24	8	13
Feared	11	18	0	0	3	5
Tolerated	21	33	25	40	22	35

More boys are popular with their peers than are girls. More of the extreme children are disliked by their peers than are ordinary boys. More girls are feared than boys. These differences are statistically significant. The behaviour of the girls, both generally and towards the other children, creates tension, anxiety and fear. They engage in more spiteful and manipulatory behaviour, setting up other children to do things – bully another child, attempt to abscond, do damage, etc. for which they will get into trouble. Although most other children are aware of the girls' tendencies, they seem unable to avoid the traps repeatedly laid for them. When victims get into trouble, they denounce the girls – sometimes with cataclysmic reactions, but go on being duped. This may be because the girls are more 'wily' or that their relatively smaller numbers amongst the boys makes them more influential. Whatever the reason, more of them are disliked, feared or at best tolerated than are boys in either of the other groups.

The stability and peacefulness of any group depends to a great extent on the ability of its members to pick up social cues about the prevailing atmosphere, dynamics of inter-relationships, and their own interaction with other group members. This is the more important in a group of severely disordered children who are unusually sensitive to stress and anxiety created by their own peers.

Both the tendency to create and to respond to stress are exacerbated by the secure and inescapable environment which throws the children together. Much of this stress is related to children's own goading and baiting of one another. The staff watch out for how far a youngster will go in hurting another, either physically or verbally, before they perceive the cues about the effect of their own actions and desist from further hurt. Obviously perception of social cues is distinct from ability or willingness of an individual to act on them. 'Psychopathic' individuals (among whom many of the seriously disordered youngsters have been traditionally classified) are thought to be deficient on both counts (Hare, 1970).

TABLE 44: ACCURACY OF SOCIAL PERCEPTION

	A		B		C	
	N	%	N	%	N	%
Good	21	34	25	40	27	44
Bad	19	31	16	26	12	19
Average	22	35	21	34	23	37

On these grounds, fewer girls are skilled in social perception than are boys. This may account in part for their greater vindictiveness, and their tendency to continue hurting even when their victim is obviously hurt.

Bringing together any diverse group creates conflict among them. With a group of disordered youngsters, each something of a star turn, kept under structured conditions, the opportunities for confrontation are legion and ever present. Because of this, there is a general expectation among the staff that the children will cut across each other. Therefore, most conflicts are regarded with mild interest by staff and not worthy of comment. Only serious and unusual conflicts are recorded. These range from lengthy or intense slanging matches, through devious manipulative acts aimed at hurting another child, to serious, open fights.

TABLE 45: CONFLICT WITH OTHERS

	A N	A %	B N	B %	C N	C %
Frequent	28	45	20	32	18	29
Rare	24	39	33	53	28	45
Not mentioned	10	16	9	15	16	26

On these criteria, girls engage in more frequent confrontation with others than do either group of boys. What is more, their confrontations are usually more intense and more frequent and quickly move on to a physical plane – from running away, shouting and banging doors to attacking the opponent or attempting self-injury. These latter forms of conflict are rare among boys in the open groups.

Whether such confrontations are due to the close physical proximity of the children, their inability or unwillingness to respect each other's private spaces, or the displacement of their anger and frustration about their personal state on to one another, is not very clear. It is probably reasonable to assume that all the above elements play a part, and that the children are likely to create conflict anywhere; but security, its inevitable result of increased face-to-face encounters and the threat to personal space, activate the potential of the youngsters for aggressive encounter and thus heighten the frequency and intensity of their conflicts.

Most people, lay and professional alike, seem to think that the major difficulty with having mixed groups is the possibility of unacceptable sexual behaviour among the youngsters. The fact that most of the girls have come to the notice of social agencies primarily for sexual promiscuity (Cowie et al, 1968; Priestley et al, 1977), encourages this view. Such a view, however, assumes that the girls are wholly indiscriminate and have no control either over their sexual urges or whom they choose for a partner.

While there are undoubtedly some indiscriminate girls (and boys), most opt for older boys or men (Marchant and Smith, 1977). This is one reason why unacceptable sexual behaviour has not proved problematic in the management of such children. The girls are somewhat older, physically more mature, and rather more experienced than most of the boys who are, in this respect, mainly novices. Most of the girls treat the boys with some contempt, though that is not to say that they would not take the opportunity were it to present itself. Opportunity is indeed a major determinant of sexual (or for that matter any other) behaviour. The high level of supervision does not allow the children much chance of engaging in such behaviour. The programme, including shower times, sitting around in night clothes, etc. is so arranged as to minimise the possibility of untoward events.

But expressions of sexuality are also accepted as a normal part of adolescence and, therefore, regarded with a benevolent attitude which keeps all overt and covert sexual expressions within acceptable bounds, as is shown by the following table. Most of both extreme boys and girls behave with what are regarded as normal limits. More girls initiate exaggerated or 'heavy' acts such as placing of hand on thighs, tight embraces, etc. than do the boys. In this study only two boys engaged in

TABLE 46: EXPRESSED SEXUAL INTEREST

	A		B		C	
	N	%	N	%	N	%
Obsessive/bizarre	0	0	2	3	0	0
Exaggerated	8	13	4	6	1	2
Normal	40	65	32	52	14	23
Not mentioned	14	23	24	39	47	76

'bizarre' acts such as swooning to get attention and exposing themselves to girls. Both were profoundly disturbed in other respects. This has been generally found with other children who do not observe the group norms for sexual behaviour. They show other signs of attenuated contact with reality, particularly and as expected, those who have committed gruesome sexual offences, for example the boy who sexually assaulted young boys and then attempted to sever their testicles with a broken milk bottle.

In general, therefore, the mixed nature of the group does not appear to give rise to any important problems of sexual misbehaviour. The fact that the staff regard some sexual curiosity and expression as normal, and that half of the staff are females and the opportunities for 'heavy' acts are curtailed, help to establish and maintain manageable group norms.

All human beings engage in manipulating their environment in order to bring about desired ends. As much of the 'desired ends' are controlled by other human beings, from an early age children learn to 'play' others to achieve their own ends. Such behaviour is regarded as so normal that the term 'manipulation' is in fact not used to describe it. The term itself has a hazy definition deriving from the action of a puppet master who 'manipulates' the strings to get his puppets to do what he wishes them to do.

In the present context and in clinical practice, the term is used to describe the actions of those people who unashamedly use others to their own ends, with little regard for the cost to those so manipulated. The term has pejorative overtones but is here used to describe rather than judge the children's actions.

In a secure setting, children's access to naturally (to them) rewarding experiences is curtailed. The rewards provided by the staff and the other children may be either inappropriate or inadequate, thus encouraging manipulatory behaviour to achieve other rewarding experiences. In this sort of setting, such experiences include the acquisition of extra cigarettes (forbidden to those under fifteen and restricted to four for those above), getting a home visit (difficult to arrange for most of these children), or getting parents to visit (most will not).

However, besides these, at least as much of the manipulatory behaviour of the children is aimed at getting one of their own number into trouble either with other children or with the staff. Many of the fights that occur as well as attempted or successful abscondings and other disruptive acts are usually set up by a girl who then sits on the sidelines and watches the show. This is dramatically borne out by the table below.

TABLE 47: MANIPULATION OF PEERS

	A		B		C	
	N	%	N	%	N	%
Considerable	12	19	7	11	0	0
Little	5	8	0	0	0	0
None	15	24	5	8	2	3
Not mentioned	30	48	50	81	60	97

Significantly more girls engage in extensive manipulation than do boys of other groups. Indeed, such behaviour is almost wholly unobserved in the control group.

The reason for these differences is not clear. It may be argued that under conditions of security a state of relative 'sensory deprivation' occurs in which the children can only relieve the deficit by manipulatory acts (see also Chapter 9). A child in an open setting has freedom of movement and can gain his goals rather more easily. Additionally, the greater contact of the children and staff in security with each other increases the opportunity for manipulation and makes observing it easier.

Alternatively, it may be suggested that the difference between the groups arises from the greater tendency of the severely disordered groups to exploit other people's weakness to their own ends without compunction. In the case of the girls, particularly, such behaviour is known to have been an important element in evoking the negative reactions of those who have had to deal with them. The girls are particularly good at using a wide array of ploys from tears and temper tantrums to self-destructive gestures and appealing to emotions from fear to pity, to achieve their ends.

The staff have to be on constant watch for such acts in order to prevent untoward events and protect other children who may be duped and used as 'fall guys'. At the same time, they knowingly allow a certain amount of less harmful manipulation to make life more tolerable for the youngsters concerned. They also use the opportunity for establishing greater contact and letting the children know that they are aware of their actions. But the children show difficulty in learning and continue in their acts, even when they result in the serious distress of other children. Why such distress should be rewarding is yet to be adequately accounted for but yet again points to the predatory nature of much of the behaviour of these youngsters.

Behaviour with Staff

In a secure facility, the staff are the fulcrum around which everything rotates for the children. They are first and foremost the sources of authority, i.e. those who open or bar the way to the children's achievement of their desires, from being taken out, to cigarettes, from arranging home visits, to being allowed to watch television late in the evening. They are also seen as the major source of care and protection against the depredations of other children. For most of the youngsters, this is their first experience of intensive, *inescapable* interaction with a group of adults to whom they generalise their feelings about other adults, including their own parents. For these reasons, the staff experience the full gamut of the children's emotional reactions.

Equally importantly, however, the children arouse in the staff a wide range of feelings and action potentials. Although the staff are generally able to separate out their private feelings from their professional task, they nevertheless react differently to different children. It is finally this interaction of staff and children which decides not only the quality of their lives within the secure setting but also the general atmosphere which affects the children's behaviour and, thus, the assessment that is made of their problems. In this context, the comments derive from the consensus of staff observations rather than individual feelings towards the child.

TABLE 48: ATTITUDE TO STAFF

	A		B		C	
	N	%	N	%	N	%
Resentful/suspicious	21	34	11	18	15	24
Normal child/adult	20	32	20	32	37	60
Attention seeking	21	34	31	50	10	16

As already indicated, children's attitudes to staff are largely predetermined by their past experiences with authority figures and other adults such as parents. These attitudes may or may not be modified as a result of their new experiences. On this basis the girls are even more resentful and suspicious of staff than either of the two boy groups. This is not helped by their greater tendency to misbehave which evokes staff sanction and in turn increases their resentment.

The extreme children are more attention seeking than the control group. Within the extreme group, significantly more boys are attention seeking than girls. The concept of 'attention seeking' is as widely used as it is ill defined. In this context it refers to behaviour which appears to be aimed at gaining

attention from staff and other children, not as a means to something else, but as an end in itself. The test is whether the
behaviour stops after appropriate attention has been given to
the child. Such behaviour ranges over a full repertory from
self-destructive gestures through standing close to a member of
staff and joking to shouting, swearing and threatening. Boys
and girls use widely differing gambits. Presumably this behaviour has been shaped by past experience, though children
also mimic the behaviour of others whom they see as gaining
attention.

Such modelling (Bandura, 1969) is prevalent and makes the
management task of staff in controlling attention seeking
behaviour more urgent and difficult. The reason is that if such
behaviour is not curbed it creates disruption and self-reinforce-
ment. On the other hand, an assessment setting should enable
the child the full manifestation of his behaviour so as to allow a
comprehensive picture to emerge. The dilemma is a difficult
one to resolve and can be seen more prominently in the next
section in children's response to management.

An assessment setting, despite the long stay of some children,
is too transient a situation for many deep relationships to be
formed. At the same time, however, its unfamiliarity presents
the children with the kind of anxiety which may impel them
to want to relate to a caring adult and the interaction is intense
and frequent enough to encourage it.

TABLE 49: RELATIONSHIPS FORMED

	A		B		C	
	N	%	N	%	N	%
Many	7	11	4	6	5	8
Few	17	27	10	16	20	32
None	21	34	16	26	16	26
Not mentioned	17	27	32	52	21	34

The results indicate that about one third of the girls and
rather fewer of the boys failed to make any relationships with

staff. Bearing in mind the deliberate diversity and presenting styles of the adults, it seems likely that these children are either deficient in ability to relate or are so suspicious and hurt that they will not allow their guards to drop because they would then become subject to the normal give and take of an emotional relationship which may leave them open to further hurt

TABLE 50: MANIPULATION OF ADULTS

	A		B		C	
	N	%	N	%	N	%
Considerable	18	29	10	16	6	10
Little	11	18	10	16	16	26
None	10	16	13	21	16	26
Not mentioned	23	37	29	47	24	39

The girls are significantly more manipulatory with members of staff than the boys in either of the other two groups. This difference is consistent with the previous one relating to the manipulation of peers, though the pattern is somewhat different for ordinary boys.

As human beings, the staff also experience a full range of emotions towards the children, however much they control these in what they do with the children. These feelings are presumably based on the children's behaviour towards them and the ease with which relationships can be formed between them.

TABLE 51: POPULARITY

	A		B		C	
	N	%	N	%	N	%
Liked	20	32	23	37	26	42
Tolerated	12	19	9	15	3	5
Disliked	2	3	8	13	5	8
Not mentioned	28	45	22	35	28	45

Surprisingly though, this does not appear to be the case. Despite the greater difficulty of the girls in making relationships with adults and tendency to engage in manipulatory behaviour, they are no less popular with staff than are their peers. Also, analysis of individual cases shows that there is no relationship between the severity of management problems presented by a child and their popularity with staff. A child can be very difficult but equally likeable. This point illustrates an important fact about severely disordered children – one which is as obvious as it is frequently forgotten. The fact is that youngsters, however disordered, are not wholly negative quantities; nor are they seriously disordered *all* the time. The peaceful interludes are not so rare and the stormy ones not always so devastating as to prevent a positive response to them as fellow human beings.

Management

The three previous sets of questions dealing with general aspects, attitudes and behaviour to peers and to staff contribute to building up a picture of the child. The present section does that but also, crucially, it gives information on the child's explicit response to various elements and techniques of management.

Management is, in this context, a broad though specific concept. It refers to attempts by the staff to foster and enforce what they see as the appropriate norms of behaviour in the group. It contains elements of curbing and controlling undesirable behaviour as well as enhancing that which is beneficial to the individual and the group.

Thus, every child and group has to be managed, particularly in settings for severely disturbed children, where otherwise predatory behaviour will prevail and the weaker will suffer. The responses of youngsters to management techniques are good guides to the pattern of disordered behaviour which has brought them into severe conflict with authority figures in the past and has resulted in their final referral. Their reactions to new attempts at management are against this background but provide crucial new guidelines regarding the types of approach which are likely to work best with them. These form a reasonable basis for the formulation of new management programmes.

In this setting, all attempts at management arise from and take place in a structured environment. 'Structured environment' denotes a setting in which boundaries of acceptable behaviour are clearly marked and enforced. The need for such a setting to ensure civilised group living is as great as it is difficult to fulfil. The children who have run amok through many previous facilities and who most need it are those who have the greatest difficulty in coping with it. This is borne out by the following table.

TABLE 52: RESPONSE TO STRUCTURED ENVIRONMENT

	A		B		C	
	N	%	N	%	N	%
Accepting	32	52	38	61	36	58
Rejecting	22	35	17	27	15	24
Variable	8	13	7	11	11	18

The girls have the greatest trouble in coming to terms with clear boundaries, though substantial minorities of the other groups continue to reject the demands of a well regulated setting. There are no immediately apparent personal characteristics differentiating the children who have the greatest difficulty in coping with the environment. Fortunately, over half the population seem in fact to welcome the clearly defined boundaries and adapt to it quickly and painlessly. This has two important implications: (1) At least half the population of even the most disordered children respond well to a structured environment which reduces the ambiguity of expectations from them and almost for the first time can enforce the boundaries it sets. Their behaviour problems, therefore, seem to reflect directly on the environments in which the disorders have been most prominent. (2) The adequate adaptation of most children to the environment does not denote any important change in their level of disorder. It simply indicates that the reception of the child into the facility has been gentle and the enforcement of boundaries appropriate enough to make it acceptable. There is, in this context, no disordered response simply because there is no trigger for it. The potential for extreme behaviour remains dormant, to be activated when the situation deteriorates.

This is a necessary corrective to those who, when faced with the amenable behaviour of youngsters in security, feel that the children have 'improved' or 'learnt a lesson', etc. It may account for the fact that when the children come out of security, their behaviour is often no better than when they first went into it, unless special measures have been taken to enable them to internalise the environmental control. Security by itself does little other than put the problem behaviour in limbo.

In work with these children considerable emphasis is laid on group work both as an aid to enhancing individual sensitivity and as an instrument of managing group and individual behaviour. To this latter end, the dynamics of the group are varied by staff to translate staff expectations into group norms. These norms then become the subject of group discussion and the spearhead of group feedback and pressure on individual children to behave in an acceptable manner.

This mode of operation is important in both management and assessment for two reasons. (1) The youngsters are much readier to dismiss staff injunctions and correctives as coming from adults – the 'them' who 'are always on at you' – than they are to reject peer pressure towards behaviour which they might not find readily acceptable; (2) a child's response to peer group pressure is an accurate indication of the degree to which he is susceptible to controlling his behaviour through strictly social cues and constraints which he understands. A child's peers are a large element of his life space, particularly in a secure setting, and his responsiveness to them is a central pointer to his construction of 'reality'.

TABLE 53: USE OF PEER GROUP PRESSURE

	A		B		C	
	N	%	N	%	N	%
Very effective	8	13	2	3	2	3
Effective	15	24	9	15	17	27
Non–effective	18	29	28	45	23	37
Not mentioned	21	34	23	37	20	32

The table shows that girls are significantly more susceptible to group pressure than are boys of either group, particularly the severely disordered ones. This is an important confirmation of the slowly emerging picture of the severely disordered boys as being distinctly more odd, even though less difficult to manage by other methods.

Much of the interaction of the staff with the children is through verbal interchanges. Much of this interchange is conversational, about generalities or particular topics of interest to individual children. A good deal of it, however, is taken up with requests of children and staff of one another. Staff requests range from 'Good morning Tina, time to get up now' through 'Your room isn't clean Dave, will you sort it out please' to 'Naomi, your shouting is upsetting the others, either quieten down and talk properly or go to your room'.

TABLE 54: GENERAL ATTITUDE TO REQUESTS

	A		B		C	
	N	%	N	%	N	%
Compliant	24	39	43	69	37	60
Token defiance	22	35	15	24	22	35
Seriously defiant	16	26	4	6	3	5

It can be seen that the girls are much more frequently and seriously defiant of requests than are the boys in either of the other groups. Furthermore, their defiance is associated with seriously aggressive and abusive behaviour. Analysis of individual cases does not suggest any particular type of request, manner, time or person by whom it is made to be specially associated with such outbursts. These episodes can quickly deteriorate into confrontations. They require the most tactful and skilled handling if they are not to escalate to explosive showdowns.

This is another aspect of the wearying and threatening impact of the girls on staff. Almost every small, normal encounter is the potential trigger to a massive explosion. Despite enormous counsel, expectation of the problem, and knowing that it can erupt at any time, the staff feel inevitably guilty and somewhat ashamed for having precipitated it. In these situations it is easy to see why the girls have been labelled as extreme and 'beyond control' by so many otherwise competent agencies.

It is gratifying (and, almost literally, a saving grace) that at least a large minority of the girls, and the majority of the boys, particularly the seriously disordered, are reasonably compliant. This confirms the earlier points that severe disorders of the boys do not often manifest themselves in explosive, acting out behaviour in a structured setting. On the contrary, if anything, the more disordered among them rarely present important handling problems.

In keeping with what is known about control of human behaviour and as established in settings concerned with disordered children (Hoghughi et al, 1977), the staff frequently use material and social rewards for 'good' behaviour rather than sanctions for misbehaviour.

TABLE 55: RESPONSE TO PRAISE AND ENCOURAGEMENT

	A		B		C	
	N	%	N	%	N	%
Positive	24	39	22	35	23	37
Nil	9	15	5	8	7	11
Not mentioned	29	47	35	56	32	52

The results do not show any important differences among the groups. There is no theoretical reason why they should differ. The largest group comprises those children whose response is 'average' and, therefore not particularly worthy of note. In view of this, the 'distribution' curve appears to be tilted towards those who respond well to encouragement. This suggests that, other things being equal, encouragement as a handling instrument is likely to find a ready and positive response in a significant number of even the most severely disordered children.

Shaping and maintaining behaviour through reward and encouragement is, however, a lengthy and tedious business. Some behaviours are so critical or disruptive that they must be curbed quickly and efficiently. In such cases, punishment or its euphemistic equivalents such as 'negative reinforcement' or 'sanction' are more effective (Bandura & Walters, 1963). In the present context, such critical behaviours range from refusing to carry out routine requests, through disruptive behaviour such as repeated banging on the table, to attacks on other children. The sanctions are less defined. The children know that they may not be hit or caned. They may be deprived of their cigarettes, put to bed early, miss out on an outing, kept in the house for their meal, stopped from watching television or, at the worst, placed in the separation room. In an environment which restricts the child's access to self-selected reinforcements, these are powerful enough sanctions and the need has not been felt for anything stronger.

TABLE 56: EFFECT OF THREAT OF SANCTION

	A		B		C	
	N	%	N	%	N	%
Challenging	14	23	4	6	3	5
Accepting	23	37	16	26	25	40
Sanction not necessary	25	40	42	68	34	55

The girls are significantly more challenging in response to the threat of a sanction than the boys in either of the other two groups. Within the boys' groups the extreme boys are less likely to invoke threat of sanction than the less difficult boys.

As with the previous items, this aspect of the girls' behaviour emphasises the difficulty of managing seriously disordered girls in a reasonably civilised and dignified manner. They do not only defy requests, voiced in suitably gentle terms, aimed at ensuring their own welfare and that of others, but also challenge the staff to enforce any threatened sanctions. This challenge is usually delivered in public, with a loud voice, suitably larded with swear words.

This presents the staff with a choice between the 'devil and the deep blue sea' – the continuation of deleterious behaviour on the one hand and a cataclysmic confrontation on the other. Such 'avoidance – avoidance' conflicts are not easy to resolve, as opting for either alternative carries a heavy price tag. Equally certainly, the conflict demands resolution. Such resolutions not only bring staff skills into sharp relief, but also provide a test of the professional support and confidence that the staff enjoy within the organisation.

A staff who enjoy adequate support and professional guidance is less likely to be threatened by such episodes, thus opting for precipitate and less cool headed approach than may be warranted. They are also likely to use more force (not necessarily physical) than may be strictly necessary to achieve the desired end, because they are fearful of a repetition. In such situations, it is the collective strength and expertise of the staff which is the surest way to an early resolution of the conflict. Children sense that they cannot get away with the defiance, perceive the determination of the staff and sooner, rather than later, become amenable to control.

Types of Children

For purpose of description and assessment, particularly one

93

that is analytical, it is necessary to look at individual characteristics of children and aspects of the dynamics of their interaction with others. Already it will have been seen that analysis of individual characteristics yields a more complex and craggy picture of the children than would have been the case had they been simply described as 'severely disordered', 'extreme' or whatever else. Indeed, these labels are at best shorthand descriptions of children's characteristics which need to be enumerated before they can form a basis for action.

Having obtained a comparative description of individual characteristics of the social behaviour of the severely disordered children, it was felt to be worthwhile to find out whether these characteristics form any configuration, i.e. go together in a way which would make it possible to describe 'types' of children.

There are numerous 'typologies' of delinquent and disordered children using a variety of statistical techniques and usually tied to some sort of theoretical orientation. They are more complex and pose more methodological difficulties than even their authors seem to realise (Clarke & Sinclair, 1974).

For the purpose of this study, a simple cluster analysis was carried out to see if any particular types of boys and girls presenting management problems emerged. The study concentrated on the severely disordered groups. To this end, nine characteristics associated with management difficulties were abstracted from the foregoing 'observation' section of the assessment report. A visual patterning of the characteristics was then carried out. Those features of children associated with easy management (that is relative to the extremes) were similarly singled out as were those of two remaining groups – one withdrawn and the other without any distinctive characteristics. In order to avoid giving impressions of undue rigour, significance levels of variations in groupings have not been presented.

The types are as follows:

TABLE 57: TYPES

		Girls N	Girls %	Boys N	Boys %
A	Very difficult to manage	10	16	1	2
B	Difficult to manage	10	16	1	2
C	Very easy to manage	14	23	16	26
D	Easy to manage	9	14	12	19
E	Withdrawn, 'in shell'	9	14	15	24
F	Others	10	16	17	27

The results above underline the general picture so far that significantly more girls present extreme management problems than even their severely disordered male peers. Fewer are consequently easy to manage. More boys, on the other hand, seem odd, peculiar, in a world of their own and noticeably out of touch with what is going on around them. It will be apparent to the statistically astute that the above would describe a peculiar distribution curve.

The characteristics associated with each of these groups are described in the following pages. The results for boys and girls are presented separately to enable a consistent comparison of each 'type' with the population or sample from which it is drawn. Although the characteristics associated with the difficult to manage are the same, the intensity with which each problem is presented is obviously different both within and between the groups. The comments presented in the preceding sections of this chapter indicate where the differences lie.

Girls

GROUP A

The following characteristics are considered to constitute a 'very difficult management problem':

  (i) Resentment towards staff (5) other 5 *all* attention seeking
  (ii) Defiance of requests*
  (iii) Challenge to sanctions imposed*

(iv) Frequent conflict with peers*
(v) Sullenness (9)
(vi) Low tolerance of frustration*
(vii) Explosive reaction to frustration*
(viii) Exhibiting intense mood swings (6)
(ix) Not affected by peer group pressure*
* denotes characteristics shared by *all*

The ten girls in Group A were all considered to possess at least eight of these characteristics at an intense level. They were, therefore, regarded as 'very difficult' to manage.

As well as these characteristics, group members had other attributes in common:

None were liked by their peers
Only two were accepting of the restricted environment and routines
Only two were not manipulative with staff
Only one was liked by staff
Seven were withdrawn or suspicious on arrival
Three exhibited odd mannerisms
Only two exhibited any overt fantasy life
None were considered well integrated in the peer group;
Five were domineering and the other five loners and isolated.

GROUP B

The ten girls in Group B were all considered to possess six or seven of the characteristics considered to constitute a 'difficult management problem'.

(i) 4; (ii) 7; (iii) 5; (iv) 6; (v) 7; (vi) 9; (viii) 6; (ix) 7.
Group members shared other attributes:
All settled easily and all responded well to praise, etc.
Only one was liked by peers
Only one was liked by staff
Two exhibited odd mannerisms
Two exhibited overt fantasy life
None were considered well integrated in peer group; five were domineering and five were easily led
Seven were manipulative with staff
Six were withdrawn or suspicious on admission

Quotes from 'Observation' Sections of Assessment Reports

Groups A and B 'Very difficult' and 'Difficult'

. . . her irritability was usually manifested in violent explosions.

Several times has had to be physically removed from the group.

Each time she has been extremely abusive and thrown objects about the room.

Likes to dominate a group . . . she can be bossy, a bully and a few of the smaller children are frightened of her.

Group pressure has not affected her behaviour . . . 'I don't care what anyone says, I'll do what I want'.

Management has had to be on an hour by hour basis and has ranged from physical restraint to nursing, as one would an infant.

Throughout her stay has seemed to be a girl of extremes; quiet, friendly, grossly affectionate or violent, rowdy and aggressive.

Much of her conversation is shouted and loaded with threats, boasts and obscenities.

Is a bully . . . and has used violence to establish and maintain ascendancy.

Appears to see adults as authority figures to be challenged whenever possible.

Female members of staff have expressed discomfort and anxiety when left alone with her.

When refused demands, shouted abuse, threw things, slammed doors and cried.

Bites her finger nails and has drawn blood on all ten, she exhibits an eye twitch, sucks her thumb almost permanently and when sitting in a chair she adopts a fœtal position; when drawn out she becomes violent.

Has tested the limits of acceptable behaviour and has pushed the situation to the point of confrontation many times.

She attacked him and he withdrew with bruised ribs and a marked face.

One disturbing feature of her behaviour has been the facility with which she has taken objects such as scissors to be used later.

In the dining hall she has surreptitiously punched boys from other houses . . . has deliberately thrown hot tea over other children.

Has been unpredictable between seeking for attention and affection and proceeding to violence and abuse.

Has exhibited a consistently positive response only to dominant and self-assured men. She regards everyone else as fair game for her threats and aggression.

GROUP C

The following characteristics are considered to constitute the group who present 'no management problems'.

- (i) Communicative 9
- (ii) Able to tolerate frustration well*
- (iii) Have good control over behaviour 13 (1 tearful)
- (iv) Well integrated in peer group 10
- (v) Pleasant general demeanour 13
- (vi) Never or rarely in conflict with peers 13
- (vii) Normal child/adult relationship with staff 13
- (viii) Compliant towards requests 13
- (ix) Does not require sanctions*
- (x) Accepting of restricted environment and routines*

* denotes characteristics attributed to *all*

The fourteen girls in Group C were considered to possess at least nine of these characteristics.

As well as these characteristics the group had other attributes in common:

Thirteen were liked by their peers
Thirteen were liked by staff
Ten were cheerful and/or co-operative on admission
Only one was considered manipulative with peers
Only one was considered manipulative with staff
All responded well to praise and encouragement
None exhibited odd mannerisms
Three were considered to be affected by peer group pressure.

GROUP D

The nine girls in Group D were all considered to possess between six and eight of the characteristics considered to constitute 'no management problem'.

(i) 7; (ii) 8; (iii) 7 (other two tearful); (iv) 1; (v) 7; (vi) 7; (vii) 4 (other five 'attention seeking'); (viii) 7; (ix) 5 (other 4 accepting of sanctions); (x)* (all nine).

As well as these characteristics the group had other factors in common:

None were considered manipulative with staff
Only one was considered manipulative with peers
Eight were liked by staff, but only
Three were liked by peers
All responded well to praise and encouragement.

Groups C and D 'Easy to manage' and 'No problem'
Her behaviour has indicated she is a tolerant child.
Has been consistently friendly, helpful and co-operative.
Has seemed an emotionally open and accessible child.
Gave the impression of a totally uninhibited tomboyish creature who took delight in things natural.
She has impressed adults as an obedient, happy girl who is, however, subject to swift mood changes.
Seems to be accepted by all the children, she has rarely been in conflict with the others.
All the staff have reported her friendliness and compliance as her prominent quality.
Her ordinariness and lack of affectation have made her presence a pleasure.

Group E

The nine girls in Group E were all considered to possess at least four of the characteristics listed overleaf. They appeared to be 'enclosed in a shell' and difficult to 'get through to'.

   (i) Withdrawn or suspicious*
  (ii) Generally sullen   (6)
 (iii) Loners   (6) other three easily led
  (iv) Not popular with peers*
   (v) Resentful or suspicious towards staff (4); other five attention seeking
  (vi) Uncommunicative*
                    * shared by all

As well as these characteristics the group had other characteristics in common:

Only three ever in conflict with peers
Only one liked by staff – others 'tolerated'

None were defiant

None challenged sanctions imposed

Four exhibited overt fantasy life (greater proportion than in any other group)

Eight were apathetic to restricted environment and routines.

GROUP E

Is, on the whole, a sad child who is uncommunicative.

Relationships have been superficial and throughout she has been suspicious of adult intentions.

Quickly expressed her sullen discontent with a down turned mouth.

Has no particular friends, relationships being mostly superficial and expedient.

Has expressed a dislike of all staff and appears to see all staff as dispensers of either punishment or privileges.

Reluctant to discuss herself or her family.

For the most part, has appeared to be a sad, resentful girl who seems to lie compulsively.

Is a moody girl who reveals profound unhappiness . . . prone to long periods of withdrawal.

Has revealed little interest in what has been going on around her.

She seemed ill at ease in the presence of adults.

GROUP F

There were no characteristics which united this group, and none of them fitted any of the previous five groups.

Boys

Only one boy fitted Group A and one boy fitted Group B as defined for girls.

GROUP C *'Very easy to manage'*

All 16 boys were considered to have at least nine of the characteristics listed previously.

(i) Communicative 9

(ii) Able to tolerate frustration*

(iii) Good control over behaviour*

(iv) Well integrated in peer group   12

(v) Pleasant general demeanour*

(vi) Never or rarely in conflict with peers   15

(vii) Normal relationships with staff*

(viii) Compliant towards requests   12

(ix) Does not require sanctions   10

(x) Accepting of restricted environment and routines   14

As well as these characteristics the group shared other attributes:

All were liked by peers and staff

Only two were considered manipulative with peers

Only two were considered manipulative with staff

Eleven were not affected by group pressure

Eleven were cheerful and/or co-operative on admission

Only two exhibited odd mannerisms

GROUP D

All 12 boys were considered to possess six to eight of the characteristics previously listed.

(i) Communicative   6

(ii) Able to tolerate frustration   11

(iii) Good control over behaviour   10

(iv) Well integrated in peer group   3

(v) Pleasant general demeanour   6

(vi) Never or rarely in conflict with peers   11

(vii) Normal relationships with staff   6 (five attention seeking)

(viii) Compliant towards requests*

(ix) Does not require sanctions   10

(x) Accepting of restricted environment and routines   10

As well as these characteristics the group had other factors in common:

None disliked by staff

None disliked by peers (not all popular though)

All responded to praise, etc.

GROUPS C AND D 'Easy' and 'Very easy to manage'

He is a mild mannered, clean and tidy young man who has not allowed himself to become frustrated even under times of extreme provocation by the girls.

Adjusted well to his peers and was soon established as the most mature member of the group.

Every member of staff likes him, however there are some who feel his behaviour is too good and that he is conforming to get a good report (this comment is very common in boys' reports).

Has seemed to be a placid, even tempered boy who is rarely sulky, worried or hostile towards staff . . .

Has no apparent difficulty in relating to adults and communicates readily, his approaches being for the most part 'appropriate' and fairly mature.

Was extremely generous . . . shared his sweets, etc.

Was invariably cheerful and active whether in company of adults or peers.

Is a sturdy, self possessed and good humoured lad . . . general demeanour is relaxed and self assured.

GROUP E

There were fifteen boys in this group.

    (i) Withdrawn or suspicious 10
   (ii) Generally sullen 11
  (iii) Loner 12 (three easily led)
  (iv) Not popular with peers 14
   (v) Resentful or suspicious towards staff 9 (four easily led)
  (vi) Uncommunicative 10

Other common attributes were:

Only four were liked by staff.
Eleven were compliant.
None challenged sanctions.
Only four were affected by peer group pressure.
Eight exhibited odd mannerisms
Six exhibited overt fantasy life

GROUP E

During the first few days, burst into tears about every half hour for no apparent reason.

He exhibits an almost permanent frown and walks with a hunched slouch. . . .

He sees himself as a failure, even when rewarded or praised he seemed sometimes to misinterpret the praise and burst into tears.

Has rarely been happy and generally does not even enjoy anything.

Does not seem to be one of the group at any time; seems to be in a world of his own.

Has never initiated contact with adults . . . even a chance meeting in a corridor sent him scurrying for the relative security of the lounge.

Adults feel that even after a prolonged period of assessment this boy remains an unknown quantity. Behaves like an automaton, complies without emotion.

Has a high pitched voice and sits for hours sucking his thumb, while playing with his right ear with his left hand.

Quickly becomes angry and tearful when faced with frustration.

Does not trust adults, he remained distant, said little and answered questions in monosyllables.

Generally impresses as ill at ease and close to tears.

For the most part appears to be in a world of his own; he sits glumly staring into open space, apparently unaware of what goes on around him . . . when upset or frustrated sits and cries, complaining that no one wants him.

GROUP F

No common features were apparent.

As the preceding pages show, there are quite dramatic differences between boys and girls in general and, within each group, in terms of their social behaviour and amenability to management. The observations from which these differences are derived are made by a staff team whose job it is to deal with very difficult children. They are not easily impressed by misbehaviour and regard much more of it as normal than do even their colleagues elsewhere in the same establishment.

Four general conclusions may be drawn from the preceding observations:

* Intensity of disorder is not always associated with management problems. Some children who are known to suffer from pathological states are not in any way difficult to handle.

* Severity of handling problems is not a general, all pervasive feature of personality which swamps all else. Even the most violent and difficult to handle children have areas of sanity and normality which enables decent human contact to be made with them.

* Difficulty to manage does not appear to be positively related to adverse personal feelings by staff. Some of the most disordered and threatening children have been those most liked and succoured by staff.

* Conformity to structured environment and compliance with demands do not denote a reduction in the problems of the children.

More specifically, the girls emerge as by far the more complex and extreme, arousing extremes of affection and threat in both staff and other children. They come in disordered and largely remain so until their assessment has been completed and they depart for a treatment setting. They do not respond much to the stability of the environment and gentle caring of the staff and are not impressed either by security or the ability of the staff to handle their outbursts. Although some achieve moderate control over their outbursts, others continue unchanged. Perhaps this is because the period of stabilisation is too short in relation to the depth of their troubles, or perhaps they are generally less amenable to intervention. Numerous other questions could be posed which would, regrettably, remain unanswered, simply because they have never been looked at rigorously enough in a management setting. This is understandable; girls present such problems of handling that most people have only enough energy to go on surviving their day to day job.

Most of the boys, by comparison, pale into insignificance – that is, as far as their management problems are concerned. Throughout they remain the more conforming and compliant group. Many are said by the staff to be presenting an amenable picture in order 'to get a good report'. And yet, they contain by far the largest group who have committed grave crimes (such as murder, arson, rape, etc.) and are those who are known to be suffering from a variety of pathological states. These boys, without being divorced from life around them, seem to operate with several alternative realities, which are not touched by their group experiences and the close interaction with a varied group of concerned adults. They simply slot into whatever life style is prevalent and yet remain fundamentally untouched by it. This should warn against interpreting their conformity as improvement.

Even setting aside their backgrounds, the social behaviour of these youngsters indicates the need for a sophisticated approach to their treatment which takes account of the complexity and intensity of their problems. Such a response would be different from anything so far attempted, which has been either a vehicle for some abstruse theorising or based on primitive, simplistic notions of the treatment needs of youngsters who have reached the end of the line.

CHAPTER 5

Problems and Needs
of Disordered Children

So far, a picture has emerged of the extreme children's backgrounds, development and aspects of social behaviour. In the context of rigorous assessment, the information provides (or should provide) a basis for rational decision making as to what should be done with the child. The child has come to the notice of the social services department because of certain critical behaviours which then become the focus of intervention.

As will be argued in Chapter 8, this focus of intervention can only be, at least initially, on the child's 'problems' – the unacceptable aspects of a child's total functioning which require intervention. This orientation has been systematically explored and has resulted in what is now an established part of the assessment report. The report writer presents comprehensive information on the child's family and social background, the previous forms of intervention, the child's views of what has been done to/with him, as well as the complete section on the observation of the child's social behaviour. Specialists complete the mosaic picture with their reports.

The information having been provided in the detail required, it is then updated and evaluated with a view to delineating the child's main problems in a predetermined order encompassing physical; intellectual and educational; family; social relationships; social behaviour; and personal. The statements within each problem area are factual, though inevitably they also entail a judgment – the judgment that given the total complex of a child's problems and the logical impossibility of enumerating all of them, some warrant mentioning more than others. This approach will be elaborated in Chapter 8.

It is important to bear in mind when looking at the following results that they only relate the *more* severe and noteworthy of a child's problems. Also, all the problems are about the child's *current* condition. Past events such as accidents, parent's death, etc. are mentioned insofar as they are thought to have a continuing effect on the child. A total of problems in each area is presented as a rough measure of the prevalence of that problem in each group.

TABLE 58: PHYSICAL PROBLEMS

	A		B		C	
	N	%	N	%	N	%
None	17	27	10	16	23	37
Eyesight	14	23	13	21	9	15
Hearing	5	8	5	8	5	8
Speech impediment	0	0	6	10	2	3
Teeth	2	3	8	13	3	5
Overweight	12	19	1	2	0	0
Physically immature	5	8	6	10	5	8
Poor physical condition	2	3	0	0	0	0
Skin disease	7	11	6	10	2	3
Poor co-ordination	4	6	1	1	0	0
Enuresis	8	13	18	29	3	5
Psychosomatic illnesses	4	6	0	0	0	0
Poor personal hygiene	5	8	0	0	0	0
Venereal disease	3	5	0	0	0	0
Other medical	7	11	20	32	12*	19
Other non medical	0	0	3	5	2	3
Total children with problems	45	73	52	84	39	63
Total problems		78		87		43

* Five of these are various deformities.

The results show that extreme boys have more physical problems than do the other groups. Fewer than one fifth of them appear to be normally healthy and without some sub-stantial disorder. What is more, analysis of individual cases shows that most have reached this stage of their development without any serious effort having been made to put right their ailments. The most prevalent disorder among the boys is enuresis, followed by poor eyesight and dental problems. The large grouping of 'other medical' include disorders such as brain damage, epilepsy, colostomy, etc.

Extreme girls present the next highest incidence of medical problems, though as indicated in Chapter 3, they make the greater demand on medical services. The pattern of their difficulties is the reverse of the boys, i.e. poor eyesight, followed by enuresis. Obesity and associated physical ungainliness is frequently witnessed in females presenting extreme disorders. It contributes heavily to their hostility to themselves as females and their tendency to denigrate and disguise their sex through both dress and behaviour. Surprisingly, only a tiny minority of girls present signs and symptoms of VD.

An unexpectedly large group of girls suffer from skin diseases. More often than not, these are associated with generally poor personal hygiene which extend from resistance to washing and changing underwear to taking appropriate sanitary and gynæcological measures. These are more extensive than indicated in the table. They seem to be yet another aspect of the girls' negative view of themselves, derived from their uncaring and abused growth into womanhood. The attempt to get the girls to look after themselves is one source of conflict with them, which they sometimes use as a manipulatory bar-gaining counter with staff.

It appears from the above, that in the context of the mass of other problems presented by these children, their physical disorders have sunk into the background and have not received the appropriate level of attention, irrespective of whether the children have been in a previous residential setting. Whether the physical problems of the children, particularly the boys, contribute in any way to the gravity of the problems they present is yet to be established. What is clear is that they are somewhat different from the stereotype of the healthy, tough and resilient adolescent preying on a weak and defenceless community.

TABLE 59: COGNITIVE PROBLEMS

	A		B		C	
	N	%	N	%	N	%
None	13	21	15	24	5	8
Retarded attainment and unable to cope	27	44	25	40	18	29
Retarded attainment but adequate for needs	14	23	11	18	33	53
Very limited ability	8	13	10	16	5	8
Others	0	0	1	2	1	2

As the results indicate, at best three quarters of the children have intellectual and educational problems. Surprisingly, the least disturbed group present as great an incidence of difficulties as the girls in this area. This suggests that being retarded at school does not by itself create social difficulties though it may contribute to the total picture of disorder which brings a child to the attention of social services. In this context it may be worth mentioning that, as shown by analysis of individual cases, most children begin to present major social *and* scholastic problems at the time of changing over from junior to secondary schools. It is suspected that this is due more to the different social circumstances prevailing in the two types of settings than to the intellectual demands made on the children.

Just under half of the girls and somewhat fewer of the extreme boys are seriously retarded in their attainments and are unable to cope with the scholastic demands of the school. Distinction should be made between 'backwardness' – which means poor attainments but in keeping with intellectual competence – and 'retardation' – which denotes functioning significantly below potential. These children have the intellectual equipment but for a variety of reasons – familial, social and personal – cannot meet the demands made on them. This bears its own seeds of disorder in the conflict it generates between the children and their teachers and parents (that is if they care about the child's attainments in the first place) and the degenerative effect it has on the child's self-respect as a person who is 'no good' and doomed to fail (cf. Hargreaves, 1967).

The majority of the less disordered boys also have limited attainments but these are adequate for most of their normal needs. 'Very limited ability' is now the preferred description of 'subnormal intelligence'. On this basis, the extreme children contain the largest group of subnormals. Indeed some of the most spectacularly disordered, given to bizarre, uncontrollable behaviours, have been from this group.

The following results on *family problems* put the flesh on the bones of the picture of difficulties presented in Chapter 3. Although the family may have certain characteristics which are deemed to be abnormal, undesirable and otherwise worthy of note, in the summing up of the kind of problems that *it* presents the child, those attributes may lose some of their force. For example, a father may be a heavy drinker or a mother may be having an affair with the lodger but as long as the partners and the children appear to be coping adequately with such problems, they would not figure as a problem worthy of intervention. This view is deliberate and somewhat contrary to the fashionable 'social reformist' attitude which seeks to put *everything* right but in fact succeeds in muddling things even more than they were before. It is worth mentioning a problem only if something should or can be done about it. Further, the assessment process takes the child as its point of reference and only comments on those aspects which seriously affect him.

As is apparent, serious family problems remain the overwhelming correlates of severely disordered and anti-social behaviour in adolescents. This has been so frequently found (e.g. West, 1967, 1969 *et seq*) that it is now almost part of folk wisdom. Judging by the total number of problems, the extreme children have more family problems than the others. Also,

TABLE 60: FAMILY PROBLEMS

	A		B		C	
	N	%	N	%	N	%
None	4	6	3	5	3	5
Material deprivation	9	15	7	11	3	5
Parents separated	13	21	17	27	18	29
Parental conflict	12	19	6	10	13	21
Inconsistent handling	9	15	12	19	6	10
Resent father/stepfather	6	10	5	8	6	10
„ mother/stepmother	6	10	1	2	3	5
„ siblings	4	6	1	2	3	5
Mother 'unstable'	5	8	6	10	4	6
Father 'unstable'/alcoholic	8	13	4	6	1	2
Lack of stimulation	6	10	8	13	5	8
Very disturbed	20	32	22	35	2	3
Neglected child	3	5	1	2	0	0
Inadequate parents	4	6	4	6	7	11
No security	6	10	4	6	0	0
No father figure	4	6	0	0	0	0
No control	2	3	8	13	9	15
Others	18	29	21	34	12	19
Number of children with problems	58	94	59	95	59	95
Number of problems	133		127		92	

apart from the surprising fact that the less disturbed boys experience more family conflict than do the extreme boys, the latter and the girls predominate not only in total but also in each individual category of difficulty, sometimes dramatically. Having said this, however, it is less easy to discern a consistent pattern of family problems for each of the groups.

More of the extreme groups seem to have been subjected to material deprivation which has a continuing effect on them. Parental separation affects more boys than girls, whereas continuing parental conflict is less of a problem with the extreme boys than it is with either of the two other groups. Seriously inconsistent handling, i.e. veering between permissiveness and punitiveness towards the child's misdeeds is more prevalent in the extreme group, as is insecurity at home. The low impact of parental instability on all the groups and of fathers' absence on the boys is surprising and contrary to much other writing.

The most dramatic difference between the extreme children and the control group lies in both the incidence and quality of family 'disturbance'. It is not possible to catalogue the quality of relationships and incidents at home which have led to this judgment. The relationships range from homicidal to incestuous and the incidents from severe beatings to suicide attempts. The effect of these on the children is to produce high levels of anxiety, confusion, severe hostility, aggression and such profound preoccupation with what may be happening at home that they become frozen with anguish and insusceptible to short term help. The fact that they are inarticulate, and because of their history have no reason to trust adults and talk through their anxiety, transforms this into the volcanic core of their disordered behaviour.

TABLE 61: PROBLEM OF SOCIAL RELATIONSHIPS

	A		B		C	
	N	%	N	%	N	%
None	21	34	30	48	37	60
Bullies/domineers peers	9	15	0	0	2	3
Hostile to adults	8	13	6	10	5	8
Gross attention seeker	12	19	2	3	0	0
Socially unaware	7	11	10	16	3	5
Very withdrawn	2	3	2	3	3	5
Difficulty making relationships	11	18	10	16	9	15
Others	1	2	2	3	5	8
Number of children with problems	41	66	32	52	25	40
Number of problems	50		32		27	

Taken as a whole, girls are significantly more inept in social skills than are either of the boy groups. More girls are prone to bullying and domineering their peers and showing hostility to adults. Their tendency to gross attention seeking behaviour is perhaps the most prominent feature of their stereotype and yet the results show that this applies to only about one fifth of them.

The extreme boys contain a large number who are obvious misfits in groups and who behave in ways which suggest poor contact with reality. Interestingly, despite the fact that they contain the physically largest (but not the most powerful – that is reserved for girls) and those who have committed the gravest crimes against person, none has been noted as a bully to other children. Between one third and two thirds of all the groups appear not to have any major relationship problems.

TABLE 62: SOCIAL PROBLEMS

	A		B		C	
	N	%	N	%	N	%
None	2	3	3	5	3	5
Truancy	21	34	14	23	19	31
Absconding	22	35	23	37	4	6
Sexual misbehaviour	9	15	5	8	0	0
Disruptive behaviour	7	11	5	8	0	0
Physical aggression	16	26	7	11	5	8
Confirmed offending	6	10	18	29	24	39
Petty offending	9	15	12	19	18	29
Serious offending	0	0	4	6	0	0
Others	5	8	10	16	2	3
Number of children with problems	60	96	59	95	59	95
Number of problems	97		101		82	

The most remarkable aspect of these findings is how few children do not show some important problem of social behaviour, a characteristic also of family problems. In general terms, the extreme groups show a higher incidence of problems in this area than do the control group. The latter contain significantly more boys who are persistent offenders engaging in what might be termed a career of 'socialised' delinquency. This group is akin to the one isolated by Quay (1966), preoccupied with delinquent values and activities, neutralisation of adult authority and correspondingly strong subcultural and peer group links. Their offences are within the mainstream of more 'acceptable' crimes, i.e. primarily group stealing. Persistent truancy is the only social problem which affects all the samples fairly evenly.

The seriously disordered group contain significantly larger numbers of youngsters who engage in disruptive behaviour – temper tantrums which result in damage to property, absconding and sexual promiscuity. Within this extreme group, many more girls are seriously aggressive than are boys and have assaulted other people, usually the police, nurses and residential workers. Also, as expected, more engage in sexually unacceptable behaviour, such as prostitution, than do boys, whose sexual problems take the form of rape, exposure, etc. Within these groups, the boys are the only ones to have committed grave crimes – murder, robbery with violence, arson, etc.

Bearing in mind that the problems are only cited here when they reach a critical level, the above picture gives some indication of why the public and most professionals are so concerned about the serious flouting of the law by extreme groups of youngsters. At the risk of distortion by simplifying, it seems that 'ordinary' boys steal as a way of life, extreme boys offend sometimes without aggression but frequently with aggression in the furtherance of an offence, and girls engage in physical assaults as ends in themselves, or at least unrelated to an offence. In all these cases, the youngsters remain a major source of threat to the community, both of person and property.

The overall results show the extreme groups to have considerably more personal problems than do the control group. Gross immaturity, or being at the level of emotional and social development of a much younger child, is the most pervasive source of difficulty for all the children, though it is more prevalent among the extreme youngsters than others. Otherwise, girls show a preponderance of severe mood swings, high

TABLE 63: PERSONAL PROBLEMS

	A		B		C	
	N	%	N	%	N	%
None	16	26	13	21	21	34
Socially/emotionally immature	21	34	17	27	10	16
Socially/emotionally insecure	9	15	2	3	8	13
Impulsive	5	8	4	6	6	10
Overt fantasies	4	6	5	8	0	0
Unstable	5	8	8	13	1	2
Severe mood swings	7	11	4	6	0	0
Depressed	3	5	2	3	0	0
Anxious	8	13	6	10	2	3
Negative self image	10	16	4	6	7	11
Suicide attempts	9	15	2	3	0	0
Others	9	15	18	29	18	29
Number of children with problems	46	74	49	79	41	66
Number of problems	72		69		52	

levels of anxiety, specially negative views of themselves and, of course, suicide attempts. Taken together with their social ineptitude and tendency to physical aggression, the above characteristics may begin to show why extreme girls generate so much anxiety and consequent incompetence among those who try to manage them.

Severely disordered boys share the girls' characteristics though to a lesser degree as, in turn, do the control group. This is the only problem area in which there is something akin to a consistent progression from 'ordinary boys' through their more disordered brethren to the extreme of girls' difficulties. Bearing in mind the paucity of psychological and psychiatric concepts and methods for enumerating and measuring personal problems, it would be reasonable to assume that most children who become extreme experience frequent internally generated stress which they can understand, articulate and cope with even less adaptively than they might with other problem areas. This is a necessary corrective to the unbounded advocacy of the notion that disordered and delinquent youngsters should be seen and treated primarily as unfeeling predators.

Treatment Recommendations

Some indication has been given so far of the range and complexity of the problems presented by severely disordered children. For most of them, despite the long and involved history of intervention in their lives, this is the first time that a systematic and relatively rigorous look has been taken at their problems in which they have been placed and evaluated in the context of other disordered children.

All this could be seen as the preparation for what is perhaps the most important stage of the whole assessment process – the determination of what should be done with a child, or the making of treatment recommendations. The main criterion governing the recommendations is that they should be addressed centrally to the alleviation of the child's problems and that they should be usable by the treatment agency. As will be shown in Chapter 8, unlike other diagnostic approaches, the classification of children's problems, as presented earlier, is directly related to the alleviation of those problems. Therefore, in this context, 'need' is seen as the action implication of the statement of the problem – thus, if 'Lynn has no secure emotional ties' the 'need' is for 'opportunity to establish supportive relationships' or if 'Kenneth is a serious bully' the need is to 'curb his bullying and make it unrewarding'. Because needs are related to problems, the conceptual difficulties about *who* exactly has the 'need' – whether the child or others, is overcome. Because all children have certain common needs (Pringle, 1975) and it is impossible to enumerate *all* the needs of an individual child, only the outstanding needs which distinguish him from other children are enumerated.

The level of abstraction and the conceptual and empirical complexity of treatment recommendations are partly a function of the professional competence of those who make them and partly a function of what they know to be available and practicable in the whole range of facilities which they may seek to deal with the child. While it is obviously desirable to state the child's treatment needs irrespective of limitations of resources, this would turn the assessment report into an academic document to which no practitioner would pay much attention. The skill of recommending, therefore, lies in achieving the best fit between the requirements of the child and slightly *more* resources than are available, so that the treatment agency has to stretch itself to cope with each new child and thereby gain greater general competence.

Another relevant point in evaluating the recommendations is that they are usually couched in general rather than specific terms required for rigorous treatment. This is because at this stage of the assessment, the venue of treatment is undecided; therefore, recommendations must be made in such general terms as to be feasible in a whole range of treatment facilities. Even when a treatment facility is decided upon, it is rare that its resources of staff, materials, access to specialists, etc. are known in sufficient detail as to warrant the detailed recommendations; the relationship of a regional specialised facility and its receiving treatment agencies is professionally (i.e. politically) a delicate one. Recommendations must not be in such detail as to tie the hands of the treatment agency who, while accepting the guidelines, wish to retain freedom of choice as to the actual methods of treatment. In any case the state of knowledge about appropriate methods of treatment for severely disordered children is so impoverished as to render rigid adherence to particular treatment methods highly inadvisable. Obviously when a treatment facility is intimately known, the recommendations are made more detailed. The fact that most treatment agencies will make little effort to deliberately choose a particular treatment approach does not make the point any less apposite. Thus, more often than not the treatment guidelines are a reconciliation of the absolute and the ideal with the relative and the imperfect real.

Since the abolition of the old approved schools system and

the assumption of through-care responsibilities by local authority social workers, there is no general information available as to how much and at what level recommendations are implemented by treatment agencies. It is, therefore, quite likely that in practice some of the recommendations are no more than attempts at emphasising the needs of a particular child and elicting resources which should be available but which are not provided in practice – intensive social work support for the family, close directiveness for the child, structured therapeutic environment, etc. They provide an empirical guide to the needs of children, which at some point in the future when the treatment of disordered children becomes less ideological, may form a basis for sensible intervention.

All treatment agencies have a legal responsibility for meeting the health requirements of the child which, as was shown earlier, has often not been met. With the general availability of health care services, there should be no problems about meeting the children's needs in this area.

TABLE 64: PHYSICAL PROBLEMS

Recommendation	A		B		C	
	N	%	N	%	N	%
None	4	16	6	10	30	48
Utilise physical skills	6	10	5	8	2	3
Diet and/or improve appearance	13	21	1	2	0	0
Eye test	12	19	10	16	7	11
Hearing test	6	10	7	11	2	3
Dental treatment	2	3	6	10	3	5
Treatment for enuresis	6	10	13	21	1	2
Improve personal hygiene	7	11	2	3	3	5
High degree of physical care	2	3	4	6	5	8
Sex instruction (contraceptive advice, etc.)	7	11	0	0	0	0
Other medical follow ups	4	6	12	19	10	16
Other	4	6	0	0	0	0

In keeping with the greater weight of their physical problems, extreme children are more frequently recommended for attention. It will be noted, however, that most of the measures recommended are not medical, but rather concerned with provision of physical care both directly and through instruction.

Given the difficulty of most disordered children in coping with the demands of school, much emphasis is laid on this section to ensure that the child's subsequent educational experiences do not further alienate him from school. Given the low employment potential of most of these children and the probability of further conflict with inappropriate educational approaches, achievement of adequate as opposed to excellent educational achievement is emphasised.

TABLE 65: INTELLECTUAL AND EDUCATIONAL PROBLEMS

	A		B		C	
Recommendation	N	%	N	%	N	%
Encourage with normal school work	12	19	14	23	11	18
Get job/job training	7	11	8	13	17	27
Careers guidance	10	16	10	16	6	10
Individual educational help	11	18	5	8	9	15
Intensive remedial help	16	26	18	29	18	29
Special education setting	3	5	3	5	1	2
Change of school	3	5	1	2	1	2
Small group teaching	7	11	9	15	8	13
Concentrate on practical subjects	4	6	2	3	2	3
Others	3	5	1	2	5	8

The only important difference here is the emphasis laid on the provision of job training opportunities or getting a job for the less disturbed boys. The amount of individual teaching recommended for the girls reflects their social behaviour problems. Over and above all the other help, about one third of all the samples need intensive remedial help to raise them above illiteracy.

Almost all the children's families have been involved with social services departments for varying, though mainly prolonged, periods. It is assumed that such involvement is programmed and proceeds from a plan of what social workers wish to achieve with the family. Even when it is suspected that no such plans exist, the assessment meeting is solely concerned with arriving at a consensus of objectives for work with the family only insofar as the child is concerned. It is not part of its purpose to prescribe for the rest of the family, hence the relatively short list of recommendations for the complex of family problems.

TABLE 66: FAMILY PROBLEMS

Recommendation	A N	A %	B N	B %	C N	C %
Find alternative home base	24	39	14	23	14	23
Social casework with family	30	48	32	52	36	58
Regulated contact with home	6	10	8	13	8	13
Others	8	13	8	13	4	6

An indication of the seriously deteriorated and damaging family life of the girls is that in a substantially larger number of cases it is thought best to find them an alternative home base. The corporate recommendation (one endorsed by the social workers present at the assessment meeting) suggests that between 25% and 40% of the children can be protected from further damage and helped only by being given an alternative home. As such it throws a worrying light on the provision of social services for these children and their families. Presumably the families have already received all the help that the local authorities can give through their social workers and utilisation of other agencies. Despite this, there is still no viable home base for so many children and an alternative has to be sought. It may be legitimate to raise the question of why social workers have not achieved this basic requirement of care for the children in their charge. This point assumes greater potency when it is recognised that social workers expend their greatest effort on trying to keep the child within the family.

About half of all the children's families are thought to require intensive casework. Bearing in mind that few new problems about the family are discovered at the conclusion of assessment and that social workers have been conversant with those problems, and yet have not provided the casework, the prospects for adopting the recommendation at this juncture are not very encouraging.

For a small group of children, it is thought that random contact with home, inadequately supervised, is likely to be damaging. The recommendation is, therefore, that any contact be carefully regulated according to its outcome for the child.

The development of adequate social skills is as important to the future adaptation of the child as it is difficult to bring about. Most agencies rely on placing the child in a group and allowing the 'market forces' of group pressure and modification to take their own course. Yet these forces are not only likely to compound the social ineptitude of the child by adding fear and suppression to it, but are also likely to generate other forms of adaptation which are contrary to the other treatment needs of the child (Polsky, 1962; Buehler et al, 1966). For this reason, the social skills requirements of the child are elaborated.

TABLE 67: SOCIAL RELATIONSHIP PROBLEMS

Recommendation	A		B		C	
	N	%	N	%	N	%
One-to-one counselling	15	24	5	8	8	13
Strong adult support	9	15	6	10	6	10
Small group setting	7	11	6	10	4	6
Firm, no nonsense handling	8	13	8	13	7	11
Behaviour modification	7	11	0	0	0	0
Strong 'model' necessary	1	2	8	13	12	19
Others	6	10	2	3	2	3
No specific recommendation	15	24	20	32	24	39

Significantly more girls are thought to need one-to-one counselling than do the boys. This appears, superficially, to be at variance with the finding of girls' greater susceptibility to group pressure. In group settings for these children, unless very skilfully managed, the pressure is covertly channelled towards non-conformity and conflict with authority. Bearing in mind the girls' penchant for such behaviour and their intolerance of group settings, it can be seen why an individual approach may be more appropriate with them. For the same reason, more of them are thought to require adult support. The need for a small group setting to minimise relationship problems applies to only a small minority, but surprisingly, so does the recommendation for 'firm, no nonsense handling'.

Living day to day with the children, the staff are no less in favour of effective measures of dealing with the children than is anyone else. Yet, from their deep knowledge of the child, the much vaunted view that 'all these children need is a good hard smack and firm discipline' does not carry much weight and is thought to be of possible benefit to only a small group.

Interestingly, only girls are recommended for social training through the use of specific behaviour modification approaches (such as teaching co-operative behaviour). More boys are believed to need the opportunity to model themselves on a strong male figure, suggesting that more of them have drifted into social deviance because of lack of strong control, guidance and affection.

As far as most of the public and social services are concerned, problems of social behaviour form the crux of the treatment recommendations. After all, whatever other problems they may have, it is frequently the youngsters' anti-social behaviour which has provoked extreme intervention. For the staff, however, conscious as they are of the totality of a child's problems and the work done in their own Training School, anti-social behaviour is more frequently related to social and environmental factors than to personal ones and is not, therefore, thought to be normally susceptible to treatment through the child. They are, therefore, primarily concerned with reducing the opportunity for further problematic behaviour by re-structuring the child's perception of what he can do, for example, with his free time.

Also, in making the treatment recommendations account is taken of the ethical, social and technical constraints in adopting specific measures (such as in *Clockwork Orange*) to curb anti-social behaviour.

TABLE 68: PROBLEMS OF SOCIAL BEHAVIOUR

Recommendation	A		B		C	
	N	%	N	%	N	%
Constructive use of leisure time	11	18	16	26	19	31
Counselling	5	8	4	6	2	3
Secure environment	2	3	7	11	0	0
Structured environment	6	10	13	21	6	10
Others	0	0	12	19	3	5
No specific recommendation	36	58	14	23	32	5

It is for these reasons that the majority of the girls and the less disordered boys are not recommended for any form of intervention aimed at reducing delinquency. There are, simply, no reliable, valid or acceptable methods that can be recommended. Boredom and inability to use leisure time constructively is clearly seen as having much to do with about one quarter to one third of the boys' anti-social behaviour but less with the girls'.

The greater tendency of the extreme group to engage in persistent absconding and serious crimes is reflected in the relatively larger number of secure and structured environments recommended for them. Even so, the proportions are smaller than would be expected from the numbers of persistent absconders and children who are major sources of risk to the public.

The reasons for this seem to be that little secure accommodation is currently available which can meet the demand for any but the most glaringly dangerous youngsters; not even all those children who have committed grave crimes are deemed to warrant it – provided the risks are understood and accepted. It is recognised that secure facilities, as traditionally run, achieve little by way of reducing the child's potential for further anti-social behaviour and do so at massive cost; if adequate attention is given to the child's other problems, his anti-social behaviour may be curbed and become more manageable.

Of all the problem areas, personal problems are the most difficult in which to make treatment recommendations to an unknown agency which, in all probability, would not have any access to the specialised resources required for effecting change in the personal problems of the child. The easiest part is to make specific recommendations for psychiatric attention or treatment. It is, however, less easy to recommend ways in which a deviant personality structure may be changed even if this were felt to be ethically permissible. Improving a negative self-concept, inculcating moral sense and teaching impulse control do not suffer from this difficulty but presume high levels of expertise and a central concern with the alleviation of the child's personal problems – qualities which are not in over abundant supply. Hence the prevalent tendency to divide this task largely between psychiatrists on the one hand and those who can give the child personalised, emotional care on the other.

A significantly larger group of girls – over one third of the

TABLE 69: PERSONAL PROBLEMS

Recommendation	A		B		C	
	N	%	N	%	N	%
Psychiatric attention/treatment	21	34	13	21	6	10
High levels of personal care	15	24	10	16	10	16
Other	24	39	21	34	22	35
No specific recommendation	7	11	18	29	24	39

sample – are deemed to require psychiatric help. This help would be aimed at both providing a check against further deterioration as well as specific treatment. The psychiatric report by a consultant usually carries the specific treatment recommendation – whether it is for a particular type of medication or for brief psychotherapy, etc.

More girls are also recommended for personal care by one or two specially selected people. The particular form of care is usually spelled out in the report, based not only on the youngster's general problem but also on what has been observed of their response to a variety of management approaches and staff. The large residual category encompasses a whole variety of measures and approaches of the kind mentioned earlier to alleviate anxiety, teach impulse control, improve self-concept, deter self-mutilating behaviour, increase empathy, etc.

Placements

Having identified the child's problems and outlined his treatment needs, it now becomes necessary to advise the responsible authority where those needs may be best fulfilled. Thus, it is not the problems *per se* which dictate the placement but the type of treatment and the resources it requires. This is important to bear in mind, because in the discussions of troubled and troublesome children, the jump is usually made from problems directly on to the presumptively related provision, e.g. 'serious offender, therefore needs locking up' rather than through a consideration of how best the problem may be alleviated.

One of the important innovations of the 1969 Children and Young Persons Act was that, at least in theory, the full range of society's resources could be utilised for the treatment of a child regardless of his area of domicile and limitations of facilities in a particular local authority. This provision, however, remains more theoretical than actual. There is no evidence that for the vast majority of problem children a wider set of resources is now utilised than it has ever been. The reasons for this are several:

(a) With the proliferation of local authority assessment centres, most children are dealt with locally. These centres are parochial both in skill and outlook. Further, they have not built up the credibility and experience which would give them access to a wider range of resources, many of which already have well forged links with other sources of referral.
(b) Local authorities prefer, for reasons of both cost and control, to provide for their children within their own patch unless it is dramatically inappropriate.
(c) High level of discrimination in choosing an appropriate treatment venue can only flow from a discriminating analysis of the child's treatment requirements.
(d) All treatment facilities exercise varying but substantial degrees of autonomy in defining the types of children they take. This would be wholly acceptable if (1) between them all the facilities could accommodate all the children and (2) the definitions remained fairly constant. But neither of these requirements are satisfied. As will be further described in Chapter 7, there appear to be an increasing number of children whom nobody particularly wants. The placement recommendation is, therefore, influenced by projection of the probable response (well known through frequent contact) of the receiving facility. The error element in the projection arises from the shifting criteria for accepting children. More often than not, the criteria move towards greater exclusiveness, so that facilities which were formerly quite happy to have a try with a particular type of problem child, find that they are no longer able to do so.
(e) There are administrative and organisational factors, such as waiting lists, rebuilding, shortage of staff, scarcity of foster parents, etc. which affect the placement of the child in a particular facility.

Another important consideration is that there are almost no facilities in the country which either possess or can arrange the provision of necessary resources to meet the *total* treatment needs of the child. Where they exist, their ability to accept particular children is limited by the age and sex of the child and his area of domicile. These latter considerations apply to practically all provisions for children.

The end result of this complex process is that children are recommended for a particular form of placement often not because that placement is best for them, but rather because it is likely to do both the child and the community the least harm.

This latter is an important consideration because as will be shown in Chapter 10, there are occasions when the interests of the child and those of the community come into conflict. Where all the treatment requirements of the child cannot be met, it becomes necessary to allow one set of considerations to predominate over the other. In the case of severely disordered children this conflict of interests is usually thrown into sharp relief, demanding an unequivocal decision, which is usually against them.

Bearing in mind the above considerations, in the present setting the placement of the child is determined by first eliminating the inappropriate forms of disposal and then 'homing in' on the particular facility within each treatment venue of penal, medical/psychiatric, educational and social services. To ensure that this process is not left to the vagaries of individual persons, the following list has been prepared as a basis for recommending placements at assessment meetings. The list is augmented by names and details of establishments and enumerates the total range of disposals available for a child.

A. *Penal Establishments*
   1. Detention Centres
   2. Remand Centres
   3. Borstals

B. *Medical/Psychiatric Provision*
   1. Outpatient Departments
   2. Inpatient Units
   3. Subnormality Hospitals
   4. Psychiatric Hospitals – Inpatient/Outpatient
                               Closed/Open

5. Special Hospitals
6. Adolescent and Child Psychiatry Units
7. Forensic Psychiatry Units
8. Hostels for Psychiatrically Disturbed Adolescents
9. Communities for the Subnormal and Disturbed, e.g. Camphill; Rudolf Steiner
10. Private mental nursing homes and hostels

C. *Educational Establishments (Local Authority and Voluntary)*
 I. Non Residential
   1. Day Special Schools:
      (i) E.S.N./S.S.N.
      (ii) Maladjusted
   2. Government Training Centres
   3. Child Guidance Clinics
 II. Residential
   1. Schools for the Educationally Subnormal
   2. Schools for the Maladjusted
   3. Schools for the Delicate
   4. Schools for the Autistic/Deaf/Handicapped Child
   5. Hospital Schools
   6. Schools run by the National Association for Mental Health
   7. Spastics Society Schools
   8. Variety of Private Special Schools

D. *Social Services and Voluntary Establishments*
 Home
   1. Return home and to ordinary day school or work
   2. Return home and to
      (i) Day Special School
      (ii) Outpatient – psychiatric unit/hospital
      (iii) Intermediate Treatment Centre
      (iv) Day boy at a Community Home
   3. Foster Parents
      (i) ordinary
      (ii) 'professional'

4. Children's Home – long and short stay
   (i) run by the local authority
   (ii) run by voluntary organisations like Dr Barnardo's, N.C.H., etc.
5. Reception Centres. Now go under the general title of local authority assessment centres. Some have long stay units.
6. 'Observation and Assessment Centres' – many of which were former remand homes.
7. Family Rehabilitation Centres
8. Specialist Units for Mentally Handicapped Children
9. Hostels – both local authority and voluntary
   (i) Hostels for children receiving special education
   (ii) Hostels for subnormal adolescents under 21
   (iii) Probation hostels – usually accommodating ex Borstal boys, ex prisoners
   (iv) Working Boys' Hostels/Homes
   (v) Community Homes used to accommodate persons over compulsory school age but under 21 who are employed or seek employment in an area where a school is provided for children who are over compulsory school age (Section 50 – Children and Young Persons Act 1969)
   (vi) Hostels (various) run by the Salvation Army
10. Mother and Baby Homes
11. Training Centres for Severely Subnormal Children
12. Community Homes with Education
   (i) Intermediate Treatment Centres
   (ii) Community Homes – normally former approved schools
   (iii) Special Units – secure and otherwise
   (iv) 'Therapeutic Communities'
   (v) Youth Treatment Centres

To put the placements of the children in the present study in perspective, it may be worthwhile to look at the list of disposals during the year January–December 1976.

TABLE 70: RETURNS FROM THE REGIONAL ASSESSMENT CENTRES 1976

	N	%				
1. Applications for admission						
(a) Boys	338					
(b) Girls	19					
2. Admitted						
(a) Boys	335					
(b) Girls	17					
3. Av. monthly admissions	29					

			Present study					
			A		B		C	
4. Placements	N	%	N	%	N	%	N	%
(a) Borstal	—	—			2	3		
(b) Detention Centre	1	—			—	—		
(c) Remand Centre	4	1			1	2		
(d) Adol. Psych. Unit	4	1			2	3		
(e) Special Hospital	1	—			1	2		
(f) Other Psych./Med.	1	—			2	3		
(g) Res. Malad. School	1	—	2	3	4	6	1	2
(h) Res. ESN School	1	—	—	—	1	2	4	6
(i) Home	80	23	14	23	4	6	16	26
(j) Children's/Foster Home	33	9	9	15	2	3	3	5
(k) Approved lodgings	1	—	1	2	—	—	2	3
(l) Hostels	8	2	5	9	3	5	1	2
(m) CHEs	175	48	19	31	35	56	25	40
(n) Special Unit	1	—			2	3		
(o) Absconders (not returned)	6	2	—	—	—	—	—	—
(p) Others	35	10	12	20	3	5	10	16

There is a dramatic difference in the pattern of placement of boys and girls and the extreme group compared with the controls. Far more of the girls are recommended for children's homes or fostering and for placement in hostels – emphasising the need for small group settings. Disproportionately fewer are allocated to CHEs, showing awareness of the girls' difficulty in coping with large group structures and the relative absence of a personalised approach. Apart from fewer placements in children's homes and fostering and rather more allocations to residential ESN schools and CHEs, control boys are much more like the girls than their more disordered peers.

Even a cursory look at the table shows how differently the extreme boys are placed from the other children. They are the only ones to be recommended for and eventually placed in penal and psychiatric settings including a hospital for mentally disordered offenders. Substantially fewer are placed back at home and significantly more in CHEs and Special (secure) Units.

The findings highlight the points made earlier about the conflicts of interests of the child and the community and the need to give prominence to one set of treatment requirements when all cannot be met. It is obvious from the above that in the final disposal of the severely disordered boys the considerations of public safety have weighed heavily with the decision makers. They are under no illusion as to the kind and amount of treatment that a youngster will receive in a penal establishment and yet it has clearly been felt that the public would be at severe risk from the child in any other placement.

The point is borne out more forcefully in looking at the judgment made of the prognosis of the child at the end of the assessment meeting. Given the form of disposal, it is possible to make some sort of global judgment about the likely outcome of a child's treatment. There is as large an element of hope and wishful thinking involved in such prognostication as there is inadequate knowledge of what *actually* happens to children when they have been through the appropriate processing.

TABLE 71: PROGNOSIS

| | A | | B | | C | |
	N	%	N	%	N	%
Good	6	10	2	3	8	13
Moderate	44	71	28	45	52	84
Poor	12	19	32	52	2	3

On this basis and for what they are worth, the results show that only a small minority of any of the groups have a good chance of making out. A surprisingly large number of both girls and the disordered boys are thought to have a reasonable chance of achieving moderate control over their problems if the treatment recommendations are carried out.

By contrast, the severely disordered boys contain, as a group, fewer who have either good or moderate prognoses. Instead they inhabit a region where despite (or perhaps because of) what is likely to be done to, for and with them, their prospects will remain bleak.

CHAPTER 6

*

Coping with Extreme Children

ALTHOUGH it is a truism, it is nevertheless worth mentioning that a youngster never blows up without reason; whether that reason is good and obvious or bad and incomprehensible is a different matter. Problems are precipitated by variations in the child's life space – that portion of reality which impinges on him, whether internally or through something happening 'out there'. The impact of the problem is felt by someone or thing and the problem must be resolved in an environment whose resources and boundaries may be redefined according to need. Thus the problems presented by a disordered child are a direct result of his interaction with the environment and the people and things that inhabit it. In this sense, if responsibilities are to be assigned, the environment in which crises occur is as 're-sponsible' for the crises as is the child. Having learnt something about the children and their problems it may now be worth-while to look at the major aspects of the environment, its resources and atmosphere in order to understand what gives rise to crises and how these may be managed.

Material Resources

All human beings have certain basic needs for survival – food, drink, warmth, shelter, sleep and bodily waste disposal. The manner and the level at which these needs are catered for are related to the culture and tradition of each society, its level of development and its economic resources. In the United King-dom because of the small size of the country and its relatively

133

homogeneous culture, there is general acceptance that children ought to be fed, clothed and sheltered well. There is sufficient variation within this homogeneity to allow for standards to range from just acceptable to excellent, with a middle ground which most people would find reasonable. In residential establishments, this middle ground is often better than the one occupied by the children in their own homes, not surprising in view of the fact that most of the children are drawn from the poorest families with the lowest standards in these areas.

The physical environment and architectural style of specialised facilities also follow the patterns prevalent in the wider society. It is, however, being slowly realised that shape, size, colour, texture and fittings of an environment have a powerful bearing on the kind of behaviour that is generated within it (Barker, 1968; Newman, 1972). These have become the subject of critical scrutiny and have resulted in a number of relevant publications (e.g. DHSS, 1972). The attempt to relate the problems and management needs of severely disordered boys and girls to physical surroundings is also being gradually carried beyond the endorsement of 'received wisdom' (e.g. Turnbull & Hoghughi, 1973). This is a relatively well explored area and will not, therefore, be described here. In the final analysis, buildings and the physical environment are simply *aids* to the management of the children. If they are well designed, they facilitate; if they are badly designed they impede, but do not finally determine the quality of the atmosphere and of the work that is carried out within them. That crucial role is reserved for the children and the other human beings with whom they interact.

Human Resources

This resource encompasses the children, the staff, the wider community of other people and the general atmosphere which their collective, constantly changing interaction creates and maintains. The uses and effects of groups of children as agents of individual change have been extensively explored (e.g. Rose,

1972; Glasser *et al*, 1974; Vorrath & Brendtro, 1976) and will not, therefore, be pursued here. Already enough has been said about the behaviour of these children in group settings to illustrate their powerful effect on one another.

The use of the community as a resource in the treatment of disordered children has received particularly close attention in the recent years with the Massachusetts Experiment (e.g. Ohlin *et al*, 1977) and the California Community Treatment Project (Lerman, 1975). In the United Kingdom the notion of community treatment has become intertwined with the ideas of professional fostering (Hazel *et al*, 1977) and of intermediate treatment (PSSC, 1977). All of these are related to but diverge in crucial respects from the notion of the use of the community in which the establishment for disordered children is based, from which it receives cues about the nature of its children and to which it in turn projects an image of those children. The quality of this interaction is centrally dependent on the establishment, the value it has been traditionally accorded in the particular community, and the strength of its contacts.

A major deficiency of most establishments for disordered youngsters has been their geographical isolation from centres of population and their tendency to develop closed, total communities, generating, feeding and in turn being fed, myths about their own children. While it may be naive, in view of the nature of the children, to suggest that 'neighbourhood' establishments (e.g. Tutt, 1974) would overcome the wider problems of total institutions for disordered youngsters and the even harsher stigmatising tendencies of the community, they would certainly provide a better basis for educating the community. Such education is a necessary prerequisite to ensuring that the community does not reject the children, thus isolating them even more than they are already, facilitates supply of staff and amenities, and provides a pool of persons who may take interest in a child and watch over his interests.

The most important human resource in any facility is its staff. It is the staff who provide for the care requirements of the child and protect him from encroachments of other disordered youngsters. Beyond this personal care and protection function, they also provide control and *public* protection as well as perform the more specialised tasks of assessment and treatment. The quality of staff functioning, their number and quality set the tone of the facility, the degree to which problems will arise and the economy and competence with which those problems will be resolved. The quality of staff is in turn dependent on the dynamic interaction of recruitment and selection, training, support and development of skills.

Staff Recruitment and Selection

Although about one hundred thousand people are employed in the residential care of slightly more children in England and Wales, little is known about their characteristics or, more importantly, what differentiates the good from the less so.

In the present context, one important difficulty is that although it is possible to speak in general terms of high calibre persons who have the qualities sought for in most normal interactions between children and adults and are capable of care giving at acceptable levels, it is not possible to evaluate them for work with severely disordered children. Before any statements can be made about the types of staff required for such a task, more needs to be known about the sorts of problems they are likely to face.

The earlier chapters of this book have shown that severely disordered boys and girls present very special handling problems. These range from the normal pattern of disruptive and threatening behaviour, including fights with their peers and destruction of property, to much more anxiety provoking events such as attacks on staff, well planned abscondings, and serious acts of violence against the other children and themselves. Indeed, one important defining criterion of such children by the time they come to a specialised facility is that other people have failed to cope with their problems. This 'failing to cope' essentially means that a number of other paid people have reached the end of their tolerance of a child's behaviour and are unable or unwilling to go on paying the heavy personal cost entailed in containing and managing the child's behaviour.

In a simple sense the characteristics of staff required for coping with these children can be seen as the extreme positive end of the continuum of those personal qualities which all care givers must possess. These include, in no particular order of priority, physical fitness. a reasonable level of intelligence, personal stability, compassion, sensitivity, resilience, and a mature outlook.

The staff, although not frequently subjected to physical attacks (that is if they are competent), need to be fit enough to cope with the taxing physical demands of the job in keeping up with and engaging physically active youngsters. In addition to these demands, however, physical fitness, the ability to demonstrate it and the capability to withstand physical confrontations is an important element in preventing these very confrontations. Staff who in some way show fear of physical contact are regarded by the children as 'fair game', and are much more likely to be subjected to physical provocation than those who look as if they can take care of themselves. Such physical competence does not prevent confrontations but its absence certainly increases their probability.

Experience has shown that this does not mean the employment of weight lifters, wrestlers, or judo experts. But even when, quite deliberately and frequently, young, light and fragile looking female workers have been employed, they have to be taught and subsequently encouraged to utilise the opportunity to show that they are capable of physically holding a youngster their own size. Physical competence of staff not only reduces damaging incidents but also gives the staff sufficient confidence to go out of their way to gentle the child out of a confrontation course. Also, dealing with these youngsters appears to have seriously exhausting and deleterious effects on staff. Experience has shown that, unless the staff have at least a day off during the week when they do not have any dealings with any children, are encouraged to take their leaves regularly and at frequent intervals and rotated with other staff so as to give them some respite from the children, absenteeism among them soars. The day to day contact with and experience of disordered behaviour seems to keep the staff at a high level of tension which tells on them physically and which begins to rebound on the children.

Intellectual competence is such a fundamental aspect of all problem solving behaviour that no special plea needs to be made for it in the staff who have to cope with extreme children. Intelligence, however, is a vague and often confused concept and its denotation differs quite considerably between psychologists and lay people. The quality of intelligence required of staff who deal with such children is an amalgam of common sense which can withstand frequent testing, ability to learn from past experience, and quickness in solving the myriad puzzles encountered in day to day work with the children. The ability to understand abstractions and discern principles underlying specific instances of behaviour is indispensable to fruitful group discussions and the training of staff to adopt constant modes of approach to a particular child. Another important intellectual aspect to be sought out and encouraged in staff is inquisitiveness. The staff members who see children's behaviour problems as puzzles to be teased out and solved, are less likely to personalise the encounters and engage in defensive and damaging behaviour with the children and more likely to survive the daily psychological battering.

Personal stability is perhaps the more difficult and, at the same time, the more desirable quality to define. It refers to a balance of personal characteristics which enable an adult to cope with stressful circumstances without adopting neurotic or other abnormal defence mechanisms as ways of coping with anxiety. If all personal characteristics were to be placed on a set of interacting dimensions, one would be looking for a state of balance between them, without any extremes of responsivity. In the present context, this would become the defining criterion of stability, namely the extent a person tends to adopt reasonably predictable and normatively acceptable reactions to variably stressful circumstances rather than show a tendency not to react at all at the one extreme, or to 'go off at the deep end' at the other. Without this quality the children have an even more difficult task of making out with a member of staff than do the staff themselves.

Compassion is essential as a motive for continuing to care when the member of staff has had just about enough or more than he can take. This is the sense in which the work comes nearest to being regarded as a vocation. This quality is what differentiates those who are lured to the job for other reasons than the care of the children from those who, although incapable of explaining why, feel that there is a job to do and they want to be among those who do it.

In day to day dealings with extreme children, every human faculty and sensibility is bombarded, mauled and stretched to the breaking point. This is the major effect of the impact of the children which has made them so intolerable to those who have dealt with them in the past. And yet, the children are often hurt, troubled and beset as much by the results of their own destructiveness as they are by depredations of others. Even at their worst, they are attempting to cope, however maladaptively, with their own fears and tensions. The staff, by being in positions of authority, crystallise the profound ambivalence most of them feel towards adults.

Staff need a high level of sensitivity, not only to understand these attempts at coping by the children, but also to be aware of the image they project and the interaction of such an image with the children's feelings and perceptions. Under stress, every one becomes defensive and adopts his favourite defence mechanism. If staff are not sensitive to such defensiveness, then *they* are likely to create a spiralling situation which will take a heavy toll of everyone concerned.

The combination of these qualities results, at best, in a state of 'balanced durability' which enables the staff to withstand high levels of repeated, frequent and variable stress without buckling at the knees, becoming brutalised and retaliating in kind.

The above qualities are much easier to find singly than in combination. They are also elemental and inherent in persons, whether genetic or as a result of their upbringing. They cannot be taught. People either have them or they do not. If they do have the qualities, training, both in terms of imparting attitudes and giving special skills, can help to enhance them. However, human beings are 'packages' and choice is made on the basis of the balance of weaknesses and strengths in relation to the job. This balance changes even within the same individual over a period of time. The best that any manager of staff resources can do is to choose the best balanced individuals from among those who present themselves for employment, enhance their strengths by training and support and minimise the impact of their weaknesses either by employing them in situations which do not put the weaknesses to frequent test or, alternatively, seek to gradually strengthen them.

The supply and demand situation of the specialised labour market is governed by a whole variety of factors outside the scope of this book. One important element, however, is the projection not only of the type of work, but also of the particular establishment in which the work is to be done. This latter factor partly accounts for the perennial difficulty of some establishments to attract staff and the relatively strong traditions of others.

The current fashion to knock residential facilities and the publicity given to difficulties experienced by them is likely to further limit their ability to recruit high calibre staff. This will then create the self fulfilling prophecy in which residential facilities can only deteriorate. When residential facilities in which the severely disordered find themselves are denigrated and devalued for their failure in achieving the aims which others have set them, they are likely to find it more difficult to obtain the staff of the calibre which is necessary for even the basic care of the children. Those attracted to the job would not be particularly concerned with the value society places on their work. If they are devoid of this central concern, they are likely to be devoid of some of the other essential attributes for the work and the quality of their performance is likely to further derogate the outcome.

Those who wish to work with extreme children are to a large extent self-selected. In any case, no establishment can always have all the staff or the exact qualities of staff it would wish. With these limitations, it has been found worthwhile to pursue a vigorous recruitment policy from a wide range of backgrounds, experience, personalities and skills. Almost the least important aspect of these, other than in specialised jobs, is the 'qualification'. In general, qualified people are not found to be any more competent in dealing with the children than unqualified ones. This does not reflect on the concept of qualification as, for example, in Scandinavian countries, but rather on the qualifications such as CQSW at present available for residential or fieldwork with children.

Experience with the use of psychologists and specialised measures has shown that there are not many reliable or valid ways of selecting the staff who will turn out to manifest the qualities which had been looked for at the time of selection. Detailed references, group screening and intensive individual interviews have all been shown to have limited utility. They are, however, the only sources of information available on the selection of staff and must, therefore, be utilised.

In practice it has been found particularly worthwhile not only to collect information from the above sources, but also to put groups of candidates in the charge of an existing member of staff who is asked to present as black and frightening a picture of the work as possible. If, by the end of this group session, a candidate still wishes to proceed with interview, then there is the probability that at least the level of motivation for the work is adequate. This has the additional merit that it involves a wide variety of staff in the selection of their colleagues. From a long range management point of view, this is useful in creating a sense of corporate responsibility for the weaknesses of their future colleagues.

Staff Training

The training of staff is centrally related to the concern for the quality of their work and the amount of importance any facility attaches to orientating its staff to its particular way of doing things. In most settings, even highly specialised ones which draw on an initially unskilled staff, the tradition and the practice is to throw in the staff 'at the deep end' and expect them to sink or swim. In part this is inevitable because staff establishments are usually only adequate if everyone is working. No spare capacity is available for training. But a more fundamental reason for the Cinderella status of training is that despite the lip service paid to it by administrators and policy makers, there is as little conviction about the need for staff training as there is about its content and the manner in which it should be carried out. Those who control the resources are unable to create better training facilities. Those who need the training are too busy surviving to dwell on the fact that training would reduce the need for exposing their survival ability. The tendency, therefore, is for staff to be appointed and to pick up an orientation to the children in the course of their dealings with their own colleagues. Their learning is haphazard and unsystematic and is likely to be so manifested in their dealings with the children. In practice it has been found necessary to give the staff who work with the extreme children systematic orientation and briefing, accompanied where possible by theoretical training and simulation exercises. The more important training, however, is done 'on the job' through analysis of problems and alternative modes of coping. This is as much a means of staff support as it is of training.

Deployment and Support

The first task of the staff is to survive, physically and psychologically, with a reasonable level of self-respect and personal satisfaction in the work they undertake. Any human being whose survival is threatened is likely to resort to defensive behaviour of various sorts which, certainly for the time being, restrict his functioning to simple survival. The most important task, therefore, is to ensure that (a) there is a minimum of occasions on which the survival of a member of staff is threatened; (b) that if such occasions do arise the member of staff is not left to feel isolated and, therefore, struggle for survival; and (c) that should the occasion arise, the support would be used for purposes of training, prevention of similar occasions, and development of coping skills. When survival has been achieved, staff can then be trained into acquiring higher levels of competence. Perhaps the most destructive tendency of disordered children is that they so frequently and unpredictably place staff under crisis conditions where survival rather than effective coping and amelioration becomes the priority. Despite some academic claims to the contrary and because of their overpowering anxiety element, crises are not very good vehicles for learning, though they may be useful for developing a thicker skin.

All human beings have some intolerance of ambiguity, but disordered children more than most. Creating a structured environment is, therefore, an early priority. 'Structured environment' refers to a set of routines, procedures, predictable responses to situations and ability to enforce them. Such structures place as much of a boundary on staff as they do on children. The important question is not whether to have structure or not, but rather how much and what kind of structure, to ensure that it does not institutionalise and reduce both the staff and the children to automatons. Structures are likely to be oppressive and, unless delicately balanced to allow for creative response, are likely to beget the seeds of their own destruction.

Experience shows that although such structure may be felt by some staff to limit their creative flexibility – their ability to respond freely to any situations that arise – in fact such creative responses in the handling of disordered children are likely to raise a great many more problems that they might resolve. This idea runs counter to the prevalent notions of need for 'human growth' and the fashionable preoccupation with unstructured 'therapeutic' environments' While it is acknowledged that human beings are not pre-programmed robots and should not fake personalities, equally it should be recognised that extreme children are not sent to establishments so that they can be subjected to creative innovations of staff and become recipients of all the fads and foibles of individual staff and victims of the inconstancy of their very human feelings. Nor are the staff in such jobs in order to simply manifest their own personalities unless their attributes can be shown to be of value in a particular setting and with particular children. An important task of the staff manager, therefore, is to set boundaries and structures for the interaction of the staff with the children, capitalising as much as is possible on individual attributes and interests.

Within such structures both children and staff need varying degrees of autonomy, not only to realise the positive aspects of their potential but also to experience new situations which, though negative, lead to learning which may be of long term benefit to them. As before, it is not a question of whether the staff should or should not have autonomy in how they deal with the children, but rather how much autonomy is tempered with what level of direction.

An important element in keeping up a high level of staff interaction with the children is to ensure that they are frequently refreshed by opportunities to express themselves, to learn from others' perception of their work and from alternative ways of coping with the children or particular problems that they raise. They need to feel that they are members of a community from which they are drawn and to which they can return. This is particularly important for staff who work with extreme children because there is a tendency for them to be either stigmatised or held in distant awe by their colleagues as are the children themselves. This leads to feelings both o isolation and of being 'special'. Neither feeling is particularly beneficial either to the children or to the subsequent development of the staff, because of its tendency to distort reality. This is one reason why specialised establishments for severely disordered youngsters are best placed within a larger set of facilities with whom they can exchange staff. An important aspect of this is that unless the staff are part of a bigger pool from which they are drawn and to which they are periodically returned, they are likely to develop practices and relationships which are of dubious benefit to the children. 'Relationship' is the sacred cow of modern social work practice. It has not been satisfactorily defined by anyone and yet it is a word more frequently mouthed than any other in discussions about dealing with disordered youngsters. It presumably refers to a set of mutual perceptions, feelings, behaviours and expectations between people who interact with each other at varying levels of intensity. Relationships are inevitable in the course of any dealings with people but this is quite different from highlighting them as ends in themselves or, even worse, the only means through which a task, particularly that of management, assessment and treatment of disordered children, can be achieved. Obviously a positive relationship enhances and facilitates these tasks just as a negative one makes them less pleasant and more difficult.

But all relationships in a specialised setting are, of necessity, transitory if the long term objective is to rehabilitate the child to his preferred community. The nature of the employment of staff and the shifting needs of the children dictate changes in the pattern of relationships. The inevitably greater isolation of both extreme children and the staff who deal with them is likely to lead to situations in which intense relationships, ranging from dependency and favouritism at the one extreme to rejection and victimisation at the other, are likely to develop. It would be hypocritical cant or simple idiocy to suggest that professional staff of *any* establishment are so regulated in their reactions that no such possibility is likely to arise. Children and staff are at special risk in such circumstances. The movement of staff and their continued links with a wider community are at least likely to minimise, if not totally obviate, this possibility.

In the present context, all staff appointments are made to a general pool rather than to any particular functional part. No member of staff is permanently attached to a particular unit. They are regularly switched around, particularly where the facility for the extreme children is concerned. Despite occasional misgivings, the staff recognise that such movement is necessary to create balanced teams of staff; give respite to those who do a particularly stressful job; enlarge the opportunity for staff to acquire a wider range of handling skills and enhance their chances of being assigned to more specialised and responsible tasks. From a longer term management viewpoint the major advantage lies in the development of a large pool of competence which can be utilised in meeting the changing needs of the children particularly at times of stress. Together with the quality of staff support, this is probably the main reason for the survival of this facility with its explosive and frequently exploding mixture of boys and girls.

The Management of Staff

A major element in the work of any facility for seriously disordered children should be that neither they nor the community which produces them remain constant, either in their problems or in their consequent requirements and that, therefore, it is necessary to remain open to change. In practice, this particular conception has been found to be crucial in enabling the staff to cope with problems and to seek solutions on a continuously evolving basis.

Additionally, the staff must accept that it is their task to cope with the most difficult children the community produces. It may be that at some point the price to the community (of which the facility is a part) is too great and that, therefore, alternative placements for a child should be sought. Such alternatives, however, are almost invariably those in the penal setting and cannot be contemplated for girls or the younger children. They are also tantamount to an act of rejection which most self-respecting and competent staff are unwilling to perform. Given these premises and the limitations of resources, both material and human, the central task of any specialised facility becomes the support of its own staff to enable them to do the job at an acceptable level of efficiency.

'Support' has two main components – enabling and

monitoring. The information provided has given some indication of the kinds of stresses to which the staff are subject and which impede their functioning. They need to be given sufficient confidence, security and skill to be able to continue when the going gets rough. But this can only be done in the context of their work with the children. Monitoring – keeping an eye on and systematically evaluating the state of both the children and the staff – is a necessary prerequisite for determining when and where special support is required.

The 'support system' for this facility comprises three components, each of which take place at a variety of different levels. These are: visits; talking to and about staff and children; and meetings.

There are frequent visits to the house from morning till night of the duty senior staff and, in the course of the week, by a large range of others from specialists to those responsible for management of the whole establishment. This ensures an open atmosphere and, because of the range of visitors, the probability that the staff would be able to talk about their problems either relating to specific children or to wider matters which enable appropriate preventive or remedial action to be taken.

More importantly, the frequent visits retain the position of both the staff and the children in the mainstream of the work of the whole establishment. This prevents the build up of a sense of isolation with all its damaging consequences. As will be further explored in Chapter 9, perhaps the worst aspect of secure provision is its insulation from a wide range of people who could witness, even superficially, the state of the children and the staff and by communicating, commenting and warning, establish a bridgehead with normality. Openness is not only compatible with but also forms an essential safeguard to security.

An important element in the support of staff who deal with disordered youngsters is the provision of frequent opportunities for talking about and through problems, as an explicit policy, to ensure that no problem festers and reaches crisis proportions. Talking by itself does not solve any problems, though it may give the impression of doing so. It does, however, ensure that a variety of viewpoints are brought to bear on the same problem. If then a solution emerges, it is likely to be more rounded and to have a greater chance of success than if it had been initiated by one person. In the absence of clearly tested and established guidelines, this is the nearest approach to an empirical solution.

Outside casual and unstructured talking, frequent meetings also take place. These range from the meetings of the Heads and senior staff with the Principal at least three times a week, the weekly meeting of the Head with his senior staff and housewardens; and meeting of the house team at predetermined times. These meetings are formal with a formal agenda and structure. The formality is deliberate to ensure that professional issues receive the most critical scrutiny. This would be less easy if close personal relationships were allowed to intrude. At these meetings, individual children and general issues relating to the management, both of them and staff, are discussed and particular actions determined.

The same intensity of communication is encouraged with the children. Severely disordered youngsters are generally inarticulate and not prone to talking. Indeed their frequent misbehaviour can be seen as an attempt at non verbal communication. The staff are encouraged to engage in frequent talking with the children, about anything, so as to maintain positive contact. There are also daily group meetings at which the children can ventilate their problems, to ensure that at least being oppressed is not the reason for their blow ups.

One goal of the staff support is to ensure that the staff remain capable of coping with a whole variety of problems which are increasingly articulated so that the solutions can be communicated to newcomers. Another important aim of this system is to ensure that the staff remain in touch with the boundaries and constraints within which the whole establishment and they, as part of it, have to operate.

One of the more frequent problems encountered in the management of a specialised establishment is that because staff are dealing with children whom previous workers have failed, they become dismissive of other agencies, complacent about their own effectiveness and demanding in their approach to their colleagues or to outsiders. Although these attitudes arise out of their care for children and the wish to do something worthwhile with them, they nevertheless give rise to unacceptable conflicts. For this reason, the considerable autonomy of the facility is described within a clearly delineated boundary.

This boundary is reinforced by not only a printed document of 'Standard Procedures' which regulate the work of the whole of the establishment, but also 'Special Procedures' relating to the particular unit. These procedures specify what the staff may *not* do with the children, precautions that must be taken in certain circumstances, the conditions under which 'separation rooms' may be used, etc. Such printed procedures are regarded as an essential safeguard both for the children and staff. The fact that they are mentioned in the staff's terms and conditions of service makes their observance mandatory.

The notion of 'boundary' is essential to effective staff performance as it is to acceptable management of the children. If the staff do not know what is expected of them and the limit beyond which they may not go, they can legitimately object to any criticism, overt or covert, aimed at improving their performance. It is, therefore, felt that staff need a setting which provides them with feedback on their performance, their weaknesses and strengths, and evaluates them for the effects of their actions on the children and their colleagues. Staff of any facility are the chief source of any good *or* harm which is done to the children and they must be held accountable for what they do. This view should be tempered with understanding of the intense stress they encounter in the course of their day to day work, and readiness to give them both the opportunity to acquire the necessary skills and support when new problems are encountered.

There is little question, certainly judging by the feelings of life long practitioners, that the problems presented by disordered children are becoming more difficult to manage. This worsening has not been matched by an improvement in the quality and competence of the staff who have to do the managing. This is mainly because no attempt has been made over the years to provide a rigorous, teachable basis for coping with the whole complex of children's problems. Even a cursory look at the syllabus of social work courses would confirm this. Also, partly due to major social changes, people's attitudes to work, their expectations of how much they should put into it and what they may be legitimately expected to do have taken a gradual but perceptible shift.

As a result of these and other reasons, there is now a notable gap between the quality of problems presented by disordered children and the ability of staff to cope with them. This in turn results in more frequent management problems presented by the children which would not have arisen with other staff, sometimes even in the same establishment. Under these circumstances, children are likely to be subjected to practices which are aimed more at staff survival than their welfare.

Because of this, it is all the more important to establish the notion of professional responsibility of staff for everything that happens to the children in their charge and not allow protectionist practices to cloud the issue. But it is futile to insist on accountability for untoward events unless steps have been taken to support the staff with adequate skills and resources that guard them against reaching the edge of survival.

Management of Disordered Children

The day to day handling and management of extreme children is awesomely complex. The age of the children can range from eight to seventeen years, their IQs from 50 to 130, their problems from persistent suicide attempts to extreme violence against others. And then, of course, there are boys *and* girls.

Thus, at any time there will be a mixed group of individuals with a constantly changing pattern of relationships as new children are admitted and others are transferred. In this fluid environment, there are three elements which have a critical bearing on the management of the groups – staff, children and the context. The interplay of these variables and the staff's perception of them leads them to adopt their particular approach amongst themselves as a means of increasing their efficiency and reducing the inconsistencies which can emerge once the programme is fully under way.

The best that can be said about management of this facility is that the same staff have not made the same mistakes repeatedly and, despite the quality of its children, it has not yet been faced with situations with which it has not been able to cope without paying an unacceptable price.

Slowly the seeds of a set of management techniques suitable for these children are beginning to emerge, based largely on the discovery that the majority of traditional skills for group management based on the exertion of staff authority, use of privileges and punishments and preoccupation with control are counter productive, inefficient and largely irrelevant.

In general, the staff are selected for maximum diversity of personal characteristics and skills. They adopt, within accepted guidelines, diverse personal and individual approaches to the children. The diversity is as deliberately aimed for as is staff constancy to increase the chances of children finding somebody among the staff who would be acceptable to them.

Routines and Programmes

When dealing with extreme children, the *individual* management of each child is of prime importance. By establishing general routines which cater for the basic requirements of all children and which become 'second nature' to both children and adults, such individual management becomes feasible. The weekly programme is well balanced to include an appropriate number of classroom sessions, art and craft sessions, visits to sports facilities, trips to swimming baths and opportunities for the children to get outside. Maximum use is made of available staff and space. Every aspect of the routine is considered so that everything the children are asked to do can be shown to be reasonable. Counselling may often be necessary in this area as individual children may perceive certain aspects if the routine as noxious. This conflict is of positive value because it may help establish with the child that there are certain prerequisites to civilised living, but also that the staff are prepared to discuss areas of apparent conflict which may unearth some previously undisclosed problems.

The programme must take into account not only the primary function of the facility, in this case assessment of new children, but also cater for the needs of those children who have been assessed and are awaiting transfer. As some children stay for considerable periods after assessment, this becomes increasingly important.

Once the routine has been established the actual management becomes the concern of the staff team on duty. There are a number of basic requirements to be met in the day to day management of the children, overlapping and sliding into one another. The children are subdivided into small groups, as small as staff availability will allow. The groups are chosen carefully to ensure that incompatibility between individual members is minimised. As well as creating more easily manageable units, this allows the staff to observe each child and interact more closely in order to contribute to the process of assessment.

All activities must be open ended to cater for the wide abilty range of the children. Staff do not have high expectations of achievement. This is particularly important in the classroom situation, as almost all these children habitually resent, reject, and avoid school. Activities are also selected so as to be appealing and, where possible, produce tangible end products so that the children gain a sense of achievement. Considerable emphasis is, therefore, laid on craftwork ranging from tie and dye through painting, doll making, batik, etc. which are displayed around the house. The majority of the children experience difficulty in concentrating for long periods of time. No activity must, therefore, require long term attention.

While most children are apathetic to start with and resent being chivvied into activities, they do become interested once pressure towards achievement and the possibility that they may be exposed to ridicule have been removed. Most children's refusal to participate in activities is part of a game they play with the staff, usually to gain some personal, positive attention. The staff must know this and play along with it until the interests of the other children begin to be adversely affected. Gentle insistence and firmness usually achieves compliance, though the resistance can easily develop into a confrontation. Staff must remain at all times sensitive to the shifting moods, particularly of the girls, which may make certain activities particularly distasteful to them. Any programme needs to have sufficient flexibility as not to have to 'push a square peg into a round hole'.

Aspects of Groups

It is reasonable to assume that as children live in groups, what is known from group dynamics about cohesiveness, group pressures and norms, performance, leadership and patterns of communication (e.g. Cartwright and Zander, 1960; Secord and Backman, 1964) would apply to them, with appropriate change, as a social system. But children are qualitatively different from adults, because of their different developmental status, and disordered children are different again from their normal peers. Until the necessary empirical work has been done (and it urgently needs doing) it would be a not particularly enlightening academic exercise to speculate on *how* group dynamics are manifested within their groups.

In the present context, the children appear more frequently to form into groupings of individual cells rather than members of a group with any kind of permanence. They slide into or collide with each other's private life spaces and move out again onto new territories. This is not to say that there are never any strong bonds of attraction or repulsion or that occasionally the individuals do not cohere as a group. Such experiences, however, are the rare exception rather than the rule and as such do not occupy a high place in the staff's consciousness of what is going on with the children. This is reserved for sensitivity to and knowledge of the current sources of stress on each individual child.

Sources of stress range from the internal – physiological, medical and emotional excesses and deficits – to aspects of the external environment – noise, overcrowding, threat, etc. To understand *all* sources of stress on a particular child would itself be the objective of more thorough assessment than is possible either theoretically or practically. It is, however, feasible to bear in mind certain central elements such as a child's medical state, intellectual competence or any particularly damaging experiences he may have had which have made him vulnerable to particular events.

Besides these overall difficulties, the staff's main concern is with the children's day to day problems. These include their current amours, vendettas, anxiety about a promised visit from parents, impending court appearances, being pressured to abscond, etc. Children's idiosyncratic reactions to such events may turn a marginally stressful situation into an explosive one. Because of the cross currents of communication between staff and children, the situation is like a dozen games of three-dimensional chess being played all at the same time. Some of the problems of inadequate management by staff arise simply because the human brain has only limited information processing capacity. The extreme alternative is to take a primitive, simplistic approach which refuses to be impressed with the diversity of children's problems and treats them all in a black and white fashion.

One of the main problems in dealing with the extreme youngsters is that while each demands personal recognition and special treatment, not many of them are prepared to have the same approach extended to others and interpret any particular interest as undeserved favouritism or leniency.

This is particularly true of the most severely disordered girls who, by definition, get very special attention. If then another girl is admitted who, because of her problems, should also be given particular care, then all 'Hell is let loose'. The girls feel betrayed and resort to sulking, tantrums and destructive acts aimed at themselves, others and property. This form of possessiveness and sense of betrayal is almost never seen in the boys. It is all the more surprising because the girls' histories do not show a significantly greater incidence of disturbed emotional ties and deprivation, nor are their relationships with the staff any deeper – indeed the opposite is frequently the case. A semblance of tranquillity is re-established when the girls are taken to their own rooms and are quieted down through gentler one to one talking, which reaffirms their status. In a long term treatment setting the approach would be very different.

Although the situation may often necessitate dealing with the children in small numbers, it is important to be able to observe the children's behaviour within the larger group setting. There are, of course, parts of the daily schedule which demand that all the children be grouped together. Staff who often deal with the children in twos and threes may experience difficulty in handling the group as a whole. Social behaviour of the children in larger groupings, as presented in Chapter 5, gives some indication of why other people have found them intolerable. It is in such situations that most crises develop.

Crises

Children and staff find the least troublesome ways of surviving one another and thereby adapt to each other's variability. From time to time, however, their pattern of variable adaptation is severely punctured by a crisis. A number of definitions of crises have been proposed (see Viney, 1976) which are not directly related to the present context. Redl (Redl & Wineman, 1957) has been centrally concerned with the therapeutic use of crises in dealings with aggressive children. His work and his insights form a particularly valuable contribution to this area but are bound up with his theoretical notions of ego psychology and do not translate easily to a setting concerned with the management of severely disordered adolescents, where the same emphasis is not laid on relationships with charismatic personalities.

An appropriate definition of crisis in this context is 'a moment of acute danger or difficulty'. Crucially, this definition leaves open the variability of individual perceptions regarding what is an 'acute' danger or difficulty, thereby allowing for the frequently observed fact that one person's crisis is another person's ordinary event.

Crises do not occur either at random or in a vacuum. As with other events, their frequency, intensity and content is the function of three elements: the children, the staff and the context. Each of these elements can be evaluated in terms of the degree to which they impede or facilitate crises. Thus, some children create a great many more crises than others, *almost* regardless of who they are with and under what conditions. The 'almost' is crucial, because even the most disastrous of children do not cause disasters *all* the time.

Some members of staff are more crisis prone than others. These can be usually related to a set of personal characteristics which interact badly with certain children: Mr X, a big, rugby playing, rather ham handed new member of staff, has more problems with the older, more moody girls than does Miss Z whose gentleness and withdrawal from normal rough and tumble makes her, on the other hand, the butt of the more exuberant youngsters.

And then, of course, certain situations are more fraught with potential for confrontation and crisis than are others; for example, when a youngster has been found out in some nefarious act, such as smuggling in knives and razors, been told off in front of a group or been 'ignored' for another child. Recently, Zeeman *et al* (1977) have applied the mathematical 'catastrophe theory' to prison riots and disturbances. So far, the application of the theory has been retrospective and concerned with mass phenomena (unlike crises in the present context) but it holds the promise of a more rigorous approach which may provide both for the analysis and prevention of crises.

Each of the above elements can be placed on a dimension, which interactively contributes to impending or facilitating crises. What makes life difficult is that not only are the potentials different between different exemplars of the same element, staff, children and situation, but also *within* them – so that Diana who seemed 'all right' when told there was no letter for her yesterday, creates mayhem when told the same thing today.

It may also be worthwhile to separate out the notion of crisis from others such as conflict, confrontation, etc. which are associated with it. Conflict is an irreducible element in all daily interaction of human beings who have different emotions, ideas, behaviour patterns and values. No one should be surprised or dismayed that disordered children come into conflict with the adults who are entrusted with their care, or with one another. Most conflict is resolved reasonably quickly and amicably through talking, use of humour, side stepping issues or other forms of peacemaking. It is not so much the conflict but rather the manner in which the conflict resolution is sought which is liable to accelerate a straight conflict into a tortuous confrontation, that is the drawing of battle lines and each side brandishing its might.

In a confrontation inevitably one side has to lose – with all the loss of face, resentment and frustration that such a defeat entails. In child-staff confrontations, the children usually lose because they are the less powerful and in the wrong, and their behaviour must not be allowed to be copied by other children. The staff, however, are conscious of the price the child has to pay and of the probability that the resentment harboured will erupt with greater force in another situation. It is for this reason that great emphasis is laid in staff training on techniques for *avoiding* confrontations and ways of recouping some of the loss as soon as the issue is resolved.

If the confrontation is not resolved, it is then likely to move along the continuum to a zone where one of the participants, either the child or the member of staff, define it as a crisis. This zone is defined by (1) projection of the present situation to its extreme – 'Janie has a razor blade in her hand now – is she likely to cut her wrist or go for my face?'; (2) how acceptable is the risk involved in the extreme events – 'Is she likely to do serious damage before I get the blade out of her hand?'; and (3) confidence in being able to deal with the crisis – 'I'll have to do what I did with Tina'. Taking these together with the variability of the constituent elements, some idea may be gained of why some people and places are more prone to crises than others and why this aspect of dealing with disordered youngsters generates as much anxiety as it has repulsed rational scrutiny.

Experience of severely disordered children in a residential context has highlighted three main types of crises: *child-child crises*; *child-staff crises*; and *self-destructive crises*.

A child-child crisis is perhaps the easiest type of crisis for the staff to cope with. It usually starts with accusations about some real or imaginary slight or threat. Unless resolved, it then moves on to threats which frequently end in a fight. Verbal and physical attacks can be terminated by separating the children and counselling them as individuals. It is important that the staff be seen to be impartial towards such confrontations as it is often impossible to ascertain who was the instigator. If the staff are careful in observing the dynamics of the group and are aware of the current moods of the children, many such crises can and will be prevented by appropriate ploys. In this way potentially explosive situations can be defused at an early stage. These conflicts are usually dealt with by the staff on duty and do not necessitate the intervention of others, unless the intervention of the staff creates a child-staff conflict due to the extreme reaction of one or other of the children involved. There does not appear to be any difference in the number of boys and girls involved in such crises.

Most of the crises with extreme children involve child-staff confrontations, usually as a result of a child refusing to do as requested. Many of these crises escalate, often necessitating the intervention of the housewarden and sometimes of the senior staff. Examination of records shows that the majority of these crises involve the girls. This is amply borne out by the information presented so far and confirms the generally accepted belief that in the extreme group girls present more serious handling problems than do difficult boys.

There is little information about what to expect from such girls and how best to cope with their potentially cataclysmic reactions where no holds seem to be barred. This tends to create a feeling of apprehension in the staff who have to handle them. The girls know this. The difficult girls appear to be very adept at perceiving the weaknesses of members of staff and using them when necessary in verbal attacks on them.

During the period of this study it has been necessary to withdraw two members of staff and replace them with others to prevent serious psychological breakdowns in them. Both were female and were particularly intimidated by the girls' gross abusiveness and tendency to resort to physically detailed obscenities. This aspect of the girls' behaviour is blood-curdlingly gross and almost never encountered in boys. This is also the aspect that, by any standards, comes nearest to suggesting why these girls tend to be regarded as 'depraved'.

One of the reasons put forward to account for the difference in the numbers of boys and girls involved in child-staff crises is the apparent difficulty of the girls in changing or halting a behaviour sequence. Boys will usually accept the chance to opt out of a confrontation with staff whereas the girls will continue with their truculence, abuse, or defiance even though they are presented with several chances to retract or reassess the situation. In general, any temper tantrums the girls exhibit are of longer duration than those of boys.

Once a crisis point has been reached another member of staff usually attempts to resolve it at as low a level as the conflict allows, using human, gentle physical touch and quiet speech as main tools. If the confrontation cannot be resolved by low key intervention, it may be necessary to isolate the offending youngster from the group. An appropriate member of staff then stays with or joins the youngster for quiet questioning and counselling. This is essential as the children, especially the girls, may become more violent towards their environment or themselves if left on their own while in a hostile mood. This counselling is a far more time consuming operation when a girl is involved than is the case with a boy, because the same ground has to be traversed from many different directions until its message has been received.

One of the problems which all staff experience in managing children is the difficulty of 'losing face' and having to retract from a confrontation. When conflict arises between a child and a member of staff, the latter is often too involved to judge best what should be done about the conflict, notwithstanding his skills and experience. The most competent staff know this and accept it with wry equanimity. To the less experienced, however, retracting from the situation and allowing a third person to intervene often threatens 'loss of face' and possibly loss of credibility. To overcome this, it may be necessary to devise a staff roster which allows teams of staff to work together consistently, thus enabling them to pool their skills in alleviating crisis situations, talking through their problems of management and recognising that there is no implied shame or slight in allowing someone else to mediate.

It is important that after the crisis has been worked through, the member of staff who was initially involved is made aware of how things stand including any sanctions which may have been imposed. Attempts are then made to quickly re-establish relations between the conflicting parties by making amends, including ritualised expressions of conciliation such as apologies, and opportunities for sharing positive experiences.

An important difference between the boys and girls is the latter's apparent inability to 'forgive and forget'. They will harbour resentment after conflict for more lengthy periods than the boys. They are great perseverators and often become vindictive and threatening. They have grown up to be so close-minded that they seem unable to accept that one criticism or confrontation need not call into question their whole meagre stock of self-esteem.

The last and the most threatening type of crisis for staff

centres around self-destructive acts. This is becoming more frequent, apparently nationally, and again is more likely to involve girls than boys. Almost all the children who engage in self-destructive acts have a previous history of similar behaviour, which is often the main reason that local authoriities send them for intensive stabilisation and assessment. Most of them do not appear sensitive to a particular set of precipitating factors, but rather attempt hurting themselves when under any form of generalised or specific stress. In a setting with other disordered youngsters they do not have to go far to find such stress in the course of any ordinary day.

Kreitman (1977) in his exhaustive survey of 'parasuicides' found illegitimacy, poverty, truancy, history of being in care, offending both against person and property, to be significantly associated with them. He also looked at the function which an attempted suicide performs for the person involved but came to the conclusion that there was not a 'suicidal personality'. From a study of self-injury among women prisoners, Cookson (1977) concludes 'Inmates in a closed institution, dependent on others for their every need, unable to do anything about problems of home and family, uncertain as to what is happening to them and theirs, inevitably suffer from feelings of helplessness and frustration which may be exacerbated by incidents. . . .' The same may be said of adolescents in a less than total environment.

Many of the self-destructive gestures are known to be attention seeking ploys but every one must be treated seriously and appropriate actions taken. Staff must be constantly alert to ensure that scissors, knives and other such objects do not go astray and that all tablets and medicines are swallowed and not accumulated to be used in suicidal gestures. It is now routine to remove all of a child's belongings from their room, if they have to be isolated and given a cooling off period, in order to minimise the chances of self-damage. When such children are placed in their rooms, a member of staff stays with them until they have calmed down. They are then visited or otherwise checked every fifteen minutes and this is recorded.

When the self-destructive crisis has been dealt with and treatment, where necessary, has been administered, intensive counselling techniques are once again employed. The happening is notified to senior staff who, knowing the children, may undertake additional counselling or initiate other measures thought necessary.

A common sequence of coping with self-destructive episodes starts with a member of staff attempting to stop the child from continuing with the self-destructive act. This seems to reverse the direction of aggression from inward to outward; attempts at self-damage are thwarted and the child becomes violent towards whoever may be present. The self-destructive crisis is then transformed into a child-staff conflict where appropriate management techniques may be employed. The cost to the staff remains high, but potential suicides brook no sparing of costs.

As with other crises, when girls are involved, the quelling of violence and the ensuing counselling may be long and drawn out. Having received the attention, they make the most of it. From a long term treatment point of view, this is probably the wrong approach. But this setting is not for treatment and, in any case, society does not yet allow professionals to risk suicide, even by default, in the interests of treatment. Apart from the fact that the girls tend to be more aggressive and thus engage in self-damaging acts more frequently, either to attract attention or to cope with stress, they also suffer from more extreme mood swings than the boys. Thus rapid changes of emotional tone often precede self-destructive acts. Particular attention is paid, therefore, to the girls' mood swings with a view to taking preventive action.

An important aspect of girls' behaviour in groups is that any critical event seems to affect them more rapidly than it does the boys. Their reactions to it are also more dramatic and uniform. For example, when one girl has been attempting to cut her wrists, in all probability the rest will follow suit and almost mimic the same behaviour, without having any apparent personal reasons or being particularly sympathetic to the other girl(s). Such behavioural 'epidemics' which are almost un-known among boys, present the staff with a serious problem of management. The facility is designed for the care and assess-ment of children under conditions maximising semblance to normality. Such an environment cannot be so clinically shorn of implements that no determined youngster may attempt or indeed succeed in committing suicide. In view of the ap-parently increasing incidence of self-destructive attempts among adolescents nationally, this problem warrants closer study to enable a wider number of people to cope with it.

Apart from the three main types of crises there is a consider-able amount of generally disruptive behaviour, such as non co-operation in activities and violent, destructive abuse of the building and its contents. There does not appear to be any differences in the numbers of boys and girls involved in such incidents. Among such problems, absconding attempts figure prominently. The girls are more likely to attempt to or threaten to run away than the boys. These attempts rarely involve any major incidents, because most children are caught by a pursuing member of staff, often before they are away from the grounds. Bearing in mind that some of the children have committed grave crimes and others are a source of danger to themselves, there is a strong temptation to curb outside activities to reduce absconding risks.

This problem and others like it show the difficulty of achiev-ing a reasonable balance between the care needs of the children (who must not be kept locked up all the time) and considera-tions of security and public safety. Rather than asking for more staff and 'resources' (whatever that may mean) it is preferable that the public should be aware of the price to be paid whatever 'solution' is adopted and to accept that, in the last resort, risks and costs may be reduced but can never be eliminated.

There is no evidence that the interaction between the girls and the boys plays a significant part in exacerbating manage-ment problems. These difficult girls would be, and many have been in the past, no easier to handle in all female environments. In fact, the general feeling is that the interaction of the sexes helps to 'soften' the behaviour of both boys and girls. The girls are often more amenable towards male members of staff, even if only by comparison with the female members of staff to whom they appear to be particularly cruel and ruthless.

Crisis Management

As suggested earlier, there is a natural course of crises to be negotiated. Some earlier work on crisis resolution is of relevance here. Caplan (1964) suggests four stages in the history of a crisis: rising tension; feelings of ineffectuality; tension reaching such a point that further resources are called for and utilised; resolution of tension and return to a state of equilibrium.

The important element in this description and others provided by, for example, Viney (*op. cit.*) is that the situation is defined as one which is beyond the expectancy and normal coping ability of the individual, which warrants the deployment of 'exaggerated' or extra defences. Obviously the tactics deployed would resolve the crisis if they are appropriate but may exacerbate it if they are not. What is appropriate to crisis resolution, bearing in mind the enormous variability of elements of a crisis, has not yet been worked out.

From the description of the crisis experienced with severely disordered youngsters, however, it appears that there is a natural progression of priorities. The first of these is *curbing*.

In aggressive and self-destructive crises the primary task of the member of staff concerned is to limit the behaviour to ensure that it does not accelerate to an even higher level of difficulty; if a girl is cutting her wrist, the staff must ensure that the girl does not attempt to cut any other part of her body or indeed go any further with her wrist cutting than she has already. This almost invariably involves physical holding and neutralisation of the child's force. In the course of this, which brings the child and the member of staff into close physical conflict and testing of strength, enormous care needs to be taken not to use any more force than is minimally necessary.

This is generally accepted among all professionals. It is, however, frequently more of an expression of hope rather than statement of a standard of practice which a person could be sensibly expected to observe. If he is unusually anxious about the situation – if there is blood pouring out of the child, or he is trying to wrest a knife – he may feel that the most sensible measure is the use of overwhelming force to curb the child's behaviour. This force may be greater than would be objectively deemed necessary to achieve its particular purpose, but crisis situations are marked by high levels of anxiety which mar objective, rational judgment.

While there is justified public concern about the possibility of adults using physical force on children in the course of altercations, no adequate alternative approaches remain which can act with the same rapidity to curb destructive behaviour towards self and others. For this reason it may be useful for all staff who deal with such children to be taught methods of physical neutralising which require more subtlety of approach than physical force. It is for this reason that the staff need considerable training in not defining situations as crises; feeling sure that once a crisis has occurred other staff and resources may become available to help them so that they do not feel they have to use overpowering force to cope; bringing about an atmosphere in which a member of staff can recognise how much force is necessary and to learn from actual encounters whether excessive or inadequate force has been used. Also, children should be safeguarded against cavalier use of force by making the recording and reporting of such incidents mandatory. Recent events in several establishments where children have been subjected to unjustified physical punishment by the staff emphasise the need for greater safeguards than provided in Community Homes Regulations (1972).

Reducing impact is the second task of staff dealing with crises. Every piece of crisis behaviour, particularly of an aggressive nature, has adverse consequences of varying extent and intensity. The most obvious purpose of intervention in a crisis is to ensure that the damage done to the child or his victim is minimised. In cases of physical hurt against self or others, all forms of first aid become paramount.

Crises in a group generate enormous anxiety in the other youngsters and it is often necessary to send the group away or ask them for help as a way of reducing the impact of the crisis on them. On such occasions there is the possibility that the witnessing of an outburst in one child may trigger off severe outbursts in other children. This is an important reason for isolating such children at the earliest possible opportunity and building in procedures for the calling of additional help should the need arise.

The spreading of a crisis from one child to another is (other than among the girls) in the context of a competent professional staff a rare occurrence. This is fortunate because quite apart from the physical hurt the staff receive, such behaviour has the most wearing and anxiety producing effect on staff and can lead to debilitating effects. At times of frequent crises staff absenteeism due to quite legitimate 'physical' ailments increases rapidly and in turn the children themselves seem to become more prone to having outbursts. Such cycles of disturbance can be accounted for only in the general terms suggested so far.

Resolution of crisis is the next priority. When its force has been spent through some form of intervention, such as taking the child to hospital, holding him until he stops thrashing about, an attempt is made to accelerate the reduction of tension and its conversion to a less cataclysmic form. In such instances, physical holding of a child is frequently accompanied by gentle, non-admonitory, soothing talk by the member of staff. To begin with, such holding, etc. elicits swear words and other vituperative outbursts, but the reaction gradually reduces both in intensity and venom and resolves into some sort of a two way conversation between the child and the adult. It is also at this time that what was originally a physical hold aimed at overcoming force with a greater force and curbing the destructive behaviour of the child becomes more of a reassuring physical contact.

Physical touch is an important source of communication with ordinary children. It has assumed particularly positive value in the course of their growth and interaction with parents and siblings. It is, however, frequently observed that severely disordered children are extremely ambivalent towards and frequently recoil from physical contact. To them physical contact seems to be associated with punishment and other forms of hurtful experience. However, even with these children it seems that after a crisis, close positive physical contact can act as a primitive form of protectiveness, communication and reassurance. There seems to be no difference in boys' and girls' response to such physical contact.

However, male staff are understandably chary of appearing to be giving girls this form of succour because of the public censure they may provoke. As long as this form of contact remains public and exercised with discretion, it is likely to continue as an important aid in establishing peace and reassurance about the human status and worth of the former antagonists. The crisis having abated, staff then tend to channel and shape it into positive forms of communication. A girl may say that she is tired and wishes to lie down; a boy may ask the member of staff if they can go out for a walk or engage in some other activity together.

Although not strictly related to coping with the particular crisis, it is important to provide an opportunity for both the child and the member of staff involved to talk through what brought about the crisis and find ways of alleviating their anxiety, not only about the hurt that may have resulted from that crisis, but also about *preventing recurrence*. With children, such talking through amounts to making positive and creative use of crises. Although on the basis of social and operant learning theories and related experiences (e.g. Bandura, 1969), there is a distinct possibility that crises beget crises, nevertheless, in settings for extreme children, crises can provide an opportunity for learning and acquisition of potentially helpful insights by both children and staff. Even though the evidence for such therapeutic use is not all that it might be, it suggests the possibility of making virtue out of the inevitability of these exhausting events.

In looking at any crisis and ways of coping with it, it is important to distinguish between short and long term objectives. In a short term setting such as the one described in this book, the primary concern of staff is with the stabilising and assessing of the children. Whatever they do is aimed at ensuring that the child is in a reasonable and stable enough frame of mind not to cause unde trouble and not to create circumstances which would make his or her assessment impossible. Long term considerations of conditioning and other influences on subsequent treatment are necessarily given a low priority. Thus, a child who engages in frequent though mild self-destructive behaviour (arm scratching, tattooing, picking at skin) is given much attention with the result that the health and other care requirements of the child are met and possible escalation of such acts into more serious ones is prevented. However, the child's attention seeking, self destructive behaviour is reinforced and is likely to recur under similar circumstances. The approach in a long term treatment setting would be quite different, based on a more thorough analysis of why the behaviour occurs and what maintains it (which is provided by assessment) and a selection of appropriate treatment methods (ignoring the behaviour, token economy, group therapy, etc.).

This point revolves around the general notion of 'costs'. Every form of intervention carries a cost, to the child, to the staff, and to the wider environment, including physical and emotional damage to persons, destruction of property and creation of environmental stresses. Dealing with crises of the type discussed here is no exception. A price has to be paid in order to stop a child from hurting himself, others, or property. Difficulties revolve around notions of who pays how much, when, how and for how long. Sadly, there are no ready reckoners available for converting costs to benefits and it is therefore, not possible to determine accurately how much or what sort of interventionis justified by what types of results. This is complicated by the fact that little is known about what forms of intervention work, so that attempts at explanation of what and why something was done become self justificatory.

Broadly speaking, however, there is general agreement that life must be preserved at all costs; that undue risks may not be taken with it in the interests of some dubious notion of treatment; and that there is a level of destruction of property beyond which the costs are unacceptable. Because there are certain broad premises upon which every culture operates, a good deal of agreement can be taken for granted in the above areas. But in dealings with extreme children, agreements are the exception rather than the rule. The more frequent occurrence is that every crisis situation can be subsequently analysed and a variety of alternative approaches put forward which, it is claimed, could have produced the same or better results. Because these are normally judgments in hindsight, it is not possible to test them and little attempt is made to set up situations in which a prospective testing may be carried out. The contention, however, causes a good deal of resentment and anxiety among persons engaged in crisis intervention, which does not help in developing a rational approach.

There is urgent need for articulating elements in the definition and course of crises and the ways in which they can best be coped with. This is a particular aspect of the general need for developing guidelines about the management of severely disordered children. This latter is a wider problem than crisis management but does not arouse the same anxiety nor does it have the same disorganising effect as do crises. If crisis management were to become more explicit and empirically based, there is a distinct possibility that fewer crises would occur and a calmer climate would prevail in which it may be possible to look at why crises arise in the first place and find ways of preventing them. Fulfilling this task may thus become the spearhead of evolving a new discipline for the treatment of severely disordered children. Bearing in mind the cost of crises, both financial and personal, incurred by everyone involved – including the wider society – it makes sense to invest some resources in investigating this eminently researchable topic. Such research may produce more beneficial long term results than the regurgitation of recycled received wisdom which currently goes under the guise of 'training and development'.

PART TWO

★

Aspects of Intervention

*

CHAPTER 7

What Makes The Children Extreme?

THE question is likely to elicit as many different answers as there are people who care to have it posed. The answers are often framed in such terms as to make it difficult to test and to determine between them. In the end it becomes a matter of choosing the answer which best fits in with one's value system. The perspective adopted in this chapter is based not on a particular theory or value system, but rather, it derives from an examination of the processes the children have been through, seen from the vantage point of the 'end of the line'. The perspective is sharpened by the total view of the child, which makes it possible to discern the cross currents of contending pressures towards the development of the child into what he is now.

Inheritance

From the moment of conception, a child starts with an endowment that sets the potential limit to his future development. Subsequent environmental experiences determine the degree to which the endowment is activated. Thus any explanation of behaviour for any group, not least the present one, merits some consideration of the interaction of biological and environmental factors. The biological influences range from the hereditary (characteristics wholly contributed by the parents), through congenital (acquired in the interim), to constitutional (changes in the body as a result of life experiences).

Studies of genetic and other biological variables have shown that neurological disorders, endocrine-related problems, and perinatal difficulties as well as genetic factors in physique, temperament and behaviour (Rutter *et al*, 1964) have an important role in accounting for both childhood psychopathology (Hurst, 1972) and anti-social disorders (Shah & Roth, 1974). The influence of temperament is particularly emphasised by Rutter (1975) who argues its crucial effect in determining a child's interaction with others, range and quality of experiences, level of social competence and vulnerability.

It is not possible to state retrospectively and without the aid of considerably more data whether and how much the behaviour of extreme children is influenced by hereditary, congenital and constitutional abnormalities. The fact that most come from the social classes and families in which a 'conglomeration of impairments' is prevalent may argue for the existence of a hereditary predisposition to their subsequent problems (Hutchings, 1974; Hutchings & Mednick, 1975).

Although there is little evidence to suggest that these children have been subject to more complications antenatally and at the time of birth, the higher levels of infant mortality and perinatal complications among problem families may lead one to expect more difficulties which have not resulted in child's death (e.g. Stott, 1977). Nor is it very clear in this context, how evidence for constitutional impairments and predispositions could be collected. If psychological arguments (e.g. Eysenck, 1964; Cattell, 1965) for hereditary nature of certain characteristics are accepted, then much of the behaviour exhibited by disordered children could be interpreted as manifesting a major inherited component. This form of explanation is particularly appealing when one looks at the differences in the behaviour of extreme boys and girls such as described in the previous chapters, which cannot otherwise be readily understood. The girls' greater intensity and range of emotional expressions, inability to accept frustration and structure, rapid mood changes, greater tendency to become verbally and physically aggressive, tendency to mimic behaviour, are more difficult to explain in environmental and sociological terms than in biological ones, though the exact mechanics of the latter also remain a matter of conjecture.

Comparative research on adolescents, particularly the seriously disordered, has not concerned itself with these areas and is not of much help (Maccoby & Jacklin, 1974). Research on their socialisation and the minutiae of parent-child interaction, shaping and modelling, has also been so scant that it does not help making any very confident comments about the relative weight of hereditary and social components in the behaviour of these children.

In any case, this issue is of essentially academic interest. By the time the children come to the attention of an official agency, they have their full genetic equipment, suffered whatever perinatal damage has come their way, and are in the process of experiencing those events which shape their temperament and behaviour. An official agency is primarily concerned with intervening in their lives so as to alleviate whatever problems they may be presenting or experiencing. The concern of the official agency is the *control* of the unacceptable behaviour. From this social control point of view, little can be done to retrospectively correct the first two elements and the third can only be observed and modified in its manifestation. While the study of 'causation' may be of general interest and may, indeed, form a part of any thorough assessment, it is not of primary concern because it cannot become the subject of modification and control, though it may help to account for and predict subsequent modifiable development.

Far from leading to a dismissal of the importance of biological factors in the problem of severely disordered children, the information available suggests that such children probably suffer from some degree of biological damage or abnormality which predisposes them to extreme forms of behaviour. Therefore, anyone dealing with them should be conscious of this predisposition and take it into account in any form of intervention contemplated. It is precisely because of the importance of biological factors that pre-emptive and preventive measures should be taken with them in all forms of disposal. If a worker with these children starts with the expectation that the 'worst' will happen (whatever that may be), then if and when it does, he would not be surprised and will not act in a panicky and precipitate manner. As will be shown later, this inadequate understanding of disordered children which leads to not allowing for their extremes is an important factor in their mismanagement by social agencies.

Development in the Family

Almost all children, even the unwanted and the unwelcome, are born in a family setting. From the moment of birth a complex process of interaction starts between the child and the total family environment, particularly the parents. While the child initially responds to its own physical needs, the adults begin reacting to its looks, behaviour and effects on the dynamics of their own relationships. The parents have their own patterns of problems and adaptation into which the child is introduced. Their expectations of the child, their initial and continuing reactions to it and the degree to which it facilitates or impedes their preferred patterns of behaviour towards one another and the family sow the seeds of how they are likely to respond to its problems in the course of its growth.

The results in this study do not make it possible to say with any certainty whether the 'first' difficulties arose with the child reacting to stress from parents and environment or vice versa. Analysis of individual records suggests, however, that these children presented more difficulties and at an earlier age than did their siblings. Even when family stresses were paramount, their reactions were more adverse than those of others. This may suggest that they suffered from a greater degree of vulnerability than their siblings. If so, this would have warranted greater care by parents in their subsequent handling of the child, but this would be unlikely due to the parents' own problems, their difficulty in knowing what to do and the child's tendency to cap and follow one piece of problem behaviour with another. The parents' inappropriate and inadequate reactions to the child's behaviour beget other behaviours in the child and an ascending spiral of action and reaction is set up, moving at different rates, with different halts and dips, but always inexorably onto ever more troubled and troublesome areas.

The parents' definition of whether a child's behaviour is acceptable or not is, of course, the chief prerequisite of whether they wish to do something about it. There is considerable research, supported by the present results, to show that the families of disordered and delinquent children suffer from a great deal of disorganisation and disadvantage, accompanied by behavioural norms and attitudes which are different from those of the mainstream of society (e.g. Wootton, 1959; Hoghughi, 1973; West & Farrington, 1973). Most parents of these children are preoccupied with their own problems against which, at least initially, the problems of their child pale into insignificance. If they regard the behaviour as at all deviant, they are likely to consider it as naughty, transitory and not worthy of serious attention. What sanctions they adopt to curb the behaviour are inconsistent in kind, content and intensity and are erratically applied. Because they cannot or do not often articulate problems, cause and effect relationships (Robinson, 1972), or regulatory feedback, the child is further confused about what he is supposed to do and what will happen if he does not.

Each society and, within it, groups and individuals have some notion of which behaviours are acceptable and which are not. While these change with time and vary in emphasis between groups, a sufficiently solid core remains to make it possible to refer to prevailing 'latitude of tolerance' of social behaviour. Children learn about these in the course of their growth. The main agents of teaching are the parents who begin, with their first admonitions, to put out behavioural markers which will eventually cohere into a *behavioural boundary*. All parents, however disordered, set out such markers by approval or disapproval of their children's self-gratifying acts. The differences in the quality of parenting come with the consistency with which the markers are applied and enforced, whether they form a coherent pattern, whether the pattern takes account of the child's problems, needs and developmental changes and how much the pattern fits into the others presented to the child by peers, teachers, and other authority figures.

Without postulating a 'need' for boundaries, it should not be difficult to see that no child can grow up to be even minimally competent in a social setting without having some notion of what is permissible. A child will behave in any fashion at all that takes his fancy unless he can recognise a boundary and accept the obligation to observe it. The 'recognition' comes from frequent and consistent pointing out and the 'observance' from appropriate enforcement, through any or all of the accepted forms of social training – classical or operant conditioning, modelling, etc. As the child becomes aware very early on that some of his actions are followed by unpleasant consequences, he begins to search for markers which will tell him what he should not do and thus avoid trouble. In this sense a child can be said to need behavioural boundaries and to direct much of his energy both purposively and incidentally at discovering them.

Thus, the major importance of boundaries lies in the degree to which they help learning of behaviours appropriate to a wide range of social settings. In the course of his transition from one setting to another, the child learns, through the recognition and enforcement of such boundaries, which behaviours are appropriate to each setting. If there are no biological impediments to his learning, the quality of his adaptation is solely dependent on the quality of his social training. All children adapt to some variability of both social training methods and conflict of behavioural standards in different settings, but by the same token there are limits to how much they can adapt to such variability. This is the source of the major differences in children's response to socialisation practices reflecting differences in probably biological vulnerability and resilience.

Against their family background and their biological make up, it can be seen that disordered children, if anything, have an even greater need than normal children for consistent marking and enforcement of behavioural boundaries. But this is precisely what they do not get. They behave in ways which will undoubtedly get them into trouble in the future – ignoring parents' instructions, wandering, throwing temper tantrums to get their own way, etc. Yet only occasionally will any of these behaviours be pointed out to them as unacceptable and even more rarely and inconsistently corrected. Even in their dim perception, the children become aware of the ambiguity of the boundaries. Because actions are followed by positive or negative consequences, they are emotionally tinged. Like all other instances of emotional uncertainty, such ambiguity leads to emotional discomfort and probable anxiety. The children, therefore, engage in 'pushing' and 'testing out' behaviour which may clarify the ambiguity. But the 'pushing' and 'testing' is inevitably a more extreme form of behaviour than even before. The parents perceive their children's behaviour getting worse. If this causes them greater anxiety but no searching for or receiving of enlightenment, then their reactions are likely to become even less rational than before.

This pattern of testing out, inconsequential and sometimes bizarre behaviour and parents' ineffective intervention is seen repeatedly in the life histories of the extreme children. If there were no intervention at all the child's behaviour is at least as likely to remit and level off as it is to accelerate. As it is, in his search for a boundary, the child sees the markings of one (in parents' reaction) but on closer testing finds that he is not stopped at it and, therefore, concludes that it was no boundary at all. Thus he becomes *habituated* to the sight of markers (acts of social disapproval) and *learns* that they have no substance. Any future markers, therefore, need to be clearly 'painted' and made of 'reinforced concrete' for the child to notice them at all and to withstand his testing out behaviour.

This account has concentrated on the social training of the child by parents, because this is the deviant and defective basis from which the child's later disordered growth continues and it forms, in all its variable incompetence and inappropriateness, the paradigm of what is done by all subsequent social agencies from the teachers and the police to the courts, social workers and specialists of various sorts.

Many children, of course, are subjected to actions or chance events at various points of their lives which decelerate the spiral of action and adverse reaction; they manage to learn observance of boundaries which in their particular context suffices. This is true of most 'socialised delinquents' who present few extraordinary problems apart from their 'normal' group thieving supported by the peer group and accepted by most people, including the police and the courts, as a reprehensible phase that some youngsters go through and get out of before adulthood.

Schools and Others

But for those under discussion, the pattern of problems of unacceptable social behaviour, poor impulse control, disregard of rules relating to property and persons and inability to accept 'no' accompanies them from home to school. School brings its own stresses – above all the need to observe niceties of group behaviour and constant opportunity for displaying poor social and individual competence. But now the behaviour is observed by perceptive teachers whose primary job it is to set out clear behavioural boundaries within which they may begin to give the children basic skills. They use a whole variety of techniques for establishing such boundaries (Morrison & McIntyre, 1969, 1972) and begin the process of reclamation of many children who would otherwise continue to be seriously disordered – that is if the teachers are good and the circumstances permit them. But teachers are as variable a professional group as any other and frequently the circumstances, such as large classes, and the number of children who require individual attention militate against them. Having used up their own internal resources, such as change of class, they refer the child to specialists such as the school psychological service or child guidance clinic. This starts the process of labelling and passing between areas of apparent specialist skills which will continue for as long as the child comes into contact with official agencies.

The child who is referred by the teacher has experienced yet another set of ephemeral boundaries. By having attempted to set boundaries and failing to enforce them it is the teacher who has failed to satisfy the child's need for control. The child is known to be deficient in his ability to observe markers and is simply doing what his endowment and life experience incline him to do. Thus if the teachers wish to set any boundaries, they should make sure that they are suitably enforced. The spiralling of testing out and boundary breaking continues from ordinary class to child guidance clinic to 'sanctuaries' and possible changes of schools.

In a different arena, the police and the social services become involved in yet another series of attempts at boundary setting with the help of courts, psychiatrists, psychologists, local observation and assessment centres, children's homes, community homes with education, etc. In looking through the children's records, it is obvious that rarely has any attempt been made to articulate the child's problems and needs in ways which might indicate how the child may be helped to discover enforceable boundaries. The end result of this process is that the child has learnt how to break boundaries and, given his characteristics, to continue to do so with increasing impunity and anxiety until he reaches the 'end of the line'. He receives many unpleasant surprises along the way, such as removal from home, being held in a police cell and going to court, but these experiences are perceived against a confused personal background which has given him little competence in understanding social causality. The anxiety associated with these experiences (and many are deliberately intended to be anxiety provoking) becomes yet another element in the maladaptive and inconsequential pattern of the child's behaviour, because he has not been taught how to avoid or cope with the anxiety.

Having eventually arrived at a facility intended as the 'end of the line' with its inevitable structure and boundaries, the

child will go through the same testing out and pushing behaviour as before with painful results both for himself and
others. The experiences are very concentrated but eventually
begin to establish the enforceability of the boundary. Much of
the early boundary setting for such children needs to be soft
and gentle in order to ensure that the testing out and the
confrontations are not (literally) bloody. The analogy of a
'rubber walled' environment may illustrate the point – the
boundary wall is there, it gives when hit so as not to break the
head that has hit it, but it comes back to its original position.

Given a lifetime of testing out and boundary breaking behaviour, it would be foolish to expect it to be transformed
quickly into compliance and conformity. The children's reactions are variable – some adjust quickly and superficially,
some slowly but at a deeper level, and some never. The attempt
to establish *internalised* boundaries requires a prolonged and
complex process which unlearns the previous testing out behaviour and replaces it with a new pattern of adaptation. But
at least the children have been stabilised and have had some
experience of an enforceable boundary which makes them
more amenable to subsequent learning.

Social Intervention

The point made so far is that observance of behavioural boundaries is the central prerequisite of social behaviour. If the
parents as the primary agents of socialisation do not establish
it others are empowered and required to intervene. The juris-
prudential justification for any form of social intervention is
that (a) without the intervention the problem will get worse
and/or that (b) the intervention will result in improvement in
the problem. The first ground is explicit in the 1969 Children
and Young Persons Act and the second very nearly so. The
same justifications, though rarely articulated, underlie individual and agency attempts at improving the child's condition.
While so far emphasis has been laid on problems created by
children, the same description applies to those cases in which

children are subjected to undesirable conditions, beating, sexual abuse, etc. by others. The focus remains on 'problems' in which the child is either the actor or the acted upon, and frequently both.

The test of legitimacy of social intervention, therefore, is whether (a) the undesirable condition has been halted and (b) the condition has improved. Bearing in mind the frequency and multiplicity of actions taken with the severely disordered children, it should be clear that neither condition has been fulfilled. The legitimacy of the actions taken with them is, therefore, open to serious question. Four outline histories of children may illustrate the point:

JIMMY

	Incidents	Intervention
1962	Jimmy was born.	
Age		
3 months	Father detained in psychiatric hospital after court appearance re indecent assault on young girl.	Police
11 months	Mother started to cohabit with another man.	
1.4	Mother served one month prison sentence for theft. Jimmy lodged with 'foster' parents.	Police Children's Department
1.9	Half brother born.	
2.0	Cohabitee left mother; parents divorced.	
5.7	Started school.	
5.10	School problems.	
6.4	Mother remarried.	
6.8	Persistent truancy.	Education Department
6.11	Half sister born. Spent three months in children's home – problem behaviour.	Children's Department
7.8	Spent two months in children's home.	Children's Department

JIMMY	*Incidents*	*Intervention*
7.10	Stepfather in court.	Police
	Stepfather left home, Jimmy and half brother taken into care again, spent two months in children's home.	Children's Department
8.0	Half brother went to live with own father.	
8.5	Spent holiday with father – indecently assaulted by him.	
8.6	Taken into voluntary care.	Children's
	Behaviour problems in children's home.	Department
	Stepfather sent to prison for two months.	Police
8.8	Half sister born.	
8.9	School problems – seen by psychiatrist.	Child Guidance Centre
	Local authority took out full care order.	Social Services
9.5	Returned to live at home.	
9.6	Mother left stepfather, taking children to live in caravan.	
9.10	Half sister died, behaviour deteriorated, truancy.	
10.10	Appeared in court – joint theft, another care order.	Police
10.11	Admitted to an assessment centre.	Social Services
11.2	Allocated to community home with education	CHE
13.3	Returned home.	
14.7	Appeared in court – burglary, robbery and arson (35 offences TIC) – sentenced to seven years' detention, detained in remand centre.	Police
14.11	Sentence reduced to five years. Admitted for assessment.	

GARY

	Incidents	*Intervention*
1961	Gary was born – father was in prison.	

184

GARY	Incidents	Intervention
Age		
2 months	Hospital after 'convulsive' fit, kept in for two months.	Hospital
3 months	Father released from prison.	
7 months	Father back in prison.	Police
1.3	Sister born.	
1.7	Father released from prison.	
2.0	Hospital for fractured skull.	Hospital
5.1	Started school – did not settle – truanted and presented behaviour problems.	Education Department
6.5	Went to live with paternal grandmother.	
7.1	Transferred to junior school – did not settle – continued to truant and behave badly.	
8.0	Father killed in car accident while escaping from police.	
8.6	Involved in burglary, arson and malicious damage – no formal action taken, supervised by Children's Department on voluntary basis.	Police Children's Department
8.7	Ascertained 'low grade maladjusted'.	School Psychological Service
9.0	Voluntary supervision ceased, behaviour deteriorated.	
9.1	Admitted to remand home, in need of care and protection.	Children's Department
9.2	Appeared in court – in need of care and protection subject of an approved school order.	Children's Department
9.3	Sent for assessment.	Children's Department
9.4	Allocated to approved school.	
12.8	Brother in court, theft, put on probation. Returned home on trial, supervised by Family Services Unit.	Police/ Probation FSU

GARY	*Incidence*	*Intervention*
12.9	Began to truant from school again.	Education Welfare
12.11	Involved in theft, received caution.	Police
13.1	Charged with breaking and entering and damage.	Police
13.2	Admitted to CHE.	CHE
	Appeared in court – breaking and entering, subject of care order.	Police
13.3	Admitted for reassessment.	Social Services
13.4	Returned home with social work support.	
13.5	Expelled from school.	Education Department
13.6	Appeared in court – several offences, sent to CHE.	Police
14.7	Expelled from CHE – general misbehaviour, moved to remand home.	Social Services
14.8	Admitted for assessment.	Social Services

STEPHEN

	Incidents	*Intervention*
1961	Stephen was born.	
Age		
1.1	Sister born.	
2.10	Brother born.	
3.11	Sister born.	
5.1	Started school.	
5.9	Sister born.	
6.2	Baby sister died.	NSPCC – Children's Department
8.0	Referred to Child Guidance Clinic – behaviour problems at school.	Child Guidance Clinic
9.10	Brother born.	
12.0	Hospital for head injury, EEG tests showed embryonic epileptic condition.	Hospital
12.1	Transferred to secondary school.	

STEPHEN	*Incidents*	*Intervention*
12.2	Placed in 'sanctuary unit' at school.	Education Department
12.3	Again referred to Child Guidance Clinic.	Child Guidance Clinic
12.6	Tried too jump from bridge.	Social Services
	Got drunk, threatened suicide, picked up by police.	Police
	Excluded from school – difficult behaviour.	Education Department
12.7	Again referred to Child Guidance Clinic.	Child Guidance Clinic
12.11	Readmitted to sanctuary unit at school.	Education Department
13.2	Warned about indecent assaults on girls.	Police
13.3	Excluded from school – more indecent assaults.	Education Department
13.8	Appeared in court – theft – fined and placed on supervision order.	Police
14.1	Readmitted to sanctuary unit at school.	Education Department
14.2	Again referred to Child Guidance Clinic.	Child Guidance Clinic.
14.3	Started to truant.	
14.5	Expelled from school following violent indecent assault on girl.	Education Department
14.6	Appeared in court – in breach of supervision order, placed on care order and sent to an assessment centre.	Social Services
14.7	Sent home from assessment centre due to disruptive behaviour.	
	Admitted to children's home.	Social Services.
	Appeared in court – theft of key, given conditional discharge.	Police
14.8	Sent home from children's home – found in girl's bedroom.	Social Services
	Admitted for assessment.	Social Services

PETRA

	Incidents	Intervention
1960	Petra was born illegitimately.	
Age		
6 weeks	Taken to live with prospective parents.	
10 months	Petra adopted.	
4.6	Parents adopted baby boy.	
5.0	Started school.	
6.0	Hospital for bowel complaint.	Hospital
7.6	Referred to Child Guidance Clinic – behaviour problems at school and home.	Child Guidance Clinic
8.0	Transferred to junior school	Education Department
8.9	Stopped attending Child Guidance Clinic – no progress.	
12.0	Transferred to secondary school.	
12.2	Referred to Child Guidance Clinic again – behaviour problems at school.	Child Guidance Clinic
12.9	Ran away from home; found drunk.	Social Services
13.0	Major problem at home – seen by psychiatrist.	Psychiatric Clinic
14.0	Ran away from home; sleeping rough.	Social Services
14.1	Ran away from home; involved in sexual activity and theft.	Police Social Services
	Hospital for 'fictitious' complaint; transferred to child development centre at hospital.	Psychiatric Clinic
14.2	CYP referral re sexual involvement.	Social Services
14.3	Took overdose; admitted to hospital; referred to psychiatric unit.	Psychiatric Clinic
14.5	Ran away from hospital; picked up by police.	Police
14.6	No longer tolerated in hospital; disruptive behaviour; moved to adolescent unit, going home at weekends.	Psychiatric Hospital
	Ran away from home; took overdose.	Psychiatric Hospital

PETRA	*Incidents*	*Intervention*
14.7	Placed in CHE.	
	Appeared in court charged with breaking a window – made subject of care order.	Police Social Services
	Made allegations against male social worker.	Social Services
	Took overdose; admitted to hospital; discharged.	Psychiatric Hospital
14.8	Involved in violent fight; remanded in custody for seven days.	Police
14.9	Admitted as inpatient to Adolescent Unit.	Adolescent Unit
	Discharged; too violent; uncontrollable; back home.	Social Services
	Took overdose; admitted to hospital.	Psychiatric Hospital
	Cut wrists in hospital; uncontrollable; discharged.	
14.9	Admitted as emergency.	

These histories are quite typical of the severely disordered children. They show that because inadequate note has been taken of their potential for creating extreme problems, each new problem has presented a crisis warranting a new form of intervention; because inadequate appraisal of their problems and needs continues, so does the process of passing them from one agency to another and back again. Thus, the number of moves made by the child (and only the grosser ones are noted in case histories), is an index of failure of social intervention. It is quite obvious that new forms of intervention have not been sought for *new* problems or as means of improving the child's condition but as attempts at primary curbing of the original or related problem, thus showing the inadequacy of the former measures.

The question may, therefore, be asked 'Why intervene in the first place?' The broad philosophical justification which may be adduced in law has already been pointed out. That justification derives from and gives rise to a number of other components which are usually tangled up.

People react favourably or adversely to the circumstances and behaviours of their fellow humans. *Public feelings* that children should be protected against social ills and treated specially mingle increasingly with reactions to disordered behaviour by very young children and alarm at the predatoriness of the older ones. Public feeling about the kind of issues under discussion are rarely subjected to scrutiny but a broad trend in them can be detected – 'We must do something about all these children' – to justify intervention. The feelings are, however, always sufficiently mixed to allow particular events, such as the notorious death of a child or the murder of two youngsters by a girl, to push them one way or the other.

What are feelings for the public, become *ideologies* – justificatory bases of actions – for professionals. Trillings's definition of ideology is particularly fitting in the present context '. . . the habit or ritual of showing respect for certain formulas to which, for various reasons to do with emotional safety, we have very strong ties of whose meaning and consequences in actuality we have no clear understanding' (1950).

Ideologies differ amongst professional groups. Priestley *et al* (1977) found such differences in relation to delinquent children among magistrates, social workers, policemen and others. Trilling's point about the 'emotional safety' of the ideologues and the ambiguity of the consequences of their views appear to be largely responsible for the dramatic changes in social and professional fashions, unrelated to any new knowledge.

Sometimes particular groups become so influential and their views so crystallised that they are able to promote *legislation* to embody it. The 1969 Children and Young Persons Act is a good example of this. The process of conversion of a set of conflicting ideologies into that particular Act is perceptively described by Priestley *et al* (*op. cit.*). While feeling and ideology may impel professionals, legislation lays duties and responsibilities on them. The simple answer given to 'Why do you intervene?' given by

Education Departments, Police, Courts, Social Services and others is 'Because we have to, we have no choice.' But the law assumes that those empowered to act have (a) the resources and (b) the competence to carry out its mandatory requirements.

Resources are a crucial element in legitimising social intervention. If there were no multiplicity and diversity of resources, there would be no justification for passing the child from one to another. Some comments have already been made about the resources required for dealing with severely disordered youngsters. The central point is that resources cannot be specified unless the problem and its requirements have been analysed and there is some reason, preferably demonstrable, for believing that the resource is relevant to the problem. On this basis serious questions can be raised about the resources available. The movement of the child from one facility to another assumes or presumes the greater relevance or competence of that facility to better cope with the presenting problem. Unless and until evidence has been produced by the users of resources regarding their inadequacy or inappropriateness, society and its individual citizens are correct in assuming that they can do the job for which they have been set up.

But no resource takes on a problem unless it has some reason to believe that it is better capable of either curbing the problem or improving it than the previous agency. This would be presumably on the basis of its greater resources, which reflects and lead to its greater *competence*. No agency is forced to take on a problem if it can show that it has no competence in relation to that particular problem, or that its competence is less than others who are able to take it on. Thus, every act of acceptance of a problem presumes the ability of the agency to cope with it. Therefore, both society and its individuals can demand that every agency delineate the limits of its competence and account for its failure to deal with a particular problem deemed to be within its purview. These latter points will be elaborated in Chapter 10. With the former, one direct result is that society, and more importantly its legislators, will learn what demands they may not make on their agencies and where they should direct the creation of new resources.

Crises of Intervention

While the above elements are implicit in legitimising social intervention, intervention itself is concerned with a different order of constraints and pressures. Perhaps the most important element in the operation of any social agency is the definition of the boundaries of its operation – who it should deal with and at what point it should stop dealing with them. Such role definition varies along a continuum from those that are fully ascribed, such as detention centres, to those that are self-designated, such as adolescent psychiatric units.

The definitions change with legislation, social pressure and the personnel concerned. The agency's ideology, perception of its resources, and of its competence determine the degree of inclusiveness of its criteria for a client population. Its inter-action with particular clients, its appraisal of its resources for coping with them, the threat to its competence, the cost involved to its self-image and to the client determine how far it is prepared to go on dealing with a client before rejecting the client as being unsuitable for its facility. The criteria for ex-clusiveness are thus also dynamic and respond to the quality of the particular client and a number of other subtle factors.

There are four broad venues of treatment of disordered children as detailed in Chapter 4 – penal; educational; medical/psychiatric and social services. The penal venue does not concern us here, not least because it is the one type of facility which has hardly any latitude in defining its own area of operation – it must simply take whoever is presented to it by the courts.

Educational facilities, while responsible for fulfilling the educational needs of all school age children, exercise almost total internal autonomy in how they are run. They are at present in no way accountable for why some of them produce considerably more truants and other problem children (Power *et al*, 1972) than others subject to the same pressures. The heads also have, and in the case of many severely disordered children have exercised, the right to exclude children from school. The reasons given for the exclusions, the criteria for setting the boundary of tolerance of difficult and disruptive behaviour, are arbitrary and inadequately stated. The fact that the local education authority has a legal obligation to provide for the education of the disordered child and someone else has to take on the exacerbated problems do not make exclusions any less likely. Undoubtedly the heads have good reasons for their action but the point about the arbitrary definition of criteria remains, as does the periodic non-education of many of the extreme children.

The heads could point out that they have no choice in which children they take. This is unless they run a special school, in which case they can refuse – and frequently do – admission to those children who are likely to be very troublesome. The head of an ordinary school can only do his best and if he still finds that the price the staff and the other children have to pay to cope with a particular youngster is too high, exclude him.

But the same cannot be said of psychiatric and child guidance facilities. Beyond the first referral, any continued work with the child is based on the frequently explicit grounds that the child presents a disorder which they can help alleviate. The grounds are some form of psychiatric diagnosis based on a current classification of disorders. It can, therefore, be assumed that a psychiatrist, having arrived at the diagnosis based on examination of records and the current state of the child, is in a position to project the child's problems and needs against his own and the facility's resources and competence. The acceptance of the child for treatment is justified on the same usual grounds that (a) he will not deteriorate and (b) he may improve.

It is, then, surprising and distressing to the child and those concerned for him that in the course of treatment and the many problems it raises, the psychiatrist decides that the child is after all not a suitable case for treatment and defines the tolerance of the facility in a way that excludes him. A large proportion of the severely disordered children have been subjected to some form of psychiatric intervention in the course of which they have picked up some of the extenuating 'reasons' for their own behaviour. By the time they reach the end of the line, all have been rejected by psychiatrists as beyond their help, despite the fact that the original diagnoses have not been withdrawn. While it is readily understood that psychiatrists are the most appropriate persons to delineate the boundaries of their own competence, the boundary is not so mystical as to be undemonstrable nor so beyond logic as to declare a child to be both within that boundary (by virtue of having a treatable disorder) and outside it.

What makes the situation more grim is that under pressure, most of it self-generated, psychiatry has come to stake out a large territory within which it claims to be able (a) to make sense of every behavioural and mental disorder and (b) to contribute to its alleviation. This has created deep dependency feelings on the part of other practitioners who cannot lay much claim to either of the above areas. They then suffer massive anxiety when told by psychiatrists that no help can be given with the most disordered children. It is less than hilarious when a girl is admitted to a psychiatric hospital after an overdose, is diagnosed as severely depressed, suicidal, and in need of treatment, but is discharged forty-eight hours later as an 'incorrigible psychopath'; or one who is admitted on an emergency order following violent behaviour, is diagnosed as suffering from a 'transient disorder of adolescence' but is discharged twenty-eight hours later as being too violent for the facility. Not only the markers and the boundary have failed to stand up yet again, but also the crisis among those who *have* to continue dealing with the children has deepened.

Those others are almost invariably the social services departments, in the person of individual social workers and their area teams who are required by law to cater for children who are being neglected or ill treated, exposed to moral danger, beyond control, not going to school, or offending. Because social workers are now the primary official agents in the processing of severely disordered and delinquent youngsters, their role may warrant a brief discussion.

The Care Order bestows on the local authority and its agents, the social workers, considerable authority for assumption of most rights over the child. This authority carries with it the equivalent responsibility. As the care order is issued by the court on grounds of inadequate care and control by the parents the clear implication is that the social services can provide for the care and control functions where parents have failed. The decision making of the social workers involved is affected by the elements of intervention outlined earlier. In the case of particularly disordered and delinquent youngsters, however, there is an important area of unease and ambiguity. This arises from the conflict between the social workers' role as the agent of social control on the one hand, and the primary guardian of the child's welfare on the other.

Having been entrusted with the care and control of the child, social workers have the task of determining the nature and extent of the problem, deciding what should be done about it and where the child should go. From this moment on, because of the vast unmapped areas to be traversed, the *ideology* of the particular social worker, his area team and of his department become his chief guide. This is inevitable because neither social work training courses nor the operation of social services departments equip the social workers with empirical guidelines or decision making grids on which to base their deliberations about the disposal of the child. Such deliberations are sometimes enacted through 'case conferences' which are beset by the same problems as individual social worker's, but multiplied by the number of people involved.

Ryall (1974, 1977) has most perceptively analysed the conflicts within social workers in their work with delinquent youngsters. He isolates three main reasons why social workers' intervention with such children is likely to fail: (1) *social work objectives*, which are primarily aimed at serving the disadvantaged, come into conflict with the socially damaging behaviour of youngsters. The conflict is not resolvable and is likely to end up with the rejection of the child by the social worker; (2) *social work practice* is based on either relationships and casework or on tangible service delivery, which end up by connivance with the children to keep their delinquent identity or the provision of services which are unrelated to the problem; (3) *social work logic* devalues the presenting problems of the child in favour of 'deeper' social and familial phenomena and, therefore, misses out on the main source of trouble, the behaviour. Ryall's statements apply with even greater force to the severely disordered children who are the subject of this book.

In addition to the above difficulties, the extreme children create crises in the family, school, clinic and the residential facilities in which they are placed. Social workers are no better able to resolve crises than are any other group of people. On the contrary, they are now the whipping boys of society and subjected to stern criticism whenever something goes wrong with a child. Their knowledge of the probable consequences of mistakes with a child actuate their anxiety and make them the more concerned to relieve the situation.

One way of achieving respite and resolution is to redefine the child's problems. Desperate as they are to find some means for curbing and possibly improving the child's behaviour, they accept readily the offers of help from any service. In the majority of instances, this help is provided by residential facilities, most of which are within the control of local authorities. Although the social worker may have misgivings about the venue offered, he is more likely than not to accept it because it relieves him, however temporarily, of front line responsibility for dealing with the child, releases his time and energy for work with the more demonstrably needy and opens the possibility that the child may be helped.

Because social workers do not pass on the problem if they can deal with it themselves, the movement of the child is yet another instance of failure of boundary setting. Most of the children see their disposal as another act of rejection – as they have so far in their meanderings from one agency to another.

This is reflected in the social worker's own deep ambivalence about placing children in residential facilities and coping with his guilt feelings by almost forgetting the child. And residential facilities know of the social workers' ambivalence and reciprocate it.

This is one reason for the frequently observed games of hide and seek residential facilities and social workers play with one another. From the time when they had to accept whichever children they were given, many community homes with education (which in the end accept most of the worst) are exercising their new found autonomy in defining their inclusion and exclusion criteria, without either publicly demonstrated or accepted reasons, concern with who else should care for the child, or increased competence to deal with those children whom their criteria do not exclude. As a result, children have to wait longer before they are accepted and their personal needs have to be frequently hawked around until someone is prepared to take them.

The treatment of severely disordered children is too wide and complex to be even hinted at here. But if residential facilities for disordered youngsters are to be regarded as *treatment* venues, they require a definition of task and access to resources – mainly conceptual competence, and facilities for monitoring of their own performance with individual children which they have palpably not achieved. They frequently misinterpret conformity as stabilisation and stability as alleviation of problems. In many cases, however, they manage to curb the disordered behaviour – at least while the child is with them. This achievement should not be underestimated, as it is more than others have done up to then, particularly as it is usually accompanied by obvious improvement in the care and welfare needs of the child. But nor should the achievement be mistaken for the alleviation of the fundamental problems of the child, deeply ingrained as they are through the processes outlined so far.

By the time the child has reached the community home, the pattern of disordered behaviour is too well established to be susceptible to the kind of mass treatment he is likely to receive.

The repeated failure of the social agencies to set and enforce boundaries within which the child can be controlled and can achieve self-control, have resulted in the self-labelling of the child as 'uncontrollable'. The repeated rejections of the child have created a fluid and negative 'I', devoid of self-respect and sense of personal worth, and shorn of responsibility for what it does or surprise at what is done to it.

For these children, this nearly extreme form of intervention has come too late. The reason for this is the prevalent ideological concern that the child should receive the *minimum* appropriate form of intervention available for his problem. This is laudable enough and would be accepted by all but the most rabid retributionists. But, as already indicated, social workers' decisions are not based on empirical evidence or other objective guidelines. For this reason, the minimum disposal is by definition inadequate for those children whose problems get worse. Often at assessment meetings the question is heard 'But why didn't you refer this child when the problem first became apparent?' with the answer 'We didn't think it would get as bad as this.' Add to these the frequent changes of individual social workers, the fact that the most disordered children are a small minority of their caseloads, the tides in the fortunes of social services departments, the fact that bureaucratic and 'industrial' concerns have divested social services of much of the vocational core of their work, and the prospects for the mismanagement of the child and his worsening condition are ideal.

Given this persistent failure with these children and the pressure on resources, it is not surprising that they should gradually become like social lepers, 'untouchables' handled gingerly by social services departments who slowly reject them, recommend them for penal sentences where appropriate and withdraw to minimum contact. Indeed some directors of social services have questioned the legitimacy of giving up scarce resources to cope with this troublesome minority. It is not clear, however, what else they popose to do with the children for whom they are legally responsible. It may instead be more profitable to look at the processes which have brought the children to this pitch and learn from them rather than relegate the children to a terminal condition.

It has been suggested that extreme children may have a predisposition to disordered behaviour which is activated and worsened by their socialisation experiences. Their subsequent treatment by various official agencies strengthens their tendency to boundary breaking and disordered behaviour. The variable and arbitrary use of specialised incompetence helps to form their identity as 'uncontrollable' and pushes them towards extreme forms of self-gratifying, testing out behaviour. The process of crisis intervention with all its muddle-headedness, results in crises of intervention. Unless the process of buck passing and redefinition of children's problems slows down, given the worsening social and familial conditions associated with the severely disordered children, there is every chance that a great many more of them will inexorably wend the same troubled and troublesome way.

*

CHAPTER 8

Classifications of Disordered Children

THE act of describing the children who are the subjects of this book is intended to set them apart from other children who are not disordered. Such acts and processes of arranging together similar characteristics of individuals into separate groupings or classes are referred to as 'classification'. This is central to all human activity, in that unless stimuli or events are classified according to some defining criterion, such as hostile-friendly, edible-poisonous, actions required for survival cannot be channelled.

Extreme children have been subjects of complex informal classification processes by everyone who has come across them almost from birth – family doctor ('poorer, more prone to risk'), health visitor ('mother can't manage'), parents ('more troublesome than the others'), teachers ('difficult at school, not very bright'), the police ('on the fringe of offending'), courts ('offender, in need of care and control'), psychiatrists ('presenting problems, not very amenable'), social workers ('a lot of trouble'), residential facilities ('troublesome, doesn't respond to treatment'), etc. All these judgments are meant to and succeed in separating these children from others and putting them into overlapping classes which eventually come together to the point at which they are made the subject of this study.

Classifications say as much about the classifiers and the attributes they consider significant as they do about those so classified. And indeed, a culture can be looked at in terms of the uniformity and extent to which its classifications are accepted and used by its members. In this sense there is a continuum of uniformity and acceptabilty of usage of classifications from the most concrete and universally acceptable to the most abstract and contentious.

This point is important to bear in mind because professions develop classificatory systems ('this child is deprived, this other is delinquent', 'this man is mentally ill, this other one is not') which give the impression that the classification is itself the reality and not an arbitrary act – albeit one that may command wide acceptance. In other words, professions tend to 'reify' or 'make a thing' out of judgments. But judgments remain judgments until through wide usage they become 'social facts' (Hobbs, 1975). These judgments are not cavalier. Their basic purpose is the systematisation of information on people so that action may become possible. As long as they remain useful (it is worthwhile to separate out epileptics from others because they can be treated appropriately), they are continued but when they are felt not to be (such as a distinction between delinquent and deprived children), they are discontinued. Such a classification is implicit in the Care Order and the social processing of severely disordered children described in the previous chapter.

Not all classificatory systems are formal, but severely disordered children are more likely than most to be made the subject of a formal classification at some stage or other of their careers. Setting aside the court procedure which operates with rules of evidence and whose decision making is outside the scope of this book, the two major forms of classification are those undertaken by assessment centres and psychiatrists, mostly separately, but sometimes together. Because both play such a crucial role in the disposal of the extreme children, their uses and abuses merit separate discussion.

Uses and Abuses of Assessment

Assessment of disordered and delinquent children as a corporate, residential activity started with the original 'Classifying Schools', the first of which was opened at Aycliffe in 1942. Since then, assessment has gone through many developments and vicissitudes until it has become one of the most contentious issues in the whole area of dealing with disordered and delinquent youngsters.

This is surprising because assessment itself is a neutral activity. It can be briefly described as a continuing process aimed at providing:

(1) Comprehensive, relevant background information on the child's context and development;

(2) a description of the child's current state, his personal attributes, the problems he presents and experiences both in natural settings and any that may be specifically constructed for this purpose;

(3) guidelines and specified measures aimed at alleviating those problems and some indication of the resources required for them;

(4) an indication of where, generally or specifically, that task may be best carried out.

This information and the manner in which it is provided can be evaluated in terms of its depth, breadth, conceptual acuity, reliability, validity, predictive ability, consumer utility and a number of other factors (Hoghughi, 1971). Thus, assessments can be placed on a variety of evaluative dimensions from the paltry and the homespun to the most sophisticated and deeply researched, from solo efforts to those involving large teams of specialists. It has, in itself, no implications for the assessment setting, whether day or residential, the child's home or a clinic. But economic and organisational factors – the scattering of specialist resources over a wide area, the undesirability of shunting the child from one place to another, or indeed of placing him away from home – may influence the application of the process.

There are two other central considerations. The history of extreme children shows that prior to reaching this particular pitch they have been seen, appraised, and classified by a whole variety of people whose judgments have been inevitably partial.

The child has been treated like the proverbial elephant by the six blind men, each describing a part without a central unifying theme – the child. This not only provides a poor guide to action but also disregards the fact that the child is an integrated entity whose actions make most sense only if they are seen as an organic whole.

The second consideration is that although there are long term behavioural constancies in all human beings – including the most disordered – much of behaviour can be accounted for in terms of immediate circumstances, as was illustrated in Chapter 6. In attempting to evaluate the child and providing a predictive picture of him, it therefore becomes necessary to maximally vary the situations under which he is observed to see how much constancy and how much variability emerge from his reactions. Thus, far from not seeing the child just in his 'natural' setting, variations of this setting, possibly including removal, become essential if valid information is to be gained about his behavioural constancies which are a necessary prerequisite of making predictions about him. The lack of such variation and the inability to reliably project present behaviour to hypothetical situations accounts for much of the predictive inadequacy of social intervention, as suggested in the last chapter.

But, 'removal' is a matter of degree. It carries a 'price tag' and must, therefore, be seen in terms of the total problems and needs of the child. Given the enormity of the suffering of these children and the damage they inflict on others, removal certainly does not warrant the torrid evangelical zeal with which it is either sought or decried.

The process of assessment is thus a dynamic one – resulting from the expectations of those who have placed the child for assessment, the assessment agency, the child and persons significant to him, and retroactive projections of those who are likely to use the outcome of assessment. To gain a glimpse of the complexity of the interaction it may suffice to look at only one of the elements, the social workers' expectations in placing a child for assessment, which range over the following:

* They do not know what to make of the child and his problems; or they know what to make of his problems but do not know what to do with him; the child's presenting problems are so serious that assessment provides objective, public 'insurance' against possible censure;
* they use residential assessment facilities as a way of getting the child out of their hair or giving him a short, sharp shock – the outcome of assessment does not seem to matter;
* they use assessment as a way of meeting the expectations of the juvenile court or public pressure;
* all or some of the above.

The variability of these expectations is normal and natural and part of the reality of a complex multi-valued society whose social agencies enjoy and operate with professional discretion. What should remain invariant is the central position of the child and the advocacy of his rights and needs in the context of public safety.

Uses of Assessment

Because assessment is carried out in a setting with its own attributes and priorities, it is not possible to totally isolate the uses and effects of assessment from those of its other concerns. Some of these, related to a residential facility, in terms of care, stabilisation, boundary setting, etc. have been outlined in the previous chapters. Most of the children and their parents seem to derive some obvious benefit from the enforced cooling of a crisis situation and the emerging knowledge that their problems will be looked at sympathetically. The assessment process, by attempting to look objectively at the total situation, frequently achieves a 'delabelling' of the child who may have been branded in all sorts of ways before. By placing him in a context of his peers, he is seen in scale and his difficulties may be deemed to have been the attempts of a 'normal' child to adapt to abnormal circumstances (cf. Cooper, 1970). On the other hand, depending on the way assessment is carried out and the way it projects itself on to the children, simply being in an assessment facility may be the bestowal and confirmation of a new label.

The main arena in which the work of an assessment agency should be evaluated is in terms of its end product – namely its report. Some criteria of evaluation have already been described. Given the variability of the assessment reports according to such factors as depth, breadth, conceptual acuity, detailed guidelines, reliability, validity, their utility depends obviously on the competence of the treatment agency which uses them, be it a social worker doing casework with the family or a residential facility teaching social skills. What assessemnt should do is to guide action and suggest focus for the use of invariably scarce resources. Whether the agency is competent to carry out those actions is no reflection on the assessment report but on the degree to which it can be utilised by a particular agency. This distinction is crucial because of the vast variations in the compentence of treatment agencies and indeed individual workers within them. The rights of the child demand that his treatment requirements be independently and objectively stated, rather than simply pander to the inadequacies of treatment.

Thus assessment of the extreme children is necessarily the most useful, valid and reliable guide to rational social policy making and the allocation of resources for them. Even allowing for its limitations in all the above areas, it is at least based on looking at individual children. Any comparison of the treatment requirements of children (of the type described in Chapter 5) and the treatment resources *actually* available, would provide a much more rational guide to action than armchair deliberations and political and ideological pressures which usually determine resource allocation.

The Abuses of Assessment

Assessment produces a great deal of information, much of it revealed and coherently presented for the first time. It requires the same scrupulous care in handling as any other private and confidential information (see MIND, 1975). But, for a variety of reasons the abuse is more frequently directed *at* assessment. This results mainly from the mushrooming (since 1971) of a vast network over the country of 'observation and assessment' facilities which are much more the embodiments of local authorities' search for status and self-sufficiency than viable facilities for children. They have little of the orientation, resources or conceptual competence to provide assessments which satisfy even low level application of the formerly mentioned criteria. Many are indeed hardly used as assessment facilities (Reinach *et al*, 1976), but rather as facilities in which social workers place children, some for considerable periods, at very high cost, until either the crisis passes or they discover some way of disposing of the children. Little thought seems to be given by the social workers or those who run the facilities to the consequences for the children of not receiving adequate education and social experience over prolonged periods and of laying down roots which have to be subsequently severed. But these are organisational and resource deficiencies which can be overcome in theory if not in practice.

A more fundamental criticism of assessment has been provided in a recent document put out by the professional wing of the DHSS (Social Work Service) and the Association of Directors of Social Services. The paper has been widely circulated, special meetings have been held to discuss it, has been frequently quoted and has proved a powerful force in the current tide against assessment, particularly residential, not least because it carries the imprimatur of the highest policy makers. It merits close scrutiny because it provides a window into how policies with far reaching consequences emerge.

In looking at the 'philosophy of observation and assessment' Tutt (1977) isolates three major assumptions: (1) '*Human behaviour is constant*'. He regards this as being based on a theory that suggests 'personality is made up of a number of traits which are common to all members of the same culture, if not to all men'; (2) '*Children in care have idiosyncratic problems open to remedial intervention'*. This assumption is based on 'the medical model' which presumes the child's problems are the result of a deep seated malady or a 'need theory', which suggests that the child is in care because 'his needs are not being met'; (3) *'The Observation and Assessment Centre is Functional'*. As local authorities have access to a number of 'specialist' establishments, assessment is necessary to choose between them.

He then proceeds to show the invalidity of these assumptions. On the first point, evidence is adduced from Hartshorne and May's (1928) classical experiments which showed that children did not cheat all the time but according to circumstances. He then goes on to quote Mischel (1968) that '. . . highly generalised behavioural consistencies have not been demonstrated and the concept of personality traits . . . is thus untenable'. Therefore, because human behaviour is responsive to situational variability, a child away from home is a 'different' child and cannot be assessed. But 'moral' behaviours, though notoriously culture bound and dependent on opportunities (Mayhew *et al*, 1976), do not negate the notion of moral differences among children (cf. Kohlberg, 1969 for an exhaustive critique). Nor is Mischel (*op. cit.*) given his considerable due, as he goes on to say later in the same book (pp. 281-2) 'It is the existence of such stimulus-free, highly generalised behavioural acts – *not the long term individual differences in response to stimuli* – that is unsupported by the data reviewed in earlier chapters' (present author's italics). The empirical evidence, therefore, when fully presented does not support the criticism which would be valid only if an extraordinarily primitive view of behaviour was held. Not to allow for a core of constancy in human behaviour, which can be evaluated in a reasonable assessment setting, would be to logically make nonsense of *any* form of intervention which is dependent on predictability of human behaviour.

The second argument is based on the contention that the difficulties of many children in care result primarily from extrinsic factors and 'cannot be rectified by isolating the child, assessing him and applying some form of remedial action'. This is corroborated by the information so far presented on disordered children. This view, however, misconstrues assessment by imputing to it allegiance to 'the medical model' and a 'need theory'. There is, to start with, not one 'medical model' but several such as 'disease entity', 'infective state', 'developmental lag', 'tissue deficit', etc. Also, it is perfectly permissible to state that a child is in care because certain of his needs for care and control have not been met, without adducing a 'need theory'. In any case, there is no reason why 'isolating the child . . . and applying some form of remedial action' should not take place at the same time as correcting the faults in the service delivery systems. It is unnecessarily crude to see children's problems as either/or rather than arising from interaction effects.

The final criticism derives from the primitive forms of assessment current in many centres and their difficulties in obtaining adequate and relevant information to make appropriate allocation to facilities feasible. But this criticism, also voiced earlier in this section, reflects on the practical and organisational limits of assessment centres. It would be logically erroneous to see it as reflecting on the conceptual rationale of assessment.

The critical conclusions presented in the document, therefore do not appear warranted by the premises. The most significant of these conclusions comes at the end and reflects the acuity with which the evidence presented has been evaluated by its authors – 'In any event, it is questionable whether we need sophisticated assessment of a clinical nature since we have only crude forms of treatment to apply subsequently'. By any standards, this is an extraordinary statement, particularly as it reflects the thinking of a group of chief *professional* advisers and policy makers. Having encouraged the indiscriminate growth of 'observation and assessment centres' they now perceive the unfortunate consequences. Instead of seeking to correct the situation, they derogate the only source of valid evidence and basis for evaluating *their* deployment of the resources entrusted to them by the community. This illustrates the point made earlier about the current bases of social policy making.

Psychiatric Assessment

This form of classification has emerged as the most potent and prestigious in dealings with severely disordered children. Although its origins are in adult psychiatry, it has sought to free itself of adult models and conceptions of mental illness and develop modes of thinking that take account of qualitative differences between children and adults (Philips *et al*, 1975). Its components are the same as any other assessment: namely the child's current state against his background; genesis or aetiology of the problem; and an intervention plan.

Unlike other forms of assessment and thus reflecting its medical origins, however, it proceeds according to a complex classification of symptoms and signs. The collection of particular indicators of dysfunction (subjective complaints of the patient and abnormalities objectively noted by the psychiatrist) cluster in a particular manner which can be seen as a distinct 'syndrome'. The formal statement of what the syndrome is forms the 'diagnosis'. Diagnoses contain within them some presupposition of the source and the course of the difficulty and the seeds of the treatment methods to be employed and the estimate of outcome (prognosis). The source and course are not frequently specified but the seeds flower in the treatment prescriptions that are made.

There are many classifications of disorders of children, each with their own special features, merits and disadvantages (see Prugh *et al*, 1975). Of these, the current classification of adolescent psychiatric 'illnesses' extracted from the International Classification of Diseases (WHO, 1967) is reproduced below. The items thus marked (*) are those which are either known to have a physical origin (e.g. 309), to respond to physical methods of treatment (e.g. 291–298), or to result in major physical change (e.g. 303). They are thus in the mainstream of physical medicine and despite variations in diagnoses and treatments, are sufficiently solid and non-controversial not to be of central concern here. The following comments apply mainly to items 300–308 alone.

INTERNATIONAL CLASSIFICATION OF DISEASE

Classification of Adolescent Psychiatric Illness

291. * Alcoholic Psychosis
292. * Psychosis associated with Intracranial Infection
293. * Psychosis associated with other cerebral conditions
   .1 with other cerebrovascular disturbance
   .2 with epilepsy
   .3 with intracranial neoplasm
   .4 with degenerative disease of central nervous system
   .5 with brain trauma (includes birth injury)
   .9 with other cerebral condition
294. * Psychosis associated with other physical condition
   .0 with endocrine disorders
   .1 with metabolic and nutritional disorders (periodic catatonia)
   .2 with systemic infections
   .3 with drug intoxication
   .9 with other physical conditions, e.g. postoperative
295. * Schizophrenia
   .0 Simple type
   .1 Hebephrenic type
   .2 Catatonic type
   .3 Paranoid type
   .4 Acute schizophrenic episode
   .5 Latent schizophrenia
   .6 Residual schizophrenia
   .7 Schizo-affective type
   .9 Other, includes Autism, childhood schizophrenia, schizo-
       phreniform
296. * Affective Psychoses
   .1 Manic depressive psychosis, manic type
   .2 Manic depressive psychosis, depressed type, includes endo-
       genous depression
   .3 Manic depressive psychosis, circular
   .9 Other, e.g. manic stupor
297. * Paranoid States
298. * Other Psychoses
   .0 Reactive depressive psychosis
   .1 Reactive excitation

.2 Reactive confusion
.3 Acute paranoid reaction
.9 Reactive psychosis other, e.g. Exhaustive delirium

300. Neuroses
.0 Anxiety Neurosis
.1 Hysterical Neurosis
    (a) Dissociative states, e.g. Compensation neurosis
    (b) Conversion phenomena, e.g. Hystero-epilepsy
.2 Phobic neurosis
.3 Obsessive compulsive neurosis
.4 Depressive neurosis
.5 Neurasthenia
.6 Depersonalisation syndrome
.9 Other, e.g. Writer's cramp

301. Personality Disorders
.0 Paranoid
.1 Affective (cyclothymic, etc.)
.2 Schizoid
.2 Explosive (aggressive)
.4 Anankastic (obsessive-compulsive)
.5 Hysterical (labile)
.6 Asthenic (inadequate)
.7 Antisocial (delinquent)
.9 Other, e.g. Immature

302. Sexual Deviation
.0 Homosexuality
.1 Fetishism
.3 Transvestism
.4 Exhibitionism
.9 Other, e.g. Voyeurs, Narcissists

303. * Alcoholism

304. * Drug Dependence

305. Physical Disorder of presumably psychogenic origin
.0 Skin (Pruritus)
.1 Musculo-skeletal (Torticollis)
.2 Respiratory (hyperventilation)
.3 Cardiovascular (effort syndrome)
.5 Gastro-intestinal (globus, dyspepsia)
.6 Genito-urinary (impotence, frigidity)

306. Special Symptoms (largely concerned with children and young people)
   .0 Speech disturbance
   .1 Specific learning disturbance
   .2 Tics
   .3 Other psychomotor disorders
   .4 Disorders of sleep
   .5 Feeding disturbances, e.g. Anorexia nervosa
   .6 Enuresis
   .7 Encopresis
   .8 Cephalalgia
   .9 Other

307. Transient Situational Disturbance, e.g. combat fatigue, adjustment reaction of adolescence

308. Behaviour Disorders, e.g. Tantrums, truancy

309. * Mental disorders not specified as psychotic associated with physical conditions
   .0 with intracranial infection, e.g. TB
   .1 with drug or systemic intoxication, flu malaria
   .2 with brain trauma
   .3 with circulatory disturbance
   .4 with convulsive disorder
   .5 with disturbance of metabolism, growth or nutrition
   .7 with intracranial neoplasm

309. .8 with degenerative diseases of central nervous system
   .9 with other physical conditions, e.g. Chromosome abnormalities

310. * Borderline mental retardation IQ 68–85

311– Mild Mental Retardation IQ 52–67

314. Profound Mental Retardation

The first point to be made is that as with all other taxonomies, the present international classification is arbitrary, though it commands a large following and is presumably found to be useful by psychiatrists. Whether it is useful to other people will emerge later. Additionally, it should be noted that all diagnoses are hypothetical, inductive judgments which go, to varying degrees, beyond the 'facts' and cannot be substantiated unless the hypothesis is tested by appropriately detailed treatment measures. This is crucial, because as will be seen later, much psychiatric diagnosis with disordered youngsters is not followed by testing through rigorous treatment and, therefore, leaves the validity of the original diagnosis open to question.

The hypothetical nature of psychiatric diagnosis also leaves it open to the vagaries and predispositions of individuals or groups of practitioners. Since the personal and professional attributes of psychiatrists are 'normally distributed', i.e. go from low, through average to high, some degree of variability in their diagnoses ought to be expected. This is complicated by the fact that, unlike physical medicine and 'hard' psychiatry, the 'ostensive definitions' of many of the diagnoses used in training ('this is a child with a personality disorder of an immature type'), are themselves extremely variable and allow for idiosyncratic learning to take place. Thus, because unlike corporate assessment, psychiatric diagnoses are carried out by individual psychiatrists, the disordered youngster is likely to receive an influential labelling judgment of his state, the reliability and validity of which is open to serious question.

This would be less worrying if the judgment was not pronounced in a form of words which is brief but mystifying enough to be repeated reverentially by the uninitiated who receive it. Thus children and parents are heard to say 'he has a hysterical personality', 'I have a mental condition'. Because of the origins of adult psychiatry and the primary preoccupation of older medicine with 'disease states', psychiatric diagnoses sound as if they refer to objects, facts or states which actually *exist* in the individual. Instead of stating that the diagnosis is a re-ordering of facts which may be elicited and observed by *everybody* (if at all), the terminology suggests the existence of a reality which can be seen only by the psychiatrist. Thus, for example, the 'reification' of a common phase in many working class adolescent careers such as persistent group thieving becomes in the context of a few other observations a 'personality disorder of an anti-social type' which an adolescent *has*.

There is little doubt that in the hands of less knowledgeable users, such labels which both devalue and distort the adolescent's condition lead to the legitimisation of measures being taken which cannot be justified on objective grounds (cf. Rains *et al*, 1975).

The presumed hypotheses regarding the origins and course of the disorders under discussion need not take much space. Suffice it to say that other than in some biologically based disorders there is hardly any consensus about the origin and development of adolescent disorders. While it may be possible to isolate the full range of possible 'causes', to adduce any of those to account for a child's disorder remains for ever hypothetical because there is no way of retrospectively testing it. Psychiatric history taking is dependent on the same information as is or can be made available to everybody else and is, as such, open to the same selective distortions as everyone else's. The error margin may be reduced by the use of special measures (e.g. Shepherd *et al*, 1971) but it cannot be eliminated.

It is in the area of treatment that psychiatry's limitations with disordered youngsters become most evident. As was suggested earlier, the diagnosis has formal implications for a variety of treatments which are scanned, the appropriate one selected, and explicitly prescribed for the patient. Because of the unsatisfactory nature of diagnosis, treatments which flow from them must inevitably suffer.

At their worst many diagnoses have no related treatment implications. The outstanding example is perhaps the categories of 'personality disorders' and 'conduct disorders' into which the majority of the extreme children fall. There are no known treatment prescriptions for personality and conduct disorders, other than those which specify environmental care and control measures which are no more within the purview of psychiatrists than they are of any other related professional group. Indeed, from a strictly psychiatric point of view, these diagnoses are tantamount to dismissal of a case and its unrelatedness to any psychiatric treatment competence.

Thus, a psychiatric diagnosis is made which excludes psychiatric treatment. But, as earlier suggested, since the validation of psychiatric diagnoses can only derive from their testing through rigorous treatment, this seems to pose a central paradox in the fundamental tenets and practice of psychiatry with disordered adolescents.

But, since much of the behaviour of these youngsters is critical and anxiety provoking, the ability of psychiatrists to prescribe drugs which enable the control of disordered behaviour to be achieved justifies, in the eyes of those who work with the youngsters, the continued involvement of psychiatrists in this area.

Other than in areas where the diagnosis indicates some form of physical intervention through drugs or other treatment with positive outcomes of known probablility that they can *and* are willing to undertake, it may be preferable that no diagnoses or other judgements should be made which are likely to adversely influence what happens to the child. Statements should be made explicitly as the hypotheses they are so that the child may not suffer from the consequences of inappropriate labelling and failure of treatment. This may also release other workers from their undue dependence on psychiatrists which impedes the development of other appropriate methods of intervention. This may help speed up the process towards a stage where in a community of professionals concerned with helping disordered children individual workers are appraised in terms of the value of their contributions to solving problems rather the deistic aura they exude.

Criteria for Evaluating Classifications

It has already been suggested that a classification should be useful. In the case of disordered children, 'use' would primarily denote the ability of the classification to direct action, to act as guide to what should be done to alleviate the difficulty. But there are many other criteria against which classifications can be judged. This topic has been the subject of a series of papers (Hobbs, 1975b) presenting trenchant critiques of classification systems and their consequences in numerous areas. Although many of the points are particularly applicable to the US setting, their relevance to anyone who deals with children and their problems cannot be under-estimated. A good classification system for children's disorders (cf. Philips *et al*, 1975) should have the following characteristics:

* Have surface validity, make sense to many and allow it to be used by as many people as possible.
* Allow for fine gradation within a few broad classes.
* Be based on experience and remain provisional, i.e. open to change with changing social and personal circumstances.
* Remain open to new empirical findings.
* Not be a disguise for a personal or cultural act of derogation, e.g. 'moral imbecile', 'psychopath'.
* Take account of fundamental differences between adults and children and thus the different significances of their disorders in the total life of each, e.g. childhood and adult depression.
* Allow for changes in persons classified, e.g. through development, in the way 'personality disorder' does not.
* Look at different levels of response in the different functional areas. Classification thus needs to be 'multi-axial'.
* Allow for both constancy and variability in behaviour related to different environments.
* Not be theory bound, as this will limit its use to those who do not subscribe to the theory.
* Not look at any isolated aspect of functioning of the child but present a succinct picture of the organic whole.
* Should have *direct* implications for intervention but allow for the use of a variety of methods.

Many attempts have been made to devise systems which satisfy all the above criteria. It is evident, however, that in the present state of knowledge, only the simplest descriptive systems which do not postulate a particular theoretical orientation or adduce any particular aetiological relationships are likely to command any sort of consensus (cf. Prugh *et al*, 1975).

Other aspects must remain strictly tentative, until more is known about the origins, development and treatment requirements of disorders. Furthermore, the classification should be couched in terms which are comprehensible to all the professional and preferably also to lay groups, the parents, and the child himself. This is to avoid the damage caused to the child by misunderstandings among the people who deal with him.

In Search of a New Approach

In the light of these and earlier comments, a classification has been developed by Hoghughi (1969, 1976, 1977) and subsequently adopted in both the assessment and treatment of severely disordered youngsters. Its applicability, however, ranges over all school age children and, with suitable modifications, to adults. It has had a long period of exposure to practising professionals, the children and their parents. It is the basis for evaluating children's needs described in Chapter 5.

The core of this approach is the concern with describing, explaining and alleviating 'problems'. The reason for adopting 'problems' as the focus of approach to the management of disordered youngsters is that they always come to the attention of social agencies and go through a particular form of social processing because they present or experience problems which are unacceptable to those around them.

A problem can be defined in a multitude of ways. In this context, it is simply defined as an *unacceptable condition*. Unacceptability implies 'undesirability' under a particular set of circumstances (time and place), thus noting the fact that what is unacceptable and undesirable in one context is not necessarily so in another; for example, it is normal and thus acceptable for one child who has lost his mother to weep without provocation, but not for another child. The definition implies that there is a person or a group on whom the condition impinges and who then regards it as 'unacceptable'. Simply logically, an undetected condition is no condition at all, though the possibility of its existence can be considered and investigated.

The definition of a condition as 'unacceptable' implies that 'something should be done about it'. This is sometimes made explicit as in a court order. What the 'something' is depends on the rights and responsibilities of those who have defined the problem.

It is possible to construe 'unacceptable conditions' from many points of view, leading to quite different classifications. In this approach the orientation is towards problems *manifested* by children in different *functional* areas. As will become clear, functional areas frequently overlap and invariably interact with one another. But this simply reflects the human condition; problems in one area impinge on the total personality and affect other aspects of functioning. A classification that takes account of this fact is preferable to one that distorts reality for the convenience of the classifier. Knowledge of 'unacceptable condition' is obtained from (a) the referral agency – which will highlight what it regards as problematic; (b) from all (or as many as possible) other persons and agencies who are thought to know about the child – primarily parents, the child, relatives, school, etc.; (c) specialist sources of information, using specialised investigative techniques, measures and approaches. These would include particular group and individual observation settings, as well as investigation by physicians, psychologists, psychiatrists, neurologists, and others.

The close scrutiny of information provided in each of these areas reveals *why* the particular condition has been found problematic – in what ways the child's functioning has been found to deviate from normal variations or latitude of tolerance within each area of enquiry. This accords with another important requirement of a classification of disorders – that it should indicate areas of normality or non-propblematic attributes. Bearing in mind the above points, the comprehensive pattern of problems is set out below. The functional attributes covered by each problem area are only set out in summary form. Detailed examples can be gleaned from the problems presented in Chapter 5.

Physical

This area includes all disorders, dysfunctions and deficits to do with the body as a whole or any of its subsystems, whether hereditary or acquired subsequently during the child's lifetime from, say, epilepsy, through diabetes and poor hearing to undescended testicles. It also includes the psychoses, as well as psychophysiological, autonomic and visceral disorders.

Cognitive

This category relates to the ability of the child to cope with the intellectual demands made on him in his daily life, particularly in school and work settings. The area also encompasses cognitive problems, such as illiteracy, which may not have risen as a result of intellectual defect but out of, say, persistent truancy. In this sense not being able to read and write fall within the cognitive problem solving area and are functionally equivalent to cognitive deficit. The problem can be general – subnormality or specific – difficulty in synthesising words. Supernormality would be a problem if it is ascertained that inadequate demands are made on the adolescent in relation to his intellectual capacity.

Family

This is the largest and the most complex category of problems experienced and presented by disordered youngsters. In tackling such a large area there is a danger of infinite regress and, therefore, the limits of how far and wide the problems should be described depend on the specific requirements of the investigator. Problems can be traced back and sideways as far as necessary if they seem to be part of the present reality of the family, for example, the mother who communes with her murdered mother's ghost or the 'uncle' who sexually assaults the child.

Family problems encompass the background of the parents

(e.g. criminal family); their socioeconomic status (e.g. unemployed labourer); neighbourhood they inhabit (e.g. slum); the home (e.g. overcrowded); their individual characteristics at a variety of levels of analysis (e.g. withdrawn, anti-authority); the pattern, content and emotional tone of their interaction with each other (e.g. submissive) and with their children (e.g. little affection), both together and singly; the style and method of upbringing of their children including methods of control (beats her; is indifferent); and children's relationships with their parents (e.g. rejecting) and one another (e.g. models on elder brother).

Social Relationships

These problems relate to the difficulties and conflicts of the child in coping with the growing demands of social interaction with both peers and adults. They refer to perception of social cues, ability to relate and reciprocate and engage in co-operative activity, amenability and response to social pressure, etc.

Social Behaviour

This is perhaps the area which causes the most anxiety in the total functioning of youngsters. It includes all infractions of laws, rules, customs and rituals of behaviour in the wider social (as opposed to small group) setting. It comprises chiefly all offences and encroachments against person and property as well as 'reflexive' offences such as drug taking and prostitution. In addition, it encompasses acts which although not strictly offences – self-destructive acts, temper tantrums, truancy and and absconding – are nevertheless seriously socially disruptive and frequently provoke dramatic intervention by social agencies.

Personal

This area covers three distinct but closely interrelated aspects:

(a) deviation in personality *structure* (e.g. severely introverted); and relatively stable personal *attributes* (e.g. rigid perseverator); (b) *emotional development* (e.g. immature); *tone* (e.g. depressive); *adaptation* (e.g. obsessive); and *control* (e.g. impulsive); (c) *identity* or *self concept*, best described as child's difficulty in answering questions like 'Who am I?', 'What am I?', 'Who cares for me?', 'What am I worth?', etc. Traditionally most clinicians have confined themselves to the first two categories. The third, however, is regarded as crucial in the understanding of the way children see themselves and make sense of their life situation, not only because it completes the picture of the child but also because it frequently helps account for *why* a child does what he does the way he does it.

As has already been indicated, each of the above problem areas can be enumerated, detailed and analysed at a variety of levels from the most general to the most specific. In the latest treatment system developed on this basis, the problems are analysed at three levels of detail: (1) *Area* (e.g. physical), (2) *Attribute* (e.g. enuresis), (3) *Behaviour* (e.g. hides sheets); or (1) *Area* (e.g. social behaviour), (2) *Attribute* (e.g. self destructive), (3) *Behaviour* (e.g. self-inflicted wounds). Each behaviour is linked with a series of possible treatments.

Parameters of Evaluation

Children differ from one another in the type and quality of problems they present. Different investigators may adopt particular evaluative dimensions but at least four are essential to evaluating any problem child for purposes of distinguishing him from others and drawing up a treatment plan:

Extent refers to the number of problems listed for a particular child. The more problem areas listed, the more problematic the child is. A child with physical, family, behavioural and personal problems presents a larger area of 'unacceptable' conditions than does one with, say, only physical and personal. The range of problems within each area also contributes to the judgment of the extent of problems, such as a diabetic and epileptic as opposed to only an epileptic. Evaluation of extent is carried out by simple counting of problems.

Intensity relates to the depth of the problem. The more intense the problem, the more severe it will be. A severely aggressive father, for example, presents a more serious problem than a mildly aggressive one; the girl who mopes and says 'I am fed up' is less of a problem than one who is suicidally depressed. Evaluation of intensity can be done either subjectively or through the development of an objective scale in any of the generally accepted ways.

Duration can be seen as a contributor to judgments of intensity. It refers to the length of time a problem has been manifested. The supposition, broadly accepted, is that the longer a problem has existed the more difficult it will be to alleviate, if for no other reason than its learned concomitants. This parameter takes note of the fact that in the course of a child's development, one problem usually generates another without the former having been resolved. This aspect of evaluation may be expanded to differentiate between problems which are *manifest* (symptoms and signs) and those which are regarded as being at the *core* of the difficulty.

Urgency. Having obtained some idea of the range, intensity and duration of a child's problems, it becomes necessary to rank them in order of priority warranting intervention. Different criteria may be used for such ranking such as 'heat' (magistrates' pressure to curb a persistent offender) or 'ease' (we can stop this boy's bedwetting in a month'). Whatever other criteria are proposed 'urgency' is likely to be the most influential in determining priorities. This involves subjective judgment, whether individual or group based, regarding the possible consequences of *not* taking certain measures and of the hierarchical order of problems ('unless we reduce her anxiety, we cannot bring the rest of her behaviour under control').

Advantages of the Problem Approach

Earlier in this chapter, a number of criteria were presented against which any classification system could be judged. They can be applied as easily to the problem approach as to any other. Over the period of time that this approach has been used in daily practice of assessment and treatment, a number of advantages over alternative classification systems have emerged. It allows for variability of the children's responses according to their age, sex, subculture and other contextual factors – an eight year old addicted to cigarettes presents a problem which an addicted fifteen year old does not. It takes note of developmental changes in children – questioning of parental authority is 'acceptable' in a sixteen year old but not in a ten year old. Because of the multiplicity of sources and levels of information, the approach provides data that are reliable over time and source of information – within limits of reliability of perceptions and measurements.

The approach explicitly allows for discrepancies in perception and judgment of problems – control of temper may be a problem to the parents but not to the school. This makes it possible to differentiate situationally variable elements from personally consistent response patterns so that judgments about behavioural constancy and variability can be made. This is helpful to both predicting behaviours and planning relevant treatment – in the way that global judgments such as 'personality disorder' are not.

It deliberately brings together and utilises different sources of approach, thus not only encouraging participation in decision making, but also ensuring that the determination of the child's problems and consequent treatment are not idiosyncratic. Children, and particularly such a socially threatening minority as the disordered, are too much at risk from labelling as to allow single individuals – however competent – to pronounce on what is wrong and what should be done with them.

The making of conditional descriptive statements, bound by time and context, removes the need and possibility of labelling. Each child carries a multi-axial description which defies the shorthand of convenience terminology. Bearing in mind the excess meanings that most labels such as 'psychopath', 'inadequate', etc. accrue, it is all the more important to make a special effort to avoid labelling a child.

This classification is particularly appropriate to a team or multi-disciplinary approach. Because learning about functional areas is part of any normally intelligent citizen's upbringing, *everybody* can contribute intelligently to the determination of each of the problem areas, though it is taken for granted that a physician can say more about the medical illness and a psychologist more about the cognitive deficits of a child than a non-specialist can.

The approach uses a language of problems which is universally applied and enables easier communication between different levels of expertise and points of view than can be achieved with any other classification. The descriptive language is common English (or Hebrew or Cantonese or whatever) and as such demystifies the disorder of the child, which is necessary if a common though differentiated approach to the alleviation of his problems is to take place.

The descriptive terminology reduces the need for inferences and as such communicates maximum information with minimum distortion. Thus a girl is said to be 'experiencing considerable conflict with parents' – a descriptive statement – rather than that 'she is suffering from an adjustment reaction of adolescence' – an explanatory statement.

The description of a disorder does not assume common aetiological factors. This is one of the major limitations of diagnostic classifications, arising from the paucity of any established and accepted evidence regarding the roots of disorders. The present approach allows for wholly different aetiologies to be associated with the same pattern of disorder. This is in keeping with common clinical experience. One girl's wrist cutting is a guilt reaction to incest with her father and mother's suicide attempt, another's a learnt, manipulatory ploy. Each of the 'causal' inferences here would themselves constitute and be described separately as problems.

One of the central advantages of this approach over others

is that it is bound to neither any particular theoretical orientation, as in the Group for the Advancement of Psychiatry classification (1966) which is heavily psychoanalytic, or an ideological one as in the International Classification of Diseases (1967) which sees delinquency as a personality disorder. It leaves open the possible use of such orientations, but only if they can be translated to problems.

Closely associated with this, the approach makes diagnoses largely redundant. The function of diagnosis is to differentiate. The configuration of one child's problems, particularly against the evaluative criteria of extent, intensity, duration and urgency, amply differentiate him from other children. Going beyond such a description is not necessary other than for purposes of developing an empirical typology. That activity can be carried out separately as research and should not, ethically, get mixed up with the alleviation of the child's problem to which any diagnosis or description of problem ought to be a preliminary step. This is related to a more fundamental point. Bearing in mind the dynamic nature of most adolescents' disorders and the multiplicity of changing circumstances associated with them, it may be argued that diagnosis is not only unnecessary but may be irrelevant and potentially against the best interests of children because it limits the possibilities of treatment.

Because diagnoses are not necessary, there will be no search for syndromes accompanied by the attempts to collect together as many syndromic signs and symptoms as possible. Because few individuals present 'textbook' pictures of disorders and many fall uncomfortably between several syndromes, it may make more sense and be more true to human diversity if an attempt was not made to squeeze them into a few doubtful categories, but rather allowed each their unique configuration of attributes. In this sense, the problem approach allows for a more complex and sophisticated approach to human problems than a syndromic one. Because individuals are not diagnosed in terms of syndromes, this obviates the need to change diagnoses in the course of treatment.

The acid test, ultimately, of any classification system is the degree to which it guides action, in this case the treatment of disordered youngsters. But despite the formal connection between diagnosis and treatment, there is little empirical connection between the two which has been established as either consistent or significant in this area. Rarely, even in physical medicine, is the total configuration of problems susceptible to only one form of treatment. Rather in almost all cases there is the need for a variety of approaches not only to deal with a particular problem, but also to mobilise diverse resources to cope with side effects of treatment and ancillary issues. But in the traditional classifications there is considerable doubt and ambiguity about both the central and ancillary approaches.

By contrast, the problem approach has direct pointers to the objective and probable mode of treatment. Because the approach is elemental, each problem demands its own alleviation, which is the least ambiguous and preferential definition of 'treatment' as illustrated in Chapter 6. The treatment options are not foreclosed by diagnosis – they are left open in all their diversity and would, therefore, allow a multi-modal approach to a disordered youngster. Thus, intensive work with the family may use a psychotherapeutic approach while the youngster's aggressive behaviour is modified by operant techniques and his anxiety reduced by appropriate medication. If the particular technique does not work with its particular problem, then that one technique needs only to be changed rather than the whole treatment – as it is at the moment. While this approach demands greater sophistication in treatment, it is likely to be more efficient than any holistic approach.

It will have been noticed that throughout this approach has been put forward as 'descriptive' rather than explanatory. The reason for this was noted earlier. Because knowledge of the origins and circumstances associated with the development and maintenance of disorders is scant, patchy, inconsistent and inadequately established, there are no *generally* acceptable explanations. Rather, there are many typologies and schools of explanations each with their adherents. Because of the difficulties, both ethical and practical, of controlling human behaviour and the circumstances that impinge on it, any explanatory statements made about their disorders do not stand up to rigorous scrutiny. At the present time, therefore, the choice of explanations says more about the preferences of the explainer than of the explained.

In view of this it would be more rational and ethical if all treatment were to be tied to a rigorous description of problems than to any inevitably hypothetical explanation that might be given for the problem. The choice of a treatment technique presumes some explanatory hypothesis on the part of the treatment agent but in a multi disciplinary team that would remain limited to one problem area of one child, and can be tested as a short range hypothesis.

This approach was developed because of the limitations of alternative classifications. It is not conclusive and does not obviate the need for explanatory systems but provides a universally workable basis for both relevant treatment and development of explanatory disciplines. Its latest developement provides detailed lists of problems at each of the analytical levels mentioned earlier and has set down procedures for the treatment of severely disordered youngsters. This provides the data base derived from actual treatment outcomes which will enable the development of explanatory models to be tested in the course of rigorous treatment. Theory can then remain a personal preoccupation while alleviation of the youngsters' problems can develop unfettered.

*

CHAPTER 9

Who Is Security For?

LOCKING up youngsters is emerging as the most controversial issue within the whole gamut of arguments surrounding the operation of the Juvenile Justice system. It has a curious allure which brings together protagonists at opposite ends of the political spectrum – the Society of Conservative Lawyers and the Howard League for Penal Reform, professional associations of social workers and the Police Federation, MPs and Government departments. Their reasons are as different as are the levels of arguments on which they are based. All are, however, agreed on the conclusion that there is a group of youngsters (estimates vary widely) who present such risks that they should be locked up. As will emerge, the heat of the argument about security has been in inverse proportion to the amount of information that is available about both the youngsters and the secure facilities.

In the United States, the detention of young people is something of a national scandal which has been largely resistant to the reforming efforts of a wide range of pressure groups.

The practices of those who are responsible for operating secure facilities are even more shrouded in secrecy and ambiguity than facts and figures about which children go into what types of detention facilities and why. Secure facilities of one sort or another have developed as a reaction to the ancient practice of placing children in the same penal establishments as adults. In the United Kingdom this development resulted in the provision of reformatories and industrial schools, borstals, and remand homes which were taken over from local police forces in 1932, approved schools which brought industrial schools and reformatories together into a new statutory service, and junior detention centres (Walker, 1965).

At present, secure facilities are provided in penal, psychiatric and social service settings. Penal provisions include remand centres, junior detention centres and borstals. Psychiatric facilities include special hospitals for those certified under the Mental Health Act 1959, and some locked wards in a variety of hospital settings. Social services departments are responsible for remand homes (now called 'observation and assessment centres') and community homes with education which between them provide secure facilities ranging from single detention rooms to large scale separate accommodation for the total care, assessment and treatment of children. The extent of penal provision changes according to demand and no information is available on the extent and use of secure psychiatric facilities for children. The extent of current secure accommodation in England, augmented by the two relatively new Youth Treatment Centres (DHSS, 1971) whose capacities are still uncertain is as follows:

Region No.	'Observation & Assessment'			Community Homes with Education		
	BOYS	GIRLS	MIXED	BOYS	GIRLS	MIXED
1. Northern	–	–	14	–	–	–
2. Yorkshire & Humberside	–	–	5	–	5	–
3. N. West	–	4	–	32	12	–
4. W. Midlands	7	–	–	–	3	–
5. E. Midlands	3	–	–	–	3	–
6. E. Anglia	6	–	–	–	–	–
7. Home Counties	5	–	2	12	–	–
8. London	10	8	–	30	4	–
9. Surrey, etc	–	–	–	–	–	–
10. Hampshire, etc	–	–	–	–	–	–
11. S. West	–	–	2	26	12	–
TOTALS	31	12	23	100	39	–

TOTAL   O & A = 67
TOTAL   CHE = 139

In Western Europe, roughly the same range of facilities for detention of children is used as in the United Kingdom. Even the most enlightened countries find it necessary to keep some children under secure conditions, but little information is available from them either about the numbers of children involved or the criteria that regulate practices within security. In Germany, for example, it is not possible to obtain even basic information about how many youngsters are in secure conditions, because responsibilities for running the facilities are divided between Federal and 'Land' (state) authorities.

In the United States, the same lack of information as well as frequently reported abuse, rape and suicide seem to have led Sarri (1974) to produce her report on the detention of juveniles. Although she acknowledges that her work only scratches the surface, she manages to draw a horrifying picture of the unconstitutional locking up of vast numbers of children without safeguards and for dubious reasons with inevitably damaging results – 'It is obvious that hundreds of thousands of children and youth are significantly impacted each year by experiences in jails, lockups and juvenile detention facilities. The deplorable condition of most of these facilities is widely known and not infrequently criticised by the media, knowledgeable professionals, and concerned citizens. But the situation continues from one year to the next with very little change.' Her characteristically forthright critique cannot be dismissed as being irrelevant to the European scene.

The lack of information and resistance to change reflect the deepest ambivalence of society to youngsters whom it regards as dangerous and predatory. The fact that these judgments are made on ambiguous grounds and through less than crystal clear procedures does not alter the ambivalence which is fed by both popular and specialist reports regarding the youngsters. It seems to be taken for granted that youngsters would not be in detention unless they were 'bad' enough to be there. In a self-evident but uninteresting sense, this is of course true. But this truth reflects as much on the judgment as on the children and does not constitute justification. As will be suggested later in this chapter, there is considerable cause for concern about the pressure to lock up more and more children and the shortcomings of the process through which they get there. The recent publication by the Howard League for Penal Reform (1977) sets out the first systematic examination of security for 'unruly' children and highlights much of the confusion in this area.

A recent government circular states:

'... it is generally accepted that a small minority of the boys and girls whom it is the present function of the community home system to accommodate have needs which staff cannot meet unless supplied with the additional facility of physical security. Moreover it must be an eventual objective to develop the community home system to assume responsibility for boys and girls who at present, on security grounds, would be committed to a remand centre or a prison on remand or sentenced to borstal training. Local authorities' regional plans for community homes accordingly provide for secure units both at some observation and assessment centres and at some long stay community homes.'

In all this, however, the concept of security, its relation to the problems and needs of extreme children and the special difficulties of operating a secure environment, have not been subjected to any form of rigorous public scrutiny. It may therefore be worthwhile to look at some of these aspects to see how far knowledge of secure facilities and practices within them can be evaluated to provide guidelines for the future development of services for coping with severely disordered youngsters.

The Concept of Security

Security can be defined as the 'condition of being safe or protected from danger'. Such a condition does not only refer to physical security but often connotes 'a feeling of being safe.' This is the sense in which people talk of 'emotional' security.

The more common sense with which workers concerned with disturbed youngsters speak of security, however, refers to a facility or conditions in which a person's freedom of movement is curbed and where he can be kept under conditions which reduce his risk to himself and to the public.

This is a relatively recent extension of the term 'security'. Its positive overtones may help to disguise a variety of purposes and methods which are less than enhancing. It is generally more acceptable to speak of 'secure provision', with its implications of care and welfare of the child than to speak of incarceration, detention or keeping under lock and key. The blanket use of the term also helps to diffuse the very different purposes for which a child may be placed in security in the first place – public protection or welfare and protection of the child. This distinction should not be blurred. Whereas the detention of the child in his interests and in the interests of the public may coincide from time to time, their departures are sufficiently frequent to warn against too glib a justification of one in terms of the other.

Implicit in both of these uses is the notion that the child is presenting a condition which, uncurbed, has or will have unacceptable consequences. The gravity of the consequences, according to society's scale of values, is 'risk'. Thus risk is a 'price' that society has paid in suffering the child's behaviour and may again have to pay unless it takes restrictive measures. An assessment of risk is, therefore, central to making any decisions about whether the child should be placed under conditions of security. But the area of presenting risks, though central to judicial and professional decision making, is one that is fraught with conceptual and empirical complications and has defined adequate definition. Although this stage of affairs is inevitable at present, it is however possible to subject the notion of risk to wider public discussion (e.g. Morris & Hawkins, 1969; Floud et al, 1977) in order to elucidate it and reduce the ambiguity surrounding discussions of young people's need for secure accommodation.

Forms of Security

In the minds of police, magistrates, social workers and others, security has become tantamount to a physical structure in which a youngster can be detained. This, however, is only one form of security. Sources of security can be broadly divided into two types, internal and external.

'*Internal Security*' refers to all attributes within the individual which reduce his ability, wish, or propensity to break bounds and behave in an unacceptable manner. Such internal curbs can be achieved through surgery – lobotomies, lobectomies and other operations on the nervous system – to render a person prone to uncontrollable outbursts no longer able to break bounds. With modern psychopharmacology, however, it is not often necessary to resort to such drastic measures. By the judicious use of various forms of medication ranging from sedatives through hypnotics and tranquillisers to narcotics, it is possible to totally control a person's ability to move. Additionally, various forms of psychotropic medication are available which substantially affect the level and quality of consciousness and volition of the subject. The third form of internal curb may be exercised by the quality of attachment to an environment, or a 'holding relationship' with a person within the environment, which for the time being reduces or neutralises the impulse on the part of the youngster to act out, run away, become violent, etc.

It is unlikely that surgery is used frequently, if at all, in order to achieve security with youngsters. Medication is commonly used in psychiatric and general practice in order to help a youngster and those around him to cope better with his problem behaviour. A youngster who is put to sleep, is heavily 'tranquillised' or has difficulty in dragging himself from one place to another, does not present much of a risk to other people. With certain rare exceptions, the use of medication to control problem behaviour hardly ever arouses public concern. It is cheap and, as a means of control, is assumed to be administered in therapeutic settings which are centrally concerned with the welfare of the individual and the healing process. Without it the revolution in recent psychiatric practice would not have been achieved and a great many more people would have remained or been put in locked wards than there are at present.

However, the benefits of psychotropic medication are attained at a price which is paid by the individual to whom it is administered. Psychotropic medication has almost always undesirable side effects and may present the youngster with longer term problems with which he may not be able to cope without the aid of *further* medication. The restriction of liberty and the alleviation of undesirable behaviour which is achieved through the use of medication is not subject to any form of impartial judgment apart from that of the medical practitioner who would be understandably as much impressed by reports of difficult and uncontrollable behaviour as he would be by any objective appraisal of the medical needs of the child (Box, 1977). The price of long term control by medication to the individual may be greater than demanded by justice.

The third type of internal security depends on the overwhelmingly positive response of a youngster to an environment or person. There are certain general assumptions about what attributes of an environment are found attractive by youngsters – openness, acceptance, trust, etc. – but these have rarely been put to the test. Although the absence of certain characteristics have been shown to be positively correlated with certain forms of disruptive behaviour (e.g. absconding, Clarke & Martin, 1971), there are no reliable guidelines as to the type of environment which would persuade a child not to run away.

The quality of a relationship with one other person or a group of other persons certainly does work, if tautologically, when the relationship is strong enough to counteract a child's urge to run away or to behave in an undesirable manner. It can be the most efficient and humane form of control, particularly as it can respond to the shifting needs and problems of the individual child. As the majority of problem youngsters seem to have suffered severely from unsatisfactory relationships, good personal bonds would appear more likely to ameliorate their problems and prepare them, yet again, for living in normal human society than any other medium.

There are, however, major limitations on this form of security. Most disordered youngsters have experienced their most severe problems in the area of making relationships. Their demands on any human contact are intense, shifting, petulant and fraught with deep ambivalence. They are not often capable of engaging in the 'give and take' which marks any satisfactory relationship. Further, all adults are not embodiments of precision engineered perfection and are not all capable of sustaining the demands that relationships make on them. The sorts of people who can and are willing to engage in such depth of interaction with youngsters are not in over abundant supply even in large professional organisations. Terms and conditions of service and other restrictions on employment of staff place severe constraints on the amount and intensity of interaction between a member of staff and a youngster. The needs of personal development outlined in Chapter 6 and increasing mobility of competent staff add additional stresses. Over and above these, staff are financially the most expensive resource. To counteract the above limitations and to create security solely through relationships, if empirically possible at all, would be more costly than many even caring societies could be induced to pay.

'External Security' essentially entails all materials and structures that are used in order to restrict the movement of a youngster. They range from handcuffing to holding by persons, to the use of a ball and chain, to shackling to a mobile or stationary object, to placement in various structures, such as a hulk moored in the middle of the sea or some form of building. All these measures have the effect of preventing escape and of confining undesirable behaviour to a limited area.

While all these measures achieve roughly the same end, they denote very different attitudes to disordered youngsters and manifest a community's ability to treat its jetsam and flotsam in a 'civilised' manner' The fact that children are not fettered with ball and chain or shackled to objects is thought to suggest that such practices, because they antedate the present ones, are barbaric and contrary to current notions of dignity of individuals, however disordered or anti-social they may be. It is interesting that these measures have not been abandoned and new ones adopted in their place as a result of any critical evaluation of arguments for and against them. It may, for example, be argued that a child whose movements are physically restricted through the attachment of a ball and chain, but who is allowed to remain ambulant, however slowly but in an open setting, is being infinitely more humanely treated than a child who is locked up in a detention room and thereby deprived of basic human contact and environmental stimulation. The argument does not have to be accepted but it merits consideration.

Buildings are the current fashionable mode of providing physical security. They enable the physical and hence the psychological environment of an individual to be so organised as to maximise the desired effect. From society's point of view they have the advantage of segregating and thereby making invisible a deviant group. They signify a solid measure of social control. On the other hand, buildings have a tendency to outgrow their usefulness quickly and, having to comply with certain standards of safety and adequacy, are inevitably very expensive. They need people to run them and in view of the practices they can encourage, they require particularly elaborate and rigorous safeguards to ensure the welfare of those inside them.

Security is also one of degree – the degree to which a person's freedom of movement is curbed. It can apply to any form of security, ranging over various dosages of medication, through variations in the level of staff supervision, to grades of physical restriction. One major reason why secure provisions of various sorts fail to have any long term benefit is that they do not take account of a person's need to be exposed to decreasing structure and security as he moves towards release to the open community. Most secure facilities are currently built in such a way that they do not provide opportunity for increasing through regulated exposure to risks of living in a free, unstructured environment. The person, after release, cannot cope with the apparent chaos and often acts in a way which will impose some structure and predictable pattern of events for him. People cannot be trained under captivity, without simulation, for living in a free society.

More often than not internal and external forms of security are used together, both singly and in combination, in a variety of settings. A youngster may be detained in a remand facility with high staff ratios where medication is used as an adjunct to controlling his temper tantrums. Bearing in mind the above forms of security, excluding the human one, it is important to recognise that in our society there are considerable numbers of people subject to some form of security as a means of curbing their undesirable behaviour. At one level this may be regarded matter of factly and said to be 'right and proper'. On the other hand, security carries a particularly heavy 'price tag' both for the individual and society, not just in financial terms but also in the erosion of personal and social values. For this reason it demands closer control and safeguarding through 'due process' than it is accorded at the present time.

Reasons for Security

At its most fundamental level, secure facilities for disordered children can be justified on the grounds that to allow a child freedom of movement would present him and/or the public with unacceptable risk. Therefore, any youngster presenting sufficiently intense problems which are also capable of being curbed could be deemed to require placement in conditions of security.

More specifically, the following groups of children are thought to warrant secure accommodation. Although security is regarded as a prerequisite for the management of these children, other assumptions, which will be brought out later, are implicit in this judgment. The groups comprise those who:

1. Persistently abscond from homes, schools and other placements;
2. Behave in a seriously disruptive fashion and act out aggressively;
3. By virtue of their behaviour are a source of danger to themselves or others;
4. Present such problems as to be beyond the help of other agencies and which a secure facility may, incidentally and by virtue of its other resources, be capable of alleviating.

Secure accommodation for the above groups would fall into one of the four traditionally established settings of remand, punishment, assessment and treatment.

Remand

Many youngsters are taken into the care of local authorities either on full or interim Care Orders. Few of them present such risks either to themselves or to the public as to warrant detention under secure conditions. However, in 1975 about 4,500 youngsters were placed in penal establishments. The figures for one day (22nd September, 1975) showed that 1,663 youngsters (including sixty-four girls) were in remand centres and an additional thirty-one in prisons. Of these the majority had been in custody for seven days or more.

This was regarded with extreme alarm and distaste by the concerned public because of the serious damage that could be done to young people by mixing them with the more established criminals, a modern echo of the concern which led to the separation of custodial facilities for children and adults. As a result of pressures both in the media and Parliament, the conditions for issuing of 'certificates of unruliness' were changed. Now as a result, no girl under fifteen and no boy under fourteen may be sent to a penal establishment on an 'unruly certificate' unless: (1) the youngster has committed a grave crime (punishable in the case of an adult by fourteen years' imprisonment or more) and for whom no suitable accommodation is available in a community home; (2) has a history of or has been charged with an offence of violence; (3) is a persistent absconder or has a seriously disruptive influence on the community home environment.

There are also certain administrative restrictions which are bound to reduce placements in penal settings, but many youngsters still find their way into establishments for remand purposes. The rest, who would normally have been so accommodated, are now either kept or newly placed in community homes and local facilities and continue presenting major problems (Hoghughi & Heptinstall, 1972). They have added a new dimension to the already serious peroblems residential establishments have of dealing with the 'heavy end' of the disordered population. Many of these youngsters present qualitatively quite different problems from their younger peers and attempt to intimidate both staff and children into submission.

This picture, unsatisfactory as it is, contrasts sharply with the American practice where practically every child who is picked up for any reason is detained in security until his disposal can be determined. Logan (1972, quoted in Sarri, 1974) found that 'dependent and neglected children' were held in jail 'when necessary'. More than 50% of the authorities reported that juveniles were put in jail as a 'deterrent' without a formal charge. Juveniles could remain in jail for indefinite periods since only a few counties or cities had procedures for controlling the maximum period a child could be held. Lerman (1975) also comments on the cavalier use of detention of children in the California community treatment project.

Perhaps the above factors account for the grim picture which emerges from Sarri's (1974, op. cit.) appraisal of detention of juveniles in the United States. She estimated that in 1974 about one million youths and juveniles were held in adult jails and juvenile detention facilities – about half a million in each. Astonishingly they included, in one census, sizeable numbers of primary school children, those below the age of six, and '181 infants below the age of two'! Many are detained in overcrowded conditions where what happens to them inside is likely to have more deleterious long term effects for the individuals and hence society than whatever induced the locking up in the first place (Cottle, 1977).

Punishment

Retribution as a response to unacceptable behaviour is among the most basic of human responses. Although punishment for disordered youngsters is not part of the official policy (Walker, 1965; Ford, 1975; cf. Cohen, 1978), it nevertheless underlies much of the police and magistrates' decision making which eventually leads to a youngster being taken into care of the local authority or his detention in a penal facility. This reasoning is implicit in the recommendation of 'secure care orders' by the House of Commons Expenditure Committee (1975). The assertion of social control over undesirable behaviour frequently includes the deprivation of liberty for however short a period. In the United Kingdom such a facility already exists in the form of junior detention centres and borstals.

However much value can be placed on the retributive element of such detention for its own sake, there is little evidence to show that placing youngsters under conditions of security has much deterrent or reformative value (Dunlop & McCabe, 1964). The majority of boys discharged from detention centres commit further offences as do those from borstals and prisons, and support the currently informed view that punishment through deprivation of liberty is rarely successful in preventing other criminal acts (Debuyst, 1967; Wilkins, 1967). This is no argument against the *efficient* use of punishment as a means of shaping behaviour, such as in behaviour modification (Stumphauzer, 1973), but it does suggest that no great claims should be made for such use of detention other than that it satisfies society's demands for retribution.

On this basis, there were in 1974 about 8,000 young people in borstals or young prisoners' facilities. In addition between three and four thousand passed through junior detention centres (Home Office, 1975). 'Deprivation of liberty' is as much a state of mind as a physical reality. Its significance depends on the wider values of both the depriver and the deprived. Because it is not for ever and can only be enforced in a relative sense, for most youngsters it is an undemanding, though unpleasant interlude in even more unpleasant and uncomprehended life histories.

Punitive placement of youngsters in traditional forms of security provides experience, tuition, and enough unpleasant experiences to prepare the youngsters to strike back more effectively against society after release. The public often forget, due to 'out of sight, out of mind' processes, that every youngster put in security will eventually return to society. The only way to ensure that he does not return as an avenger is to have done something with or for him to make him a happier and better adapted person than the one who went in.

Assessment

The first part of this study was about an assessment facility for disordered youngsters, showing the dramatic nature of most of the children's, particularly the girls', disorders. Many of them have presented serious problems which have demanded assessment under security before appropriate disposal can be made. Apart from the risk they present, they cannot be assessed if their movements cannot be controlled.

The extent of the demand for such a facility is related to its supply. The more such facilities exist the more they will be used (Sarri, 1974 op. cit.). The particular problems of assessment attributable to security have been outlined in the first part of the book and will not, therefore, be repeated here. They are important enough to urge considerable caution in setting up secure facilities for 'observation and assessment' and to hope that they would manage to achieve their objectives at an acceptable cost.

Treatment

Many of the severely disordered youngsters (though by no means the majority) present such problems that any treatment intended for them can only be carried out, at an acceptable level of risk, in conditions of security. These do not only include children who have committed grave crimes such as murder, rape, arson and other premeditated forms of violence, but also those who are such a source of danger to themselves as to require the kind of close supervision and curtailed movement that can only be reasonably guaranteed in a secure environment. What should be pointed out quite categorically is that whatever other problems may be susceptible to treatment, delinquency is not one of them (e.g. Wilkins, 1967; Debuyst, 1967 *op. cit.*). This is despite the many and varied claims that have been made for typological systems with presumed efficacious treatment implications (e.g. Ferdinand, 1966; Quay, 1975; cf. Clarke & Sinclair, 1974).

The focus of intervention must, therefore, be on other problems snch as serious physical and cognitive deficits, family disorder, difficulties of relationships with peers, and personal problems of various sorts. This point, however, highlights the major area of weakness in all discussions about seriously disordered youngsters. Put at its briefest, very little is known about organising environments for the alleviation of problems of the type presented by extreme children. Claims have been made for a whole variety of theoretical approaches ranging from 'therapeutic' communities (Redl, 1969) to behaviour modification systems (Stumphauzer, 1973). Most of the available literature is exceedingly superficial and many of the claims made for treatments are either obvious or dubious. Many establishments are designated as serving the treatment needs of the child but few show any awareness of the complex requirements (e.g. Street, Vinter & Perrow, 1966; Solberg, 1975). Hardly any of them have the complex monitoring facilities to show the types of youngsters they are best able to help, or produce results which show what elements or configuration of elements in their treatment have produced the claimed therapeutic results. Indeed, many treatment agents, particularly those using 'dynamic' methods regard their work in a mystical fashion and beyond empirical evaluation. Where monitoring of a treatment has been carried out, it has been done in relation to delinquency and recidivism rather than other presenting problems of young people (California Youth Authority, 1974).

This state of affairs need not necessarily persist. There is no reason why schemes should not be developed which enable the monitoring of the alleviation of children's problems in a complex enough fashion to show effectiveness of particular, treatment approaches to a configuration of problems (Hoghughi, 1978).

Of the many elements of an environment and resources which can be brought to bear on the treatment of disordered children security is only one. There are other elements which are at least as important. Put as dimensions they include: open–secure; tightly–loosely structured; short–long term; general–specialist provision; intensive–low level; large–small; 'hard'–'soft'; low–high resource provision; etc. It is thus misleading to talk of secure accommodation as if it were an end in itself or that it could stand by itself shorn of the other attributes which give it the potential for destructiveness or enhancement.

Little is known about the effect of security on treatment. While it may be deemed a necessary factor in achieving the required treatment goals, it certainly is not sufficient and is likely to be seriously counter-productive unless used with a high degree of sensitivity and awareness of youngsters' needs to experience growth and opportunities for developing internal control.

It therefore appears that secure facilities may be provided to fulfil different roles but that, apart from the obvious and sometimes necessary function of restricting movement, their value remains primarily hypothetical, totally dependent on context and, as yet, to be demonstrated.

Secure facilities are the extreme end of the spectrum of social services provisions for the severely disordered. Most of the ordinary criteria for evaluating efficiency and effectiveness of other facilities can be applied to them. They are the most expensive form of provision. At current rates they range from about £200 to £500 per week per child in purpose built secure facilities and do not take account of the high capital costs. While some secure provision is obviously necessary to cater for the types of children described earlier, any large scale provision of security must result in major diversion of funds from other types of intervention. As with all other services rendered by helping professions, it is not possible to place a *generally* acceptable value on them. Also, personal social services have proved remarkably resistant to any form of cost-benefit analysis, largely because any such analysis brings into focus the value placed on human welfare and dignity. It is, therefore, not possible to state whether secure facilities provide 'value for money' (Howard League, 1977 *op. cit.*).

A variant of the above argument concerns 'efficiency' – namely how well a facility achieves its task. Because of the ambiguity surrounding the purposes of any one particular secure facility, it is not possible to speak of the efficiency of secure facilities in general terms. However, the evidence on re-offending available so far does not suggest greater efficiency of more complex forms of security than of simpler ones as aids to prevent further delinquency. The argument is vitiated by preoccupation with re-offending as a criterion of success and the tendency of authorities and government to provide for what can only be regarded as the basic care requirements of children and staff who inhabit secure facilities. If the facilities had clearer notions of their task and had sought and been given the appropriate competence, the evaluation of efficiency would be more appropriate.

Effects of Security

It would seem from the foregoing comments that a child should not be placed under conditions of security unless he is a major source of risk to himself or the public or manifests such problems as can only be alleviated in a particular facility which requires restriction of movement. Such evaluation of the child's treatment needs should proceed from a thorough assessment of the child in a facility which has a large enough intake of extreme children from a wide enough catchment area to be able to form adequate judgments of which children are indeed extreme enough to warrant this extreme form of social control.

Shut away from the rest of society, the children are subject to particular anxieties and stresses and are likely to experience an increasing attenuation of their identities. If the intention is to place them back in the community as reasonably well adapted individuals, it is then essential to maintain sufficient links between them and the community to ensure that by the time of their return they are not total strangers. This requires more active effort than simply arranging for the writing and receiving of letters and the occasional visit by some possibly interested person. It suggests, instead, deliberate attempts to create for the child a strong social nexus which may include interested outsiders from the community who will provide an unofficial window to the outside world. The incursion of outsiders into such surroundings may be met with suspicion and possible resistance by the staff, and yet this is as essential to their welfare, safety and sanity as it is to the children's.

The emotional needs of a young person vary according to his personality, upbringing and the situation in which he is likely to find himself. Exposure to security has dramatically different effects on extreme children; some become liberated by no longer having to spend all their energies worrying about how to cope with frustration and about the consequences of their own uncontrollable and uncontrolled behaviour. Almost for the first time they begin to bloom as a plant placed in a hothouse. Some become terrified of the feeling of closure and the fact that they can no longer run away. They bend all their energies on trying to find a way out of what they regard as an intolerable source of threat. Still others remain indifferent; having no particular expectations, they are unsurprised by this further intervention. In the first case, there is the enormous danger of institutional dependence and an addiction to the predictability and limits of security. In the latter, the child bends all his forces on testing the chinks in security and finding ways of enlarging them sufficiently to get out. All are likely to suffer further anxieties if for no other reason than that for the first time they come face to face with the severity of the problems that have brought them to the facility and thus become subject to new pressures. They therefore demand particularly high levels of sensitivity in the staff who deal with them. If, in addition, a compassionate, warm and gentle approach can be extended, then there is at least a possibility that the child would not be further damaged by the experience of security.

All children need high levels of physical, emotional and social care. Because of the visibility of the open environment and relatively greater access of children to the community it is not difficult to see whether children in open facilities are being adequately cared for. But special measures need to be taken to ensure that the care requirements of children under secure conditions are being adequately met. Of these the least difficult to fulfil are physical care needs.

But in secure conditions the child is deprived of the even inadequate sources of emotional succour that he may have enjoyed in an open environment where contact with others would be more frequent. Special effort needs to be made to counteract the 'out of sight, out of mind' effect of placement in security. A good body of staff will inevitably provide the child with much emotional support. In time, however, they may become invested with the child's frequently unfulfilled desire for a close relationship. Such a relationship is an aid to emotional development, but unless it is public and carefully modulated to fit in with the child's growth towards independence from the secure facility and the staff, its failure or severance will be yet another source of damage, much intensified by the effects of security.

This form of emotional deprivation and attempts to meet it, though dramatic, are probably less damaging than the effects of relative social deprivation resulting from the isolation of the child from the normal diversity of social experiences. Secure facilities are almost always highly structured. As such they operate with all-pervasive routines, which though initially necessary for transforming individual chaos into group order, engender a high degree of predictability of sequences of events and expectancies. The direct result of this is boredom and its correlate of lowered activity level. In secure facilities, it is possible to observe that children's movements are slower, less animated and more uniform. This latter characteristic results from the ritualised behaviour which accompanies so many of the routines in most institutions but particularly secure ones, pervading practically all aspects of daily living from getting up, doing chores to taking meals, going to classes, and other activities.

In all types of residential facilities (Weaver *et al*, 1977), however, the effect of such routines is reduced activity level, ritualised actions and dependence on a predictable environment which saps initiative, reduced demands on problem solving and personal adaptive ability, all of which makes future adaptations to a normal environment the more difficult. The staff become as dependent on these routines as do the children. Both seek change to relieve boredom as actively as they resist change. The paradox and the ensuing tension results in a series of modulations around the same ground base of predictability, where the changes themselves become ritualised.

The longer a secure facility has been in existence and the more its security has been defined as its criterion function, the more rigid and resistant it will become to change. This is because the staff see their primary job as the maintenance of security, just as the children aim to find a way out of that security. This leads to a mutually reinforcing spiral whereby the tighter the security, the more bizarre and outlandish the attempts to breach it, and this in turn confirms the worst suspicions of those responsible about the nature of their wards and the need for still greater security. This is the most important reason for not giving security considerations pride of place, but instead for placing them in the context of an overall balance sheet of costs and benefits.

To counter this, it is necessary to maintain an open aspect to secure establishments – open in the sense that they can be visited by not just those related to the children but also other bona fide individuals and groups. While there is obviously a price to be paid for this in terms of inconvenience and possibly ogling of the children, the benefits considerably outweigh the costs both to the staff and the children. The children will not feel isolated and caged and will have the safeguard of being visible to outsiders. The staff will similarly not feel cut off and will have the opportunity of exploring the reactions of interested visitors to their work.

This will not only keep them open minded to the outside influences but will also be their greatest safeguard against possible allegations of malpractice. Over and above this, routines and structures need to be subjected to frequent and hard headed criticism, if need be with parents and social workers, to ensure that no more than the minimum structure needed for security and any other functions of the facility are imposed. Opportunity needs to be provided for the children to acquire self control. This implies the reduction of external structure and control on a phased and predetermined basis and its replacement by the exposure of the child to variable stress and increasing unpredictability and reliance on impulse control.

The personal encounter with problems that cannot any longer be avoided may be an important and perhaps necessary beginning to the process of treatment. As has already been indicated the alleviation of problems of severely disordered youngsters resembles more a mythological saga than an empirical discipline. This mythology says a great deal more about the wishful thinking of the treatment agents and their ideological preoccupations than about any valid and effective ways of ameliorating the problems of the extreme children in order to fit them out for return to the open community. Because these children are extreme, it may be found easier to justify marginal and extreme forms of treatment which may not otherwise be acceptable in an open setting. In open settings not only can the child react by running away, but, because open establishments are relatively less total and more open to outside inspection, dubious practices may become subjected to wider scrutiny. In a secure setting the children are at particular risk from the therapeutic zeal of their caretakers. While fairly frequent case reviews involving the child's social worker may act as reasonable guarantees against unacceptable practices, these reviews do not provide adequate details of the forms of intervention to enable an interested person to form an accurate picture of what may be happening to the child. Nor do the Community Homes Regulations require the kind of detail that would make such evaluation possible. It, therefore, becomes imperative not only that the child should have frequent visits from his social worker, parents and others, but that the whole operation of a secure facility should be closely monitored, documented and opened to knowledgeable public inspection to ensure that practices of dubious merit do not take root.

To obviate the negative aspects, however, does not guarantee positive results. Because secure accommodation is currently the ultimate form of social control for severely disordered youngsters, there is an obligation on the part of the secure facility to do everything that is humanly and empirically possible to maximise the treatment of the child and expedite his return to the open community. No child should stay a day longer in a secure facility than is dictated by his special and publicly demonstrated needs. This does not suggest that the kind of hard and fast criteria exist which would make such a demonstration possible, but rather to claim that it is not beyond the wit of skilled workers to present cases which carry a high degree of consensus by a group of reasonable persons. One implication of this claim is that no child should be admitted to a secure facility for purposes of treatment unless a treatment plan can be shown to exist for him and the secure facility can demonstrate that it has the ability to meet the needs of that particular child. This may not be possible to start with but it suggests that at least initially no pretence should be made that children are admitted to secure facilities other than for a very basic level of protective care and custody which may not in the long run be acceptable from the viewpoint of justice.

As set out in this chapter, secure provision is likely to satisfy the needs of society for protecting its self-destructive children and being protected from their depradations. It can also satisfy the basic and extended requirements of children and staff for viable mutual enrichment. If, in addition, the facility provides for the training of specialists and the necessary monitoring research which can be extended to other facilities which deal with difficult youngsters, it will have more than adequately justified its existence. What would crown its work would be the possibility of learning sufficiently from its own practice to be able to evolve prescriptions for preventing the development of extreme forms of disorder due to inadequate intervention. Such guidelines can then be used either for preventing the emergence of children who have such extreme problems as to warrant admission to a secure facility, or at least stem the tide in the extent of problems that might justify the proliferation of other secure facilities. Each facility should provide for the totality of the treatment of the extreme children of its own catchment area. As with every other helping facility, it should also be capable of extending its own work sufficiently backwards in the chain of intervention as to make its own existence unnecessary. Until that ideal day, however, there is a long, long way to go.

CHAPTER 10

Do Disordered Children
Have Rights?

THE rights and responsibilities of children can only be seen in the context of the responsibilities and rights of society. Society is the organisation, norms, and collective behaviours of groups of people. But groups comprise individuals, and each individual has responsibilities and rights in relation to others. Because society is a large collection of individuals, in any conflict of interests, the rights of the majority take precedence over the rights of the individual to either positive experiences or unbridled harmful behaviour.

It is, therefore, taken as axiomatic that society's first task is the protection of its members from harm – whether done by children or adults. What form this protection takes reflects the values prevalent in society at any given time. Society, through its politicians and other standard setters, arrogates to itself many rights over the individual. These are sometimes codified in law, such as the 1969 Children and Young Persons Act, but often remain as traditions – teacher-child relationships – and general attitudes – 'the poor will always be with us'.

These laws, customs and attitudes are manifested in three objectives of social intervention: to enhance positive aspects of society and the functioning of its individuals, such as the encouragement of sports and cultural activities; to maintain, in their present state, certain aspects of society, such as the fabric of the family; to curb and reduce the impact of negative influences experienced or presented by portions of society, such as crime, poverty, ill health.

Even though these objectives are particularly explicit in the

251

philosophy of the welfare state, there is widespread belief that some of its aims are incompatible with the freedom and dignity of the individual.

In the UK as with many other western European countries, comprehensive legislation has established a form of services for children which should ensure that their care and welfare requirements are adequately met. These include care from before birth to protection from abuse and neglect, physically, educationally and socially as well as inadequate control and guidance. However, critics believe this form of all pervasive legislation, particularly in the case of delinquent and disordered children, has had the effect of: (1) giving massive power to the executive; (2) making children into even more dependent subjects than they would normally be; (3) without giving them adequate redress against the executive; (4) increasingly divesting parents of the sense of responsiiblity for and direction of their children's lives, and thus (5) undermining family life in a more insidious manner than can be resisted by disadvantaged and dependent families.

What is undoubtedly true but not always apparent is that there is now a great labyrinth of legislation relating to disordered children encompassing health, education, penal and social services which only experts can find their way through. The arms of official intervention reach far and wide into the lives of its youngsters. Because its good intent is generally taken for granted, its intervention is not seriously or often successfully challenged. As the above general criticisms indicate, however, the wisdom of state intervention is not universally acknowledged, particularly when, as in the case of disadvantaged groups and minorities, the *results* of its interventions do not match the professed intentions. In view of this there is a need to protect citizens (on the basis of whose collective interests its actions are justified) against encroachment upon their rights unless absolutely inevitable. It is necessary to set up safeguards to ensure that individuals are properly dealt with once caught up with the machinery of state intervention, its systems, organisations and bureaucracies.

This is all the more important in the United Kingdom where there is no written constitution or 'bill of rights' as known in many countries such as the United States. Even the existence of such formal documents does not appear to wholly safeguard the individual against the weight of official power as shown by Sarri (1974). Because so much of the use of official power is discretionary, and those who are entrusted with safeguarding rights are often those who exercise power, such as police and social workers, individual rights are likely to become subjugated to organisational or personal interests.

Severely disordered children, such as those described in this book, show up the values of a civilised society in particularly sharp relief. The way society deals with them reflects the extreme reaches of its welfare orientation. Since these are the children who are manifestly under-privileged, troubled and troublesome, the extent of its concern for them illuminates the genuineness of its other welfare preoccupations.

All human beings have certain rights, and minorities have special need for the protection of these rights. Children, as a minority, have recently become the subject of intensive discussion and attempts have been made to define their rights in different settings (e.g. Bittner, 1976; Mercer, 1976; Rosenheim, 1976; BASW, 1977; Knight, 1978). In general terms, children have the same right to the protection of life and limb, and access to normal growth opportunities and nurturance as other human beings. They have the right to be treated with the same dignity and the same notions of fairness as have others. However, because children are powerless, inarticulate and incapable of exercising foresight they have need of much more sensitive advocacy and protection than is the case with adults.

To put the issue in its proper context it may be useful to recapitulate the bases of official intervention with disordered children: (1) there is a problem; (2) without intervention the problem will get worse; (3) with intervention the problem is likely to improve. These bases are acknowledged to varying degrees of explicitness in the legislation concerning children. Thus, responsibility for the child and his condition is in varying degrees transferred from parents to officials, employed by and acting on behalf of the community. To enable them to carry out their responsibilities, officials are given corresponding authority. This authority is unchallenged and, in the case of disordered children, within the bounds of relevant laws, pretty near total. The authority is further reinforced by the administrative and financial resources provided for and by the officials with legislatively sanctioned moneys. In strictly juris-prudential terms, therefore, officials cannot be exonerated from their inappropriate management of problem children on grounds of inadequate resource, though this indeed may be the correct explanation of the particular impact made on the child's problems.

If the above arguments are valid, it seems to follow that a child's problems in any one area should not be *worse* at the end or as a result of an episode of official intervention than they were before. The child and the persons (the parents) from whom powers of care and control have been wrested have a right to the halting, at least, of the unacceptable condition if not to its improvement. As was shown in Chapter 7, this right is clearly unfulfilled in the case of disordered children whose problems go from bad to worse to extreme and eventually result in the massive curtailment of their liberties at heavy cost to society. This process of deterioration is accepted with frightening insouciance, reinforced by society's deep ambiva-lence to miscreants and its glib assumptions that the best has been done for these children, and that their deterioration re-flects, paradoxically, their bloody-mindedness or impervious-ness to any form of treatment, rather than the failure of official intervention.

The paradox illustrates the power of officialdom to safeguard itself against censure and relates in turn to the central notion of 'accountability'. Accountability in this context means that official intervention should be responsible, and open to examination by interested bona fide persons, official and other-wise, to showing what has been done, why, and how the outcome has matched up to the original intention.

At the present time, the only form of intervention that has accountability is to be found in the judicial setting – when a care order is taken out on a child, or in quasi-judicial enquiries in particularly publicised cases of possible official ineptitude, such as the Maria Colwell case. Social workers and other professionals who make decisions about children do not operate in a judicial framework, do not arrive at their decisions after collecting evidence in a particular manner, and have at present no way of ensuring or showing that their decisions have not been influenced by any other than relevant or valid forms of evidence. What is done with the children is often lacking in coherent theoretical or empirical foundations and has no demonstrable regard to the notions of justice or individual rights. Many of these 'rights' have been incorporated into general notions of 'care', 'welfare', etc. But the degree to which even these considerations are observed remains unknown.

As a result of official decisions, children are often removed from their homes and placed in establishments with dubious relevance to their problems. Some are locked away for substantial periods, and subjected to treatments of unknown utility without any form of check on the rights and wrongs of the decisions, other than the opinions of social workers and their fellow professionals. In this sense, juvenile law, as it stands, denies children the same protection of a 'due process' that it gives older persons who fall foul of its standards, despite the powerlessness of children, and hence their greater vulnerability to oppressive exercise of official power.

The result of denial of such protection may not necessarily be inimical to the interests of the child. Indeed, the major argument put forward by social workers and the myriad other professionals who make decisions about children is that they are capable of evaluating the problems and needs of the child outside the formal constraints and pressures of a court setting. This is the argument put forward by a variety of people (e.g. Priestley et al, 1977; Rea Price, 1978) who advocate the abolition of the remaining powers of juvenile courts in England and Wales. But these arguments arise out of difficulties in resolving the conflict between the protection of the public and the child welfare functions of the court. They do not advance any good reason for denying the need for due process. Nor are they in any way based on examination of an alternative system (other than the Scottish Panel System) which gives adequate protection to the child.

The notion of due process does not necessarily imply judicial involvement. A good example of this is the aforementioned Scottish Panel System in which a child, having pleaded guilty to offences and having been deemed worthy of referral to the Panel by the 'Reporter', is then involved in the 'due process' of decision making about himself with a group of lay Panel members and his parents. Another example is that of an assessment meeting at a competent centre in which up-to-date, cross-checked information is presented on the child, his problems evaluated, and decisions made about his treatment on explicitly stated grounds. In this sense the notion of due process is as much an attitude of mind, and its organisational concomitants for safeguarding the interests of the children and protecting them from vagaries of individual preferences, as it is one of demonstrating the validity of any decision made in the light of available evidence.

In a study of Norwegian Child Welfare Boards, Benneche (1967, quoted in Dahl, 1976) has shown that even rigorous legal safeguards laid down against removing children from their homes do not work in practice outside a judicial setting. This is despite the explicit feelings and experiences of the Norwegians regarding the possible influence of prejudices in decision making about problem children by specially constituted groups of lay persons and professionals. Dahl (*ibid.*) continues 'the gap between the law in books and the law in action is partly due to social workers' neglect of the value of due process'. If this is the case in a system where explicit legal safeguards for children have been set up, it gives cause for concern in others such as the United Kingdom and the United States (as shown by Logan, 1972, *op. cit.*) where no such safeguards are available.

The six monthly statutory reviews and the legal right of applying for revocation of care orders by parents in England and Wales are seriously deficient in protecting the interests of the children. The reviews are attended by social workers, both field and residential, and occasionally by other interested specialists. Although there is no reason to imagine that such groups can and do take anything but an impartial view of the child and attempt to evaluate his problems and needs objectively, there is at present no check or established procedure of decision making to show that this is indeed what happens.

In the case of children in secure accommodation, the Review Committee must, under certain circumstances, contain an 'Independent Person' within the meaning of the Children and Young Persons Act 1969 (Sec. 24). Little information is available on the operation of this section of the Act and it is, therefore, possible that in practice such persons may provide an adequate guarantee that the rights of the child would be safeguarded. However, even at their best, such persons do not command a professional vocabulary and range of arguments which are based on intimate knowledge of the child. It is not, therefore, possible to state how effective their role in decision making about such children can be.

The right to apply for revocation of care orders places the parents of the child in an adversarial role against the social services departments. Although legal aid is available to the parents, it is often difficult to show that the risk factors which led to the child being taken into care in the first place have been sufficiently ameliorated to warrant the revocation of the care order. This, of course, takes for granted that the parents are inclined to, and know how to set about, getting the care order revoked. But the majority of severely disordered children come from such rejecting families that most parents cannot be bothered to actively fight for the return of their child; the children cannot, therefore, count on the natural protectiveness and possessiveness of the parents to safeguard their interests and bring up a judicial review of their case.

One important reason that professionals resist accounting

for their actions is that it would reduce their professional autonomy. In the definition of a professional role, autonomy is one of the hallmarks of the strength of a profession and one which is staunchly defended by every group which has achieved or aspires to achieve professional status. Apart from certain general requirements both of politics and economy, which require that each agency be seen to be dealing with *some* children which it has deemed to fall within its purview, there are no checks on the validity or the utility of the roles adopted either by groups or individuals within particular groups. Thus, individual professionals evolve idiosyncratic conceptions of their own roles, modes of operation, capabilities and limits of tolerance. Every child coming within their purview is yet another arena for the exercise of their professional role play. Should the child fail to respond to their measures they define their function in such a manner as to exclude him. This exclusion may be either physical or psychological but it is tantamount to the same outcome, being defined as beyond help. While this process reinforces the professionals' identity which may have come under stress, it certainly does no good to a child who had been deemed to be an appropriate subject for their services but who is now made to understand that his problems are too serious to be alleviated by that particular agency.

In this respect, professionals tend to adopt the appropriate distance and to provide reasons from their own professional perspective for their inability to help a particular child. Thus, their allegiance and responsibility appears to be much more to a system and profession than to the child. System maintenance becomes of paramount importance. As long as there are some children with whom they are working and to whom they are offering services of some demonstrable benefit, they do not have to account for why a particular child has not been deemed to be appropriate for their care. Their allegiance to the system overrides their allegiance to the child whose existence justifies the existence of the system.

'*Due process*' is the means through which justice is not only done but is also seen to be done. It is, as such, the appropriate basis for accountability. It entails the notion that intervention is not justified unless it can be shown that the decision to intervene has proceeded from certain formal steps. More specifically, the steps should include (1) records of decisions made about the child; (2) on what grounds the decisions were made and with what evidence; (3) with what expected outcome; (4) what is done to achieve outcome; (5) how the outcome matches the expectations; (6) the reasons for any discrepancy.

This recording of due process and the purpose of accountability which it serves make it possible to discover what has happened to a child and why. It helps to show how much effort has been made to make decisions on the basis of sound evidence rather than on personal feelings and opinion. One of its important implications is that it makes it possible to see whether everything that could have been done for a child by a particular service or agency has been done, before failure is declared and he is moved to another facility.

It is thus suggested that no child should be excluded from school or taken into care on grounds of truancy or bad behaviour unless the Head can give evidence to satisfy the magistrates that the school has taken every necessary step (remember the argument about inadequate resources) to stop the child from behaving that way. A Child Guidance Clinic would not simply cease to deal with a child it had accepted for treatment without being able to show that it had done what it could within its power to ameliorate the child's problem. A psychiatrist would show why he had taken on a child for treatment and then declared his inability to help. The magistrates' own decision making and their expectations of the agencies would become more explicit. The social services would be expected to be much more punctilious in going through every one of the steps outlined above, particularly the requirement that they state what they did and why they did it. The same would extend to their agents – the specialised facilities, both day and residential – who would be required to show that their dealings with the child proceeded from an explicit plan based on the hardest (possible and available) evidence, that they did what they were supposed to do and did not cavalierly redefine their criteria to exclude a youngster who continued to present the same problems as the one for which he was admitted and which they should have anticipated.

It would, thus, become established practice that agencies would, as a matter of right, satisfy themselves that everything possible had been done for the child, according to publicly demonstrable due process before they accepted the change of means and venue of treatment.

One result of such a process is that most agencies with the powers to give or withhold services are likely to make more conservative decisions about their capabilities than they do at present. However, unless they exercise great discretion, they are likely to be without adequate clients which would leave them open to alternative deployment. On the other hand, the practice of accounting would ensure that damaging rejection of children on dubious grounds is minimised and service givers begin to become more critical in defining their own areas of professional competence and perhaps increasing their efforts and tolerance with the children.

One side effect of this is that society would then have a much clearer picture of what it can and cannot expect of its agencies and decide how best to order its priorities. A regrettable effect of the present situation, arising from ambiguous definition of roles and limits of competence, is the perpetuation of the misguided feeling on the part of most people that they have adequate services for most types of social disorders.

Children placed under conditions of security present special problems and are subject to particular risks which were outlined in the previous chapter. They are deprived of their liberty and placed in establishments which are in one important respect, at least, the functional equivalents of imprisonment for adults. Some of them (Section 53 cases) have ended up there as a result of the judgment of a Crown Court and the judicious exercise of the Home Secretary's powers. However, the majority have been through no relevant judicial process, other than the one that resulted in the issue of a care order to the local authority. These children go through a tortuous series of consecutive failure as a result of which they become extreme and are deemed to 'need' a secure facility – either for their own protection or for that of the public.

But, other than in rare instances, this chain of labelling and decision making is not subject to any sort of due process. Crises occur in which social workers desperately try to do what they feel is the best for the child. They have little choice but to go along with any competent recommendation, particularly if it comes from a specialist agency and if it presents a chance of curbing or improving the child's condition. They and the people they deal with rarely concern themselves with such niceties as distinction between feelings, opinions, and facts. As a result of such a process, it is currently possible for a youngster to be taken into care on grounds of persistent truancy, to be sent to a community home from which he may abscond persistently, probably for the same reasons that led to his original truancy, be transferred to another community home and continue his behaviour, and eventually find himself locked up for a substantial period, with the full concurrence of the local authority. This is done to him in the name of treatment and, therefore, such notions as fairness, justice and proportionality do not obtrude into the decision making.

In view of this, placement of all children in security, which is currently the ultimate form of social control of children, should be subjected to judicial decision and review, regardless of whether placement is for the protection of the child or of society. This would encompass only those children who are placed for treatment or those whose secure assessment exceeds a particular period, say two months. The decision makers would be required to satisfy the court that the steps in the due process outlined earlier had been complied with. The court would not be able to direct the secure placement of a child (as recommended by the Magistrates' Association and the Expenditure Committee Report 1975), but it can refuse to grant permission for such placement. This power combined with the court's ability to ask for an accounting of what has happened to the child up to then would provide a powerful safeguard for the child against inappropriate curtailment of his liberty. It would also return to the court one of its major functions, eroded over the years, of becoming a defender of the child's rights against undue official intervention.

The authority to keep a child under secure conditions would be renewable at frequent, say three monthly intervals, on the same judicial basis as above. This would foster the idea that the incarceration of an individual ought to be accompanied by some demonstrable and proportionately reasonable benefit to the child and the community. This may be augmented by wider involvement of responsible members of the community (like, for example, Scottish panel members) in the non-judicial review of the child's treatment and the advocacy of the child's rights and needs by someone akin to a children's advocate.

All the above arguments derive from the simple premise that children are a minority, and disordered children a particularly vulnerable one, who require special advocacy. Because of their risk potential to the community and to themselves, they have a right to being protected from further deterioration of their problems due to inappropriate official intervention. Because they are subjected to the exercise of power, they have, like every other citizen, a right to the accountability of those who wield the power. The only means to such accountability is diligent adherence to a due process which regards the troubled and troublesome as deserving of no less.

Appendix

THE following report is included as an appendix, not only to illustrate the points made in the body of the text about the format of the report, but also to give some indication of the type of problems presented by a particularly difficult girl. All identifying details have been removed from the report.

CONFIDENTIAL

AYCLIFFE SCHOOL — REGIONAL ASSESSMENT CENTRE

REPORT ON: J. Daisy

DATE OF BIRTH: 1961   RELIGION: R.C.

NAME AND ADDRESS OF PARENTS   M..........................
OR PEOPLE RESPONSIBLE: ....
                               ....

ADMITTED TO AYCLIFFE ON: ....

ADMISSION NUMBER: ....

BASIS FOR ADMISSION: Care Order dated ....

LOCAL AUTHORITY RESPONSIBLE: ....

SOCIAL WORKER RESPONSIBLE: Mrs........................

                 ADDRESS: ....
                               ....

               TELEPHONE: ....

TRANSFERRED TO: .... Hospital   ON: ....

AGE ON TRANSFER: 16

Pen Picture

Daisy is a slender, agile, and generally graceful girl with hazel eyes, gaunt pale face, and slightly bulbous nose, the result of an accident when she was a child. Her behaviour is both volatile and unpredictable and she is subject to abrupt changes of mood. She is suicidal.

Daisy comes from a broken home, and both parents appear rejecting of her. She has experienced considerable instability throughout her life, through family problems, changes of home and numerous residential placements.

She has presented behavioural problems in the form of explosive outbursts, temper tantrums and prolonged rages from a very early age. These outbursts appeared less frequently and were of shorter duration in early adolescence but are now more intense. She is occasionally enuretic and was encopretic until the age of eight.

She was made the subject of a care order in 1975, was admitted to the Regional Assessment Centre and subsequently returned home, attending a residential school initially as a day pupil although she was later admitted on a full time basis. Daisy was employed as a cook in the summer of last year and was eventually sent home on trial from the school although she frequently returned to the school when unable to cope with problems at home.

In December of last year Daisy swallowed a quantity of Amoxil tablets and was admitted to the local general hospital. After her discharge from the hospital, she swallowed a mixture of Dettol and Thawpit, was readmitted to the hospital but later transferred to a mental hospital. Ultimately she was transferred to a special, small psychiatric unit where she swallowed a quantity of paracetamol. After a period of observation in another hospital, Daisy was returned to the psychiatric unit. Her uncontrolled and disruptive behaviour presented management problems which aggravated the nursing staff. After a case conference held in February 1977 and a further suicide attempt, when Daisy consumed a quantity of aspirin, she was admitted to Aycliffe Regional Assessment Centre on an emergency basis at the request of the Social Services Department.

MEDICAL RECORD

Aycliffe School
Regional Assessment Centre

Name *J., Daisy*   Date of birth *1961*

Family Doctor's Name and Address

PERSONAL HISTORY		PREVIOUS MEDICAL HISTORY (Yes/No)			
Age of walking	*'Nearly two'*	Whooping Cough	No	Bronchitis	No
Age of talking	*'two'*	Measles	Yes	Asthma	No
Bowel control	*Normal*	Scarlet Fever	No	Otorrhoea	No
Bladder control	,,	Mumps	No	Chickenpox	Yes
Age of Menarche	13	German Measles	No	Bed wetting	Yes

PROPHYLAXIS (Yes/No)		
Diphtheria	Yes	Injuries *Numerous superficial self*
Smallpox	Yes	*inflicted cuts to wrists and arms since*
Whooping Cough	Yes	*admission. Also ears pierced, self*
Measles	Yes	*inflicted since admission.*
Tetanus	Yes	Operations *Appendicectomy 1974*
Poliomyelitis	Yes	
B.C.G. Vaccination	Yes	

CONDITION ON ADMISSION TO AYCLIFFE (including medication)
Nail biter. Depressed, drowsy, subdued, tearful.
Largactil 100 mg IM prior to admission.
Admitted from ——— adolescent unit.

FAMILY MEDICAL HISTORY
Father *Alive*
Mother *Alive*
Siblings
Others

General appearance and		Posture *Normal*	Nose &	
physique	*Small*		Throat	*Normal*
Nutritional state	*Good*	Limbs ,,	Ears	,,
General condition	*Good*	Eyes *Hazel 6/12 6/9*	Speech	,,
Sex development	*Normal*	Hearing *Normal*	Teeth	,,
Heart and circulation	,,	Hair *Blonde, short*	Urine	*NAD*
Lungs	,,	Skin *Normal*	Genitals	*NAD*

TREATMENT WHILE AT AYCLIFFE *Seen in Royston, admitted direct from
———— unit, tearful, depressed, subdued, drowsy. Barbiturate level and liver
function tests normal. Complained of nipple discharge, prolonged periods,
constipation (LMP ————).
Routine medical by school medical officer – satisfactory.*

Medical Report (cont'd)

24.2.77 Eneria very good result, no complaints re nipples.

25.2.77 Seen briefly by consultant psychiatrist. Medication reviewed, sanctioned by school medical officer.

3.3.77 Neulactil 2.5 mgs TDS. Tofranil 25 mgs increasing to 50 mg over one week (recommended by consultant psychiatrist).

7.3.77 Complained of painful micturition urinalysis. NAD Encourage fluids.

10.3.77 Dressing to wrists – attempted to remove tattoo herself.

11.3.77 Requested to speak to Sister in confidence. She stated she was very ill tempered and vicious, very afraid in case she did someone an injury, then be sorry afterwards. Daisy stated medication not doing her any good.
She absconded from her escort and gave herself up to Sister in sick bay. Returned to Royston by Mr. H, later returned to sick bay by Mr. G (found wandering along the drive by Principal). Feels suicidal, Mr. G informed by Sister re Daisy's suicidal feelings. Seen by consultant psychiatrist. Medication reviewed. Valium 2 mgs × TDS and Ospolot 200 × TDS sanctioned by school medical officer.

12.3.77 Daisy used abusive, foul language. Suicidal tendencies persist. Commenced reviewed medication. Old SI re-opened wound. 8.15 pm I.M. Largactil 50 mgs I.M. given by Sister. Daisy fighting injection effects. Did not fight when injection administered.

17.3.77 Wrists re-dressed. Ear cleansed. Urinalysis NAD (psychiatrist's request).

20.3.77 Infected (L) forearm, had attempted to remove SI tattoo from arm. Forearm cleansed and dressed.

21.3.77 Sister to Royston. Daisy had broken a window. Hysterical, settled after counselling.

24.3.77 Cut (L) wrist and forearm and graze (R) arm with broken nail polish bottle. Same cleansed and redressed.

25.3.77 Dressings and sutures dumbbell removed by Daisy. Same redressed. Refusing evening medication 8.30 p.m. School medical officer informed. IM Valium 10 mgs given by Sister 9.40 p.m. Refusing more medication and meals.

26.3.77 Sister to Royston 10 am requested by Mr P. On arrival in Royston Daisy looked pale, drawn, shaking. Asked Sister to accompany her to her room. Talked until 11 am. Still reluctant to take medication, eventually did so. Spent from 2 pm until 6 pm with Sister in sick bay, escorted back to house 6 pm as requested by Mr P. Appeared brighter although still looks poorly. All meals and medication taken in sick bay pm. Still suicidal.

27.3.77 Daisy still pale, looks miserable this am. (R) ear redressed. Had pierced same herself with old ear ring.

29.3.77 Dressing renewed in Royston. As reported by housemother, Daisy had not eaten for five days. Ate her tea and mid-afternoon break Saturday with Sister. Tattoo much improved, lacerations nearly healed.

Family List

FATHER	Tom J	aged 50	Unemployed. Separated and living in digs somewhere in the area.
MOTHER	Dorothy J	44	Housewife.
HALF BROTHER	David	24	Married and living locally. Engineer in the Merchant Navy.
BROTHER	Gary	20	Serving a sentence at HM prison.
SISTER	Daphne	17	At home. Recently discharged from a mental hospital.
SISTER	Gloria	13	Schoolgirl.

Family Setting

Mrs. J lives with her two younger children in a three bed-roomed council house, situated in a poor area of a development estate. Conditions inside the home have been persistently described as 'chaotic' and on at least one occasion Mrs. J has received help in trying to clean up her home and make a fresh start. She shows little interest in her home, preferring to spend her time at the local bingo hall or at the home of a friend.

Father's Background

Mr. J has one younger sister who lives locally. His father died when he was about five years old and he and his sister were brought up by their mother. There was barely enough money to cover the essentials but he remembers his childhood as a fairly happy one. He went to the local secondary school and left at the age of fifteen. After the war he joined the Navy and eventually qualified as a fitter, but since then has had little regular employment, preferring to work at odd jobs when he needs the money. Mr. J admits to having been in trouble with the police in the past, but only for 'simple matters', i.e. breach of the peace. His mother is still alive and lives with his sister. He visits her occasionally, but she has no contact with her son's family.

Personal Characteristics

Mr. J is a short, slim man with curly hair, who seemed anxious at interview. He is reported to be a heavy 'all day' drinker who gets into frequent fights. His extensive use of foul language, coupled with his violent temper made him disliked and feared both within his home and outside. Mr. J is well known to the police for his frequent fights and his 'anti-authority' attitudes. While frequently aggressive and rejecting in his behaviour towards his children, he has simultaneously 'protected' them from all official agencies which he claimed were persecuting and victimising his family.

Father's Attitude and Behaviour towards Daughter

Mr. J is said to have beaten Daisy often in the past, and to have been more punitive towards her than his other four children.

It appears that he expected her to act as a servant, making little effort to stop the other children from treating her in the same way. Frequently drunk, he would often beat her for no apparent reason. Daisy has claimed that she has been sexually assaulted by her father and although the Social Services Department are unable to substantiate this claim, they consider it may well be true.

Mr. J has sometimes visited Daisy and written to her since she has been in residential care, but has never been present when she has appeared in court. Social Services reports indicate that he was unconcerned about Daisy's behaviour and did not show any interest when told of Daisy's recent troubles.

Daughter's View of Father

Daisy's feelings about her father are very simple. She states that although he has visited her and she has written to him she does not love him. She feels that he loves her because he cries when he sees her. When Daisy meets her father, she is nervous and has said she dislikes him for the way he used to hit her mother. Her views of him are confused but generally negative. She only reaches out for him when she is at her lowest ebb.

Mother's Background

Mrs. J was born in the North, the second girl in a family of two. Her mother died shortly after her birth and she and her stepsister were brought up by her mother's elder sister, whom they looked upon and referred to as 'mother'.

Mrs. J describes her childhood as 'hard but happy'. She attended the local school and left at the age of fourteen to work in a factory. She went from there to work as a chambermaid in a residential school and had a variety of short term jobs until the birth of her son David in 1954. She remained at home with her aunt until her marriage to Mr. J in 1956.

Personal Characteristics

During the interview Mrs. J seemed a warm, affectionate person, anxious to help. She offered information readily but delicately skirts around and refuses to be drawn on personal issues. She is a poor housekeeper and generally dislikes domestic chores.

Mrs. J claims that she is a mild and even tempered woman but also states that when placed in a situation where she loses her temper she can 'raise the roof'.

Mother's Attitude and Behaviour towards Daughter

Mrs. J claims to have a close relationship with her children, but particularly so with Daisy. She appears to set great store by the fact that she treats Daisy more as a friend than as a daughter. She states she has few problems controlling Daisy within the home and claims to have used a counselling technique, except on one memorable occasion when she 'walloped the girl hard' in the presence of the police. Other reports, however, indicate that she may well have used the latter method more frequently and Daisy may have suffered non-accidental injuries inflicted by her mother. Mrs. J describes her daughter as 'a deep girl who bottles up her problems' and refuses to discuss them. She states that her daughter's violent temper and behaviour have been in evidence since her early childhood. She says she could not explain them and that is why she referred her daughter to 'doctors', but she blames their acceleration on the pressures of home and the girl's academic difficulties.

Daisy's more recent behaviour, including incidents of drug overdose and self-mutilation appear to have both worried and confused her mother who claims not to be able to understand this aspect of her daughter's behaviour.

Mrs. J appears to share to some extent her husband's views on the family being victimised by the authorities, for when Daisy was excluded from her last school, Mrs. J promptly withdrew her other daughter from the same school.

Child's View of Mother

Daisy, in the interview, maintains that she loves her mother and although she has said that she believes her mother does not want her, or love her, she finds this very difficult to accept. Mrs. J thought she was a friend to Daisy and she agrees with this, but thinks her mother would only chat to her as a friend and not help her with her problems. Daisy states that her mother was out most of the time, playing bingo; at home her only interest was knitting. She disliked Mrs. J's untidiness and often felt the need to tidy and clean the house. This attitude often, she feels, caused arguments which would lead to major rows and on some occasions, to blows.

Daisy's uncertainty about her mother has led, on several occasions, to bizarre behaviour: hitting her head against walls, screaming abuse at her mother and then subsequently saying how much she misses her mother and how much her mother cares for her. At times, it appears that her insistence that she is loved by her mother is almost an attempt at convincing herself of this.

Parental Relationships

Mr. and Mrs. J were married in 1956 after a courtship lasting two years. The relationship appears to have been beset with problems from the start. According to Mrs. J, she and her husband spent very little time together as he was always out drinking. He often came home to eat and wash and would go straight out to the pub again.

During their marriage there have been a number of separations in which the mother left home, largely because of her husband's violent behaviour, bad language and excessive drinking. When she attended her eldest son's wedding in 1973 she remained with him due to her ill health and 'anxiety state' brought about by domestic conflict. On her return to her family early in 1974 she reportedly found the house in a 'filthy state', all the furniture sold and her children running wild outside. It appears that the father was almost permanently drunk during this period.

In May 1975 she made a final separation from her husband, taking the two younger children with her, and stayed with her friend, subsequently moving into a council house with the children. In August of that year she obtained a legal separation from her husband through which he was ordered to pay maintenance for his dependents and was also ordered not to visit his wife's home. However, it is reported that he frequently disregards the terms of his separation and has been disruptive and violent towards his wife and two younger children during his frequent visits to them.

Social Service reports indicate that the mother is now seeking a divorce from her husband as she wishes to remarry.

Siblings

Daisy's half brother David was born illegitimately and appears to have presented few problems at home. He is now happily married and has a child of his own. He is presently employed as an engineer in the Merchant Navy.

Daisy's brother Gary is reported to be a bad tempered young man with a long history of stealing and physical violence. He is currently serving his second prison sentence for taking and driving. He remained with his father when his parents separated and offered Daisy £1 per week to stay in order to keep the house clean and attend to the general domestic duties. It is reported that Gary has been frequently violent towards his younger sisters, particularly Daisy.

Daphne appears in many ways to share her sister's problems. She had been a 'disruptive influence' at school and in 1973 was made the subject of a supervision order for two years following an assault on a teacher and being drunk and disorderly in school. In January 1975 she spent seven days in a remand centre and was bound over for one year following an assault on the police which occurred when she attempted to help Daisy who was being removed by them from an infant school playground where she trespassed and was using offensive language.

On leaving school she found employment in a local amusement arcade but left home shortly afterwards to live with mother's relations in Staffordshire. It is reported that in December of last year she was admitted to hospital following a drug oversode, but has since been discharged.

Reports indicate that at one time Daisy was very close to her sister Daphne but she now claims she does not care for her sister. She appears to be slightly bitter at the fact that her mother managed to travel to Staffordshire to visit Daphne regularly when she was in hospital, but found it almost impossible to visit her when she was in a local mental hospital.

Daisy's younger sister Gloria is also giving cause for concern. Daisy claims to feel closer to Gloria than any other of her brothers and sisters.

Girl's Development, Behaviour and Attitudes at Home

Daisy was born at home, six weeks overdue. It is reported that she was born face down and Mrs. J's aunt, who helped at the delivery, 'had to hold her head up to prevent her from drowning'. Mrs. J claims not to have had any pains or contractions during the birth and therefore could not push the baby out.

Daisy was a bottle fed baby, who ate well and slept well, but was slow to walk and talk. She was also slow at toilet training. Daisy was six years old before she was dry during the night. She was also encopretic until around the age of eight.

According to Mrs. J, at about nine months Daisy began to have temper tantrums. She would scream and fling her body around while kicking out. The family reacted by laughing at her as they thought she was being funny. These outbursts were infrequent and only happened when Daisy was very upset. After the initial burst of tantrums, Mrs. J does not remember any other incidents until Daisy was about two years old.

The tantrums became worse and Daisy began screaming and biting at her clothes. Mrs. J would undress her but this only resulted in Daisy clawing at her body. She would be left alone in bed until she cried herself to sleep. These tantrums then became a regular feature if Daisy could not have her own way. Mrs. J thought that she was suffering from a 'split personality' because she would run from room to room rushing at her mother as if to claw but would end up loving her instead. She would frequently tear at her own body when in a rage.

At about two years old Daisy was taken into hospital for a few hours to have a birth mark removed. When she returned to the hospital to have the dressing replaced she caused such an outburst that it was decided a nurse would come to the home. This type of incident was repeated a few months later when Daisy was taken to the dentist.

Following further problematic behaviour and temper tantrums Mrs. J took Daisy to the local GP, who advised her to leave the child alone when she was upset. She tried for a while but the neighbours did not like the noise, and often complained. Mother says she tried various methods of discipline, including slapping, but 'nothing worked' and all she could do was put up with it.

About twelve months later during one of Mr. and Mrs. J's periods of separation, Daisy went to live with her grandmother. Reports indicate that her behaviour improved; there were no temper tantrums and Daisy appeared happy. The only problem was her encopresis which offended her grandmother so that she threatened to 'put her out'. Mrs. J says she felt the girl often soiled herself deliberately because Daisy could control her bowel movements when she wanted to.

At the age of five Daisy attended the local infant school. Her early schooling appeared to be quite happy and she ceased soiling herself. But by the time she was nine years old her tantrums had started again at home. On one occasion during a temper trantrum Daisy smashed her face against the kitchen floor, fracturing her nose. On another occasion she rolled about in the road biting her feet in front of passing cars. She began presenting problems again at school and was accused of stealing there. Mrs. J asked the police and Social Services Department for help and Daisy was eventually received into care under Section 1 of the 1948 Act. After a short period at a family group home Daisy was admitted to a local assessment centre. This included a short spell at a hospital for 'observation'. After assessment it was decided that Daisy was in need of long term care and she was admitted to a children's home where she remained for about fifteen months. Following apparent stabilisation of behaviour and temper outbursts, Daisy was returned home. She resumed schooling, but once again her behaviour deteriorated. At about this time the relationship between her parents deteriorated rapidly and Daisy's behaviour both at home and especially at school became increasingly unreasonable, unpredictable and violent.

In March 1975 Mrs. J separated from her husband and went to live with her aunt. She took her daughters with her. A few weeks later Daisy was excluded from school following violent attacks on other pupils which resulted in the headmaster needing the assistance of the police in escorting her from the school premises. Following exclusion Daisy was referred to an educational psychologist who thought that she was functioning within a normal range of ability, although test results were below average. No evidence of deep psychological disturbance was apparent.

Daisy first appeared in court in June 1974 charged with breach of the peace. She was fined and bound over for twelve months. One week later she again appeared before the court charged with a similar offence and was bound over for two years and fined. In June of that year she was remanded in custody having been charged with a further breach of the peace and having an offensive weapon in a public place. She was remanded to a remand centre for seven days. In July 1975 Daisy appeared before the court on the same charge and was made the subject of a Care Order. She was then admitted to Aycliffe Regional Assessment Centre. Daisy was seen as a sad, lonely, anxious and reflective girl of volatile temperament but who showed little hostility towards the world. She seemed a gross attention seeker who displayed poor social judgment when dealing with her peers. Daisy continually reported a stream of minor ailments which required attention and psychiatric opinion indicated that she was likely to continue to present psychosomatic illnesses.

As Daisy's mother had created a 'new home environment' for her daughters which with Social Services support could provide a stable home base for Daisy from which she could attend a small remedial teaching group within a day school, she was returned home in August 1975 in accordance with the treatment recommendation.

In October of that year she began to attend a residential community home with education as a day pupil. Despite initial difficulties it is reported that she settled fairly well but the increased tension and violence at home, exacerbated by her father's visits, resulted in her being admitted to the school in November on a five day a week basis, returning home at weekends. In December of that year Daisy appeared before the court charged with breach of the peace and was bound over for two years.

In May 1976, Daisy was suspended from the school following an assault on a member of staff. After a cooling off period of one week, she was readmitted to the school where her disruptive, demanding and attention seeking behaviour continued to give cause for concern. Daisy's menstrual periods were very irregular during this time for which she received considerable medical attention.

In June of that year after working as a nursing assistant in a hospital for two weeks, Daisy found employment as a cook with Community Services. Although it is reported that she was warned about her behaviour on several occasions and following one incident at work received a two day suspension, Daisy appears to have settled well and was reported to be a good worker.

In October of that year Daisy returned home on a full time basis. It is reported, however, that she frequently returned to the school when she found life at home unbearable.

In December of last year Daisy swallowed a quantity of

Amoxil and was admitted to the local hospital. She was discharged and went home after two days' observation. It is reported that Daisy became increasingly depressed at home throughout this period and made incessant demands on both her social worker and on the staff of the school. On Christmas Eve 1976, having left home to spend Christmas at the school, Daisy was admitted to hospital after swallowing a mixture of Thawpit and Dettol. She was seen by a consultant psychiatrist, who described her as a chronically deprived and unhappy girl who was likely to be successful in killing herself at some time in the future. A long term placement in an accepting environment was recommended. There was also some concern expressed about the possibility of liver damage.

In December 1976, Daisy was admitted to a mental hospital under Section 25 of the Mental Health Act. She was seen by a psychiatrist who reported that she was progressing satisfactorily. Daisy was discharged from the hospital to return home after eighteen days. She was readmitted the following day as a voluntary patient as she claimed that nothing at home had changed. It is reported that she settled fairly well, although she was involved in an attack on another patient.

In January 1977 Daisy was transferred to an adolescent unit which was considered to be a more suitable placement for a girl of her age. Later on the day of admission she was admitted to a general hospital after having apparently swallowed around fifty paracetamol tablets. Due to the possibility of liver damage, she remained in the hospital for six days for observation. She then returned to the unit where it is reported she became increasingly disruptive and presented serious management problems to the nursing staff.

A case conference was held in February 1977 attended by a large body of psychiatric and social services experts. No treatment recommendations were made. The following day Daisy consumed a quantity of aspirins and was admitted to the Regional Assessment Centre at Aycliffe on an emergency basis at the request of the Social Services Department.

Observations at the Assessment Centre

General Behaviour

Daisy is a slightly built young woman of medium height. She has a pale, rather stark rectangular face with a slightly low forehead. Her hair is of an attractive blonde colour, while her eyebrows and eyelashes are very fair. Daisy's rather long, gaunt face frequently drains of all expression save a rather sullen vacancy, her large hazel eyes staring fixedly before her. However, Daisy has an attractive smile but this only appears on rare occasions and her facial expression is predominantly characterised by a scowl.

Daisy is very agile and can walk, run and perform cartwheels and handstands in very neat and graceful movements. However, most of the time she moves in a rather clumsy, weary manner, frequently appearing to resemble a sick old woman mustering all her strength to move about the room.

Much of Daisy's behaviour and her reaction to social situations seem to be dependent upon her moods which have become increasingly changeable and unpredictable since her initial few weeks in the house. She vacillates between sullen withdrawal and quite elated gaiety several times within the hour. Unfortunately, as her moods seem unrelated to the events taking place around her, it has been increasingly difficult to predict her response. While at times she will shrug off a disappointment with a scowl and a subsequent glimmer of a smile when teased, at other times she becomes violent and uncontrolled when her wishes or demands are denied. At times Daisy will involve herself in a situation which concerns another child apparently using this as an excuse to have what she later describes as a 'fiji'.

Daisy has been involved in many incidents involving abusive threats and assaults on both staff and children and has attempted to leave the school without permission on several occasions. On two occasions her behaviour appeared to be so beyond control as to warrant an injection of Largactil. However, it has been observed that some of this ill controlled behaviour is quite theatrical in nature and is designed to suit the audience present.

Much of her attention is devoted to obtaining materials for self-mutilation and schemes of self-destruction. The scarring on her right forearm and wrists and the stitches on her left arm attest to her success at procuring sharp implements in her present carefully supervised environment. Despite her claims that she cuts herself only when very depressed, these incidents are premeditated and planned to the extent that Daisy enlists, or more often extorts, the help of other children in procuring the necessary implements. She quickly discovered the value of self-mutilation as an attention seeking ploy and began to procure sharp objects in order to tease members of staff. This game quickly ceased when she did not receive the attention she desired. However, some of her self-mutilation was far from this superficial level and careful supervision was required to avoid serious damage.

Daisy, rather contrarily, appears preoccupied by the state of her health and makes frequent requests every day to be taken to sick bay in order to have the nursing sister attempt a further diagnosis based on her spurious symptons or more recently to check the dressing on her self-inflicted wounds.

Daisy claims to be afraid of the dark and although she says she prefers falling asleep with the light on, she falls asleep just as quickly in the dark. She enjoys sitting on the knees of staff, both male and female, and will sit as long as she is allowed.

Daisy is a very tense girl who seldom allows herself to relax. She frequently withdraws into a tight bundle in one corner of the room with her knees drawn up to her shoulders, her hand in her mouth biting her nails. After a few minutes in this position, from which she refuses to be drawn by conversation or sympathy, large tears well in her eyes and she looks thoroughly miserable. She has often been eventually winkled out of her corner by a warm physical and maternal approach by a housemother. More frequently it is from this perch that she eventually swoops down on the group and takes issue at some imagined slight or insult, becoming increasingly abusive and irate.

In the interview and in frequent talks arranged at her request she is rather withdrawn, often tearful and generally unforthcoming. When asked about her future she claims to be unable to answer questions. She has claimed that she does have a reason for wishing to kill herself, and has mentioned the death of her 'boyfriend' in a road accident in December of last year, but there is no evidence to substantiate this incident. She also claims to have 'a different reason' for her further violence directed towards herself, but would not reveal this.

Daisy seems a very tense, immature girl who is completely lost in the chaos of her past and present life. Much of her behaviour appears to be attention seeking but unfortunately she does not appear to have learned how to handle the attention she does receive, which results in her spurning staff approaches and embarking on a repertoire of even more extreme behaviour.

In the increasingly rare moments of calm reflection, Daisy expresses quite genuine remorse for her behaviour and laughs at herself saying, 'Anyone would think I'm nuts.'

Response to Peers

Daisy's behaviour appears to be generally self-centred as she rarely considers the needs of others or accommodates them in her actions. She is socially nomadic and wanders between groups and individuals. She has managed to make a few friends within the house group but these friendships have proved to be ephemeral.

Although frequently isolated and withdrawn within the group, she spends as little time as possible outside the physical proximity of others. Her ill controlled and unpredictable behaviour has led many of the present house group to distrust and even fear her.

Until recently she has shown little interest in any of the boys in the school. However, she now claims to have a boyfriend in the school in whom she has expressed a superficial but overt sexual interest. She claims, however, to be afraid of close physical contact with people of the opposite sex, which is a result of being 'raped' at the age of eleven, but she claims not to be able to remember anything about it. Daisy also is most reluctant to be seen naked by the housemother when supervising her showering and always attempts to cover herself with a few towels.

Daisy is an insightful enough observer of her house group to be able to carry out a number of machinations within the group at the expense of her chosen victim. However, this insight also enables her to be quite understanding and, in rare moments, even affectionate when another child is distressed.

Response to Adults

Daisy's response to staff seems to be determined largely by her moods. She rarely avoids staff and takes a delight in being the centre of their attention. She frequently makes requests to speak privately with a member of staff. However, when arrangements are made to make this possible she often does not say anything.

Daisy seems to live in an idealised world of childhood in her relations with staff, seeing the different members of staff in terms of almost total perfection or 'rottenness'. She prefers to have the individual attention of a member of staff and makes frequent requests to leave the group in order to help another member of staff in another part of the house.

She understands the instructions and intentions of staff very well, as has been shown by her behaviour when in a cooperative mood. But when she is in low spirits she becomes increasingly defiant and obstinate.

Response to Management

Daisy's behaviour has been at times so abusive and defiant that she has required quite forceful physical restraint in order to contain her violent, uncontrolled tantrums. Generally, however, most requests and directions are received with a scowl and an accompanying defiant profanity. A refusal to take this display of aggression seriously by laughing and parody usually encourages her to laugh at her surliness. In more tense and volatile situations many housemothers have soothed her by a quiet approach and a cuddle, and when she resumes a more rational frame of mind it has been found that she responds well to an appeal being made to her maturity and commonsense.

Daisy threatens at times to have a tantrum in order to get her own way despite staff demands, at which a blank refusal to take her seriously is usually enough to eventually reveal to her the ridiculous side of her behaviour. Daisy also responds well to the withdrawal of the privilege of smoking and, although all such sanctions are met with defiance and verbal abuse, this has proved to be an effective measure in regulating some of her behaviour.

In general Daisy is well accustomed to the routines and restrictions of the house and apart from getting up in the morning and her belief that all school work is beneath a sixteen year old, she has been nudged, hugged, pushed and at times almost dragged through the daily activities of the house group. It is, however, worthy of note that due to her disruptive and often violent behaviour, it has been necessary to restrict her to the security of the house on a number of separate occasions.

Educational and Practical Assessment

Daisy has refused to attempt any academic school work during her stay in the school. She has based her refusals on the fact that she is now sixteen years old and has no further obligation to attend educational classes. All attempts to persuade her otherwise have been useless and are met with either a stream of abuse or utter passivity. Only during craft sessions has she made any effort and even this has been minimal. Her cooperation is geared to seeking an opportunity of working one to one with the staff and when their exclusive attention has been won, she can be reasonably polite and will take full advantage of the situation to talk about herself. Daisy has very little interest in any other children she may be working with except as objects of abuse. Occasionally she will attempt to dominate the group or use them as an audience for her tirades. During her periods of lethargy, she is quite willing to comply with any request as long as it does not disturb her relaxation.

Daisy dislikes reading and has very little confidence in her ability in this area. Her hands tremble when reading aloud, and her voice is devoid of expression. Her facial distortions of scowling and frowning reflect the difficulty she experiences. Although punctuation is observed, she has a tendency to confuse word order in sentences but the sound order in individual words is usually correct. She has a limited vocabulary and finds difficulty with words such as 'pale', 'soon', etc. – silent and final 'e's proving to be something of a stumbling block for her. Unfamiliar words are attempted phonetically and only with tri-lettered, centrally vowelled words is she reasonably articulate.

Daisy's writing is neat. Her letters are well formed but not cursive, and while she can copy accurately out of a book or off the board, she has refused to attempt anything else. Even her letters home are always written by somebody else, with Daisy rarely even offering a suggestion as to their content.

She is quite familiar with the four basic arithmetical processes and has a good knowledge of her multiplication tables. She is familiar with the basic principles of fractions and can carry out subtractions and additions with fractions but is not capable of multiplication or division in this area. She is thoroughly competent with problems involving decimals and money. She has no difficulty with calculations involving time or area but is rather hazy in her grasp of percentage and ratio. She appears to have reached a reasonable functioning standard in her maths and is able to apply it in a practical way in some of her work with Community Services. It is difficult to keep her involved in problems or revision as she sees no reason to do any more mathematical work. She is very defensive about being tested and compared with her peers.

Although Daisy can sew neatly, she is reluctant to demonstrate her skill in his field, and is more interested in using a needle to either remove old tattoos or inflict fresh ones. Most planned activities she objects to and alternatives are never to her satisfaction either. In fact, directing her energies in a positive way educationally, practically, and artistically has been exceptionally difficult and only during house cleaning, physical exercise or sports, has she shown any real involvement.

Psychological Report

Educational Attainments:
 Wide Range Reading: Standard Score 71
   „   „   Spelling: „   „   66
   „   „   Arithmetic: „   „   72
 GAP Reading Comprehension: 8 years 4 months

Daisy is functioning at a below average ability level. She finds particular difficulty with verbal tasks. Her verbal skills in this area are not well developed, reflecting her unstimulating home background. Her poor attention span and seemingly high level of anxiety resulted in poor performance at certain tasks. On the other hand, she was reasonably competent at certain other practical tasks obtaining slightly above average scores suggesting that she is potentially of average ability, although unlikely to reach this potential.

Daisy is considerably retarded in basic attainments. On the present occasion she lacked persistence and showed little interest in the tasks presented, reflecting her generally depressed demeanour. At reading she succeeded with words of up to about six letters in length, and at spelling with words of up to about five letters. At number work she appeared unable to succeed with anything beyond simple examples of the four basic processes, although once again she gave up easily.

Daisy's extreme depression seemed to be deepening on each successive occasion on which she was seen. There can be no doubt that she is, at the time of writing, a great suicide risk insofar as she wishes to do away with her own life. Increasingly frequent incidents recorded by the staff suggest that her attempts to carry out this wish are more than manipulatory gestures. Additionally, she is a gross attention seeker. Daisy is extremely depressed and this is at present a central and all pervasive personality feature. In her own words, life is 'not worth living'. Considerable mood swings are, however, apparent and at times she can become elated. Similar observations were recorded by the consultant psychiatrist, a month previously when she saw Daisy at the Assessment Centre. She reported that Daisy 'wishes that she were dead', and that there was a risk of suicide.

Her temper continues to be a serious problem. Revised medication was prescribed for her but Daisy remains depressed. Other significant personality features include her poor social relationships and lack of social skills. She has never really learned how to form a meaningful interpersonal relationships with others, nor how to give or accept affection, and she is extremely shallow emotionally. Her sometimes violent temper almost certainly reflects a stormy upbringing in a family where violence was and is all too common and became a learned response of most members of the family. Daisy is aware of her own difficulties in relating to other people but has not responded to help in this direction, which despite the considerable efforts of those concerned, has probably failed because it came too late in her life, and because of the tremendous and recurrent domestic problems and crises. Daisy has a high level of anxiety and a low level of self-control. She follows her own urges impulsively. She has come to live increasingly in a world of her own, and her growing depression seems related to an increasing withdrawal from reality, often characterised by fantasies.

Daisy has an exceptionally negative self-image and seems to believe that her *only* positive qualities are that she is clean, tidy and unselfish. This lack of self-esteem may be associated with her tendency to be grossly self-critical and her exaggerated feelings of guilt and unworthiness particularly in relation to her relationships with others. Daisy wishes to change nearly every aspect of herself in directions which will gain social approval. Although this desire might provide motivation to respond to therapy it is rendered maladaptive because Daisy's ideal self is unrealistically virtuous, popular and removed from her present personality; for example, she would like to be a detective but refuses to read Agatha Christie as it might make her want to kill someone. She has no faith in her ability to control herself or her life and is lightly overdependent on social service agencies, although personality testing would suggest that this is not a basic trait but more likely the result of the restrictions imposed by institutional life.

There is a history of encopresis and enuresis, the latter still occurs occasionally. Psychiatric treatment has been necessary on four occasions for these problems and temper tantrums. The girl complains of vague aches and is convinced she will get cancer. She is very particular about personal hygiene and house cleaning, is particularly careful of her physical appearance before leaving the house, and checks and rechecks the safety of her environment before going to bed.

Daisy has ambivalent feelings about her family, which appear to vary from one day to the next. She has no regard for her father, whom she fears, although some emotional ties are present with her mother and some siblings, especially her youngest sister Gloria. The most meaningful family member, according to Daisy, is her grandmother. At times, however, she will verbally 'write off' all her family.

Daisy has few, if any, developed leisure time interests and shows little enthusiasm for any activity. At present she is pessimistic in the extreme. She does, however, appear to have had at least some success with a job as a cook and was mildly enthusiastic about this.

'Offending' as such is not Daisy's problem, but rather her failure to adjust socially and emotionally to the world in which she lives. The primary and immediate aim must be to ensure Daisy's physical survival, and this will require, at least initially, an environment providing physical security and intensive care. Her violent responses often make her a danger not only to herself, but also to other people. Counselling might be attempted on a regular individual basis, with the object of developing some sense of purpose without which her life will remain meaningless; new behaviour patterns and responses of a non violent nature must also be developed. She requires regular psychiatric oversight and treatment. She should learn to become independent of her family.

Psychiatric Report (I)

I saw this girl briefly on 11th November. Daisy has a very poor relationship with her mother and the latter has demanded the girl's removal from the home. Despite the girl's 'acting out' behaviour she does show a response to structure. On reading the social, psychiatric and psychological reports concerning her, I am impressed by the mother's consistent rejection and inclined to the view that Daisy was the victim of non-accidental injury. She should not, in my opinion, have been returned to her mother's care. Although she shows some ambivalence about her parents, she dissociates about her mother's behaviour and is still dependent upon a fantasy of home life.

I understand that the girl's early development was abnormal and she was noticeably apprehensive when commencing school. Neurotic traits included fear of the dark and she was both enuretic and encopretic. She was given to temper tantrums and attention seeking behaviour which culminated in allegations of cruelty. Even now she will state that she was 'knocked about' when younger. Anxiety on this topic is suppressed as she does not yet feel sufficiently independent to make progress away from home. She wept when talking about her mother.

She seems to be an alert, attractive girl, but shows a great deal of tension. There is intolerance of frustration and she is only of dull intelligence, requiring very clear instructions. She denies any 'blackouts' or any family history of epilepsy. She presents extensive depressive symptomatology and is a real suicide risk. Her sleep and appetite are disturbed, and she shows marked anxiety and severe mood swings. Her present state is marked by possibly severe personality disorder. In my opinions she requires psychiatric treatment and long term residential placement in an accepting environment. I suggest pericyazine 2·5 mg tds, Trimipertofran 25–50 mg nocte (gradual increase 1/52) but care should be taken if there is any suspicion of permanent liver damage.

Signed: N.K.T.
Visiting consultant psychiatrist

(II)

Seen as requested. Daisy is aware of and unhappy about her own problem of excessive temper outbursts. Relevant factors –

(a) Experiences 'blank' periods.
(b) Sometimes does not remember an outburst.
(c) Irregular and heavy menses, anything up to ten days usually; the loss lasted for a month some time ago.
(d) Suffers from premenstrual tension, restlessness and instability. This was at one time improved by taking 'the pill'.
(e) Background and family setting is relevant.
(d) No interest in boys – dressed up as a non female.

Suggest:

(1) Repeat EEG.
(2) Valium 2 mg tid. Ospolot 200 mg tid. Suspend present medication.
(3) Check urine for glycosuria.

(4) A more clinically oriented placement.
Will see again Monday.

M.N.O.
Visiting consultant psychiatrist

(III)

Review:

Daisy is no better, not surprisingly. She is still upset, depressed and unable to control her temper, saying she tried and failed, and this makes her more unhappy. She has attempted suicidal gestures again ('I got depressed') and has generally remained unsettled and uncooperative. Daisy has attempted to abscond a few times and has succeeded once or twice (was away earlier today).

Daisy claims that she will be happy if another family gave her a proper home. She admits, however, that her past record and doubts about her future conduct seriously preclude realisation of such wishes. Clinically, Daisy does not present typical depression.

Symptoms:

Her sleep and appetite pattern reflect secondary depression and her volition is subject only to impulsiveness, possibly due to suspected cerebral disturbances.

I do not feel a formal extra, psychiatric report will be required. I suggest that the investigations requested be completed. Meanwhile, Valium may be increased to 5 mgs tid. I reiterate that a more 'clinical' setting is required to offer help and treatment for this girl.

M.N.O.
Visiting consultant psychiatrist

Personal History

1961 Daisy was born, allegedly six weeks late.
1962 Began to throw temper tantrums, but after the initial outburst these subsided.

1963 Once again Daisy began her temper tantrums.

1964 Sister Gloria was born.

1964 Daisy was taken into hospital to have a birthmark removed from her buttock.

1965 Mr. & Mrs. J separated for a short while and Daisy went to live with her grandmother during that time. Prior to this, more 'severe' tantrums. Daisy would bite at her clothing and claw her naked body.

1967 Daisy began her schooling – initially she was enuretic and encopretic.

1967 Daisy was no longer enuretic. She was taken to her GP by her mother re her encopresis, but during the examination Daisy threw a tantrum and the doctor could not carry out his examination.

1968 Daisy continued to throw temper tantrums. On one occasion she banged her head deliberately on the kitchen floor and fractured her nose. Shortly after this her encopresis subsided and apart from the odd occasion, Daisy was now clean.

Jan. 1970 Accused of stealing from both home and school. Taken into care under Sec. 1, 1948 CYPA. Admitted to local assessment centre.

Feb. 1970 Admitted to local hospital for observation.

April 1970 Admitted to ——— children's home.

July 1971 Returned home having made good progress in the children's home.

Sept. 1971 Daisy transferred to comprehensive school.

Oct. 1971 Daisy referred to the Social Services Department due to temper tantrums following minor frustrations and dramatic behaviour designed to promote attention. The family were supervised by the Social Services Department.

1972 Daisy claims to have been raped aged eleven years but there are no reports to confirm this.

Sept. 1972 Daisy was seen by a psychiatrist.

Daisy missing from home overnight.

Oct. 1972 Mrs. J again took Daisy to the Social Services Department as she felt she could not control her daughter. Daisy received into care under Sec. 1 of 1948 CYPA. She was placed in a family group home.

Nov. 1972 Daisy admitted to an observation and assessment centre.

Dec. 1972 Seen by a consultant psychiatrist.

Jan. 1973 Seen by Area Senior Educational Psychologist. A case conference was held and efforts were made to gain admission to a hospital and to a special school. Both were unsuccessful.

July 1973 Daisy was admitted to a psychiatric hospital on a short-term placement. An EEG was carried out but results were inconclusive. Drugs were considered to be of little use.

July 1973 Daisy was discharged from hospital and returned to the assessment centre.

Sept. 1973 Spent ten days on holiday at home with her mother. Admitted to a community home. Reports indicate an initial difficult period while settling in followed by a prolonged period of calm when reasonable progress was made in all areas. Occasional outbursts were reported. Leaves were spent at home.

Jan. 1974 Had appendicectomy.

Mar. 1975 Daisy was returned home.

Mar. 1975 ——— Juvenile Court – Daisy and her sister Daphne appeared on charges of breach of the peace. Daisy had a temper tantrum and was using foul language in an infant school playground. Daphne went to her aid when police were trying to remove her from the playground. Both spent seven days in a remand centre and were bound over for one year.

April 1975 Daisy returned to school and was severely disruptive, openly abusive to staff and pupils and required the attention of three or four teachers and headmaster to restrain her. The class had to be cleared of other pupils and Daisy proceeded to throw chairs about. She stated that she intended to misbehave until she was put out of school. She refused to leave the school premises and the police had eventually to be called as she was waiting for another pupil to 'kick his bloody head in'. Two policemen, a police inspector and a sergeant, had some difficulty in removing her. Daisy was excluded from the school until further notice.

April 1975 She visited the school based youth club and was refused entry. She entered via a window, used foul language to a youth tutor and the police were called to escort her from the premises.

May 1975 Daisy entered the school in the afternoon. She was asked to leave but refused, using foul language. Police called to escort her from the premises.

May 1975 Daisy was referred to an educational psychologist who did not observe any signs of deep psychological disturbance. Test results were below average but within the normal range of ability.

June 1975 ———Juvenile Court – Daisy appeared before the court on a breach of the peace – bound over for 12 months and £20 fine.

June 1975 ——— Magistrates Court – appeared on a charge of breach of the peace and she was bound over for two years and fined £50.

June 1975 ———Juvenile Court – Daisy appeared before the court having been remanded in custody since 10 pm the evening before. She was charged with breach of the peace and with having an offensive weapon in a public place. Her friend had been carrying a large wooden mallet and Daisy a 'stout cane with a 6" nail'. She was sent to a remand centre for seven days.

June 1975 ——— Juvenile Court – Daisy reappeared before the court on the same charge, was remanded in the care of the local authority for a further seven days and after many unsuccessful attempts to place the girl, she was allowed home.

July 1975 ——— Juvenile Court – Daisy again reappeared on the same charge and was made subject of a Care Order.

July 1975 Daisy was admitted to Aycliffe for assessment.

Aug. 1975 The assessment meeting concerning Daisy took place. She was seen as a sad, lonely, anxious and reflective girl of a volatile temperament but showing little hostility towards the world. As it was held that Daisy's mother had created a 'new home environment' for her daughters which, with Social Services support, could provide a stable base for her, it was recommended that she return home.

Aug. 1975 Daisy left Aycliffe to return home.

Oct. 1975 Daisy began attenting a residential CHE as a day pupil. Despite unruly and often disruptive behaviour, she settled quite well and came to rely on the support of staff.

Nov. 1975 Due to the difficulties Daisy was experiencing at home, she was admitted to the school, being granted leaves each week-end. At around this time Daisy's sister Daphne, left home to live with her brother David.

Dec. 1975 ——— Magistrates Court – Daisy appeared before the court charged with breach of the peace, allegedly using loud and offensive language to an old woman outside a youth club from which she had just been excluded. She was bound over to keep the peace for two years.

April 1976 Following a prolonged persectuion of one particular member of the staff which culminated in Daisy's assaulting her, Daisy was sent home from her school.

April 1976 Daisy returned to the school after a 'cooling off' period.

June 1976 After working as an auxiliary nurse at a hospital for two weeks, Daisy found permanent employment as a cook. She apparently settled well at work and despite one suspension for her disruptive behaviour she was reported to be a good worker.

October Daisy returned home.

Nov. 1976 Daisy received a caution on being charged with riding a bicycle on the pavement and using obscene language.

Dec. 1976 Daisy was admitted to ———— hospital after swallowing a quantity of Amoxil tablets.

Dec. 1976 Daisy was discharged from ———— hospital and returned home.

Dec. 1976 Due to increasing conflict at home Daisy returned of her own volition to the school where she later swallowed some Thawpit and Dettol. She was admitted to ———— hospital where she was later seen by the psychiatrist, who reported that Daisy was a chronically deprived and unhappy girl who was likely to be successful in killing herself some time in the future. It is reported that around this time Daisy's sister Daphne also took a drug overdose and was admitted to a hospital in Staffordshire.

Dec. 1976 Daisy admitted to ———— hospital, under Section 25 of the Mental Health Act 1959.

Jan. 1977 As the psychiatrist was reportedly satisfied that Daisy was progressing well she was discharged from the hospital and returned home.

Jan. 1977 Daisy was voluntarily admitted to ———— hospital when she returned claiming nothing at home had changed.

Jan. 1977 Daisy was transferred to ———— adolescent unit. Later that day she swallowed approximately fifty paracetamol. She was admitted to the hospital where the possibility of damage to her liver was investigated.

Jan. 1977 Daisy was transferred back to the unit where she proved to be boisterous and disruptive. She presented serious management problems which generated concern among the nursing staff, visitors and fellow patients.

Feb. 1977 A case conference was held to discuss the problems which Daisy presented. This was attended by consultant psychiatrists and representatives of the Social Services Department.

Feb. 1977 Daisy consumed a quantity of aspirin and was admitted to the Regional Assessment Centre at Aycliffe on an emergency basis.

April 1977 Daisy was admitted to hospital after taking an overdose of Ospolot and Valium. She spent the night in hospital and returned to school at 5 pm the next day escorted by the senior housemaster and the nursing sister.

Summary of Problems

Physical

In view of the family history as well as her many early difficulties, the possibility of genetic predisposition to disordered behaviour cannot be ruled out. There is no evidence of neurological abnormality though her rapid and unexpected mood changes may have a physiological basis. Daisy suffers from many physical manifestations of psychological stress. Her periods are particularly irregular and troublesome.

Intellectual and Educational

Daisy operates at a below average intellectual level although her potential is somewhat higher. Her educational attainments are severely retarded. She has no job aspirations although she appears to have enjoyed her previous employment as a cook.

Family

The family situation is grossly disturbed. There is a long history of severe marital disharmony manifested in persistent violence by the father to the mother and Daisy and frequent separations. Daisy has been subjected to prolonged physical abuse and deprivation as well as ambivalent and increasingly rejecting relationships with other members of her family. The family are neither interested enough nor capable of containing her behaviour. She is particularly fearful of her father and one of her elder brothers and incapable of not precipitating head-on conflicts with her mother. For all practical purposes there is no longer a home base for Daisy.

APPENDIX

Social Relationships

Daisy's relationships with her peers are highly superficial and marked by manipulatory acts aimed at gaining dominance over them. She is disliked and feared and has become increasingly isolated from her own mates of the same age and their culture. With adults Daisy is variably dependent, suspicious and hostile, frequently testing the boundaries of acceptable behaviour and precipitating confrontations. She evokes pity rather than liking. She is not even capable of sustaining a superficial relationship which is of obvious emotional and material benefit to her.

Social Behaviour

Daisy has become a severely disruptive influence in any setting in which she is placed. Her acts include drinking, violence, absconding and offending. Her assaults have taken on an increasingly violent and uncontrolled tinge. She generally, and apparently deliberately, disregards standards of acceptable behaviour and tests out to the limit any social structure within which she is placed.

Personal

Daisy is a basically introverted, emotionally immature and unhappy girl who is profoundly confused about herself and the world around her, prone to seeing everything in a negative light and resorting to fantasies which support her view of the world. She is in a state of high, generalised and almost constant anxiety, though the severity of this anxiety frequently changes and may be associated with her unpredictable mood swings.

She presents the picture of a severe 'neurotic depressive' with associated suicidal behaviour. Her self-destructive acts are extreme, both in intensity and frequency. She knows the effect of her attempts on others and now uses them, in part, as attention seeking ploys. This feature is the most critical of Daisy's problems and has so far not only failed to respond to a variety of management techniques (including medication and counselling) but has, in fact, deteriorated. Daisy is a highly impulsive girl and does not seem to be particularly concerned with the consequences of her behaviour, either for herself or for other people. Her ideas of what she wants to do are fluid and short term.

295

Treatment Recommendations

1. In view of the multiplicity of Daisy's physical problems, a high level of medical provision would be necessary to cope with them. Neurological and metabolic examinations may be deemed worthwhile for the sake of greater sophistication in explaining her condition.

2. It is unlikely that much improvement can be made in Daisy's intellectual or scholastic state by further teaching. Effort should instead be concentrated on giving her worthwhile work skills after a variety of avenues of possible employment have been explored.

3. It is unlikely that casework, however intensive, will improve the state of the family. Every effort should be made, however, to protect Daisy from the depredations of her father and elder brothers. She needs an alternative home.

4. It is unlikely that Daisy's social relationships will ever become particularly satisfactory and no specific intervention in this area is indicated.

5. Daisy's social behaviour is likely to remain a source of major concern, particularly in view of her potential for inflicting hurt and damage on other people. Her offending is not yet serious enough to warrant custodial care but her effect on others should be closely regulated with a view to minimising the damage she can cause. A very firm but gentle approach, setting out and enforcing boundaries of acceptable behaviour, is likely to be the most successful. If Daisy commits further offences it would seem best that she should be charged with them in order that the legal process may take its due course.

6. Every effort should be made, through intensive supervision and use of a variety of management techniques, to prevent Daisy from committing suicide either deliberately or by default. However, in the nature of this behaviour Daisy will probably succeed in killing herself, unless appropriate psychiatric and psychological interventions succeed in calming her emotional state and training her to use alternative methods of coping with stress and gaining her desired ends.

Treatment Venue

Daisy is not currently on a charge. Penal treatment is, therefore, inappropriate as is educational placement, due to her age. No social services facilty exists which can either contain her behaviour, do better than those she has already experienced, or meet her treatment needs. Only a psychiatric hospital, geared to the care and treatment of self-destructive patients is likely to be effective in alleviating Daisy's problems in the long term.

Placement

—— Hospital.

References

Andry, R. *Delinquency and Parental Pathology*, London: Methuen, 1960.

Bandura, A. 'A social learning theory of identificatory processes' in Goslin, D. A. (ed.), *Handbook of Socialization Theory and Research*, Chicago: Rand McNally, 1969a.

Bandura, A. *Principles of Behavior Modification*, New York: Holt, Rinehart & Winston, 1969b.

Bandura, A. *Aggression: a social learning analysis*, Englewood Cliffs: Prentice-Hall, 1973.

Bandura, A. & Walters R. H. *Adolescent Aggression*, New York: Ronald Press, 1959.

Bandura, A. & Walters, R. H. *Social Learning & Personality Development*, New York: Holt, Rinehart & Winston, 1963.

Barker, R. C. *Ecological Psychology*, Stanford: Stanford University Press, 1968.

Belson, W. A. *Juvenile Theft – the Causal Factors*, London: Harper & Row, 1975.

Benneche, G. *Legal Safeguards in Child Welfare*, Oslo: Universitetsforlaget, 1967, quoted in Dahl, T. D. (1976), *The Scandinavian system of Juvenile Justice: a comparative approach*.

Bittner, E. 'Policing juveniles, the social context of common practice' in Rosenheim, M. (ed.), *Pursuing Justice for the Child*, Chicago: University of Chicago Press, 1976.

Bloch, D. A. 'The family of the psychiatric patient' in Arieti, S. (ed.), *American Handbook of Psychiatry*, New York: Basic Books, 1974.

Bowlby, J. *Maternal Care & Mental Health*, Geneva: World Health Organisation Monograph, 1951.

Box, S. 'Hyperactivity: the scandalous silence', *New Society*, Dec. 1, 458–60, 1977.

British Association of Social Workers. 'Children in care – a BASW charter of rights' in *Social Work Today*, vol. 8, No. 25, 1977.

Brown, F. 'Depression and Childhood bereavement' in Annell, A. L. (ed.), *Depressive States in Childhood and Adolescence*, Stockholm: Almquist & Wiksell, 1972.

Buehler, R. E., Patterson, E. R. & Furniss, J. M. 'The reinforcement of behaviour in institutional settings', *J. Behaviour Res. & Therapy*, vol. 4, 157–67, 1966.

California Youth Authority. 'A Review of Accumulated Research in the California Youth Authority', Sacramento: California Youth Authority, 1974.

Campbell, A. 'What makes a girl turn to crime?', *New Society*, Jan. 27, 172–3, 1977.

Caplan, G. *Principles of Preventive Psychiatry*, New York: Basic Books, 1964.

Cartwright, D. & Zander, A. *Group Dynamics: Research and Theory*, London: Tavistock Publications, 1960.

Cattell, R. B. *The Scientific Analysis of Personality*, Harmondsworth: Penguin Books, 1965.

Children & Young Persons Act 1933, London: HMSO.

Children & Young Persons Act 1969, London: HMSO.

Clarke, A. M. & Clarke, A. D. B. *Early Experience: Myth and Evidence*, London: Open Books, 1976.

Clarke, R. V. G. & Martin, D. N. *Absconding from Approved Schools*, London: HMSO, 1971.

Clarke, R. V. G. & Sinclair, I. 'Toward more effective evaluation' in *Collected Studies in Criminological Research*, vol. XII, Strasbourg: Council of Europe, 1974.

Cohen, S. 'Back to Justice' review of *Doing Justice: The Choice of Punishments* by Hill & Wang (New York), *New Society*, Feb. 16, 380–1, 1978.

Community Homes Regulations (1972), London: HMSO.

Cookson, H. M. 'A Survey of self-injury in a closed prison for women', *Brit. J. Criminol.*, vol. 17, 4, 332–47, 1977.

Cooper, J. D. 'The responsible society' in *Residential Care and Treatment*, Advisory Council on Child Care, 1970.

Cooper, J. D. et al. *The Family in Society*, London: HMSO, 1974.

Cottle, T. J. 'The return of the bat lady', *New Society*, May 5, 222–4, 1977.

Cowie, J., Cowie, V. & Slater, E. *Delinquency in Girls*, London: Heinemann, 1968.

Dahl, T. S. 'The Scandinavian system of Juvenile Justice: a comparative approach' in Rosenheim, M. (ed.), *Pursuing Justice for the Child*, Chicago: University of Chicago Press, 1976.

Debuyst, C. 'The standpoint of experimental psychology and clinical psychology' in *The Effectiveness of Punishment and Other Measures of Treatment*, Strasbourg: Council of Europe, 1967.

Department of Health & Social Security. *Community Homes Design Guide*, London: HMSO, 1971.

Department of Health & Social Security. *Youth Treatment Centres*, London: HMSO, 1971.

Dunlop, A. & McCabe, S. *Young Men in Detention Centres*, London: Routledge & Kegan Paul, 1964.

REFERENCES

Expenditure Committee of the House of Commons. *Report on the Children and Young Persons Act 1969*, London: HMSO, 1975.

Eysenck, H. J. *Crime and Personality*, London: Routledge & Kegan Paul, 1964.

Ferdinand, T. N. *Typologies of Delinquency – a critical analysis*, New York: Random House, 1966.

Floud, J. (Chairman) & others. *'The Dangerous Offender' a consultative document*, Cambridge: Institute of Criminology, 1977.

Ford, D. *Children, Courts & Caring*, London: Constable, 1975.

Gibson, R. *Violent Children*, DAES Dissertation, School of Education, University of Newcastle upon Tyne, 1967.

Glasser, P., Sarri, R. & Vinter, R. *Individual Change Through Groups*, New York: The Free Press, 1974.

Greer, S. 'Parental loss and attempted suicide', *Brit. J. Psychiat.*, vol. 112, 465–70, 1966.

Hare, R. D. *Psychopathy: Theory and Research*, New York: John Wiley, 1970.

Hargreaves, D. H. *Social Relations in a Secondary School*, London: Routledge & Kegan Paul, 1967.

Hartshorne, H. & May, M. A. *Studies in the Nature of Character*, vol. 1, *Studies in Deceit*, New York: Macmillan, 1928.

Hazel, N., Cox, R. & Ashley-Mudie, P. *Second Report of Special Family Project*, Maidstone: Kent Social Services Department, 1977.

Hobbs, N. *The Future of Children*, San Francisco: Jossey-Bass, 1975a.

Hobbs, N. (ed.). *Issues in the Classification of Children*, San Francisco: Jossey-Bass, 1975b.

Hoghughi, M. S. 'A Conceptual model for a comprehensive child care system', *Child Care*, vol. 25, 2, 41–57, 1969.

Hoghughi, M. S. 'Assessment: purpose & practice', *Child in Care*, vol. 11, 1, 10–16, 1971.

Hoghughi, M. S. *What's In a Name? some consequences of the 1969 Children & Young Persons Act*, Aycliffe: Aycliffe Studies of Problem Children, 1973.

Hoghughi, M. S. *The Aycliffe Report*, Aycliffe: mimeo, privately circulated, 1974.

Hoghughi, M. S. *Conceptual Model of a Treatment System for Problem Children*, Aycliffe: Aycliffe Studies of Problem Children, 1975.

Hoghughi, M. S. *Organising for Treatment*, Aycliffe: mimeo, privately circulated, 1977.

Hoghughi, M.S. *Monitoring Treatment in the Special Unit*, Aycliffe: mimeo, privately circulated, 1978.

Hoghughi, M. S. & Heptinstall, J. 'Recommittals: a continuing problem', *Community Schools Gazette*, vol. 65, No. 10–13, 1972.

301

Hoghughi, M. S. & Porteous, M. A. *Manual of Aycliffe Data Card – Mark II*, Aycliffe: Aycliffe Studies of Problem Children, 1976.

Hoghughi, M. S., Cumiskey, P. D., McCaffrey, A. & Muckley, A. *The Franklin Token Economy*, Aycliffe: Aycliffe Studies of Problem Children, 1977.

Home Office. *Report of the Work of the Prison Department 1974*, London: HMSO, 1975.

Howard League for Penal Reform. *'Unruly' Children in a Human Context*, Chichester: Barry Rose, 1977.

Hurst, L. A. 'Etiology of mental disorders: genetics' in Wolman, B. (ed.), *Manual of Child Psychopathology*, New York: McGraw-Hill, 1972.

Hutchings, B. 'Genetic factors in criminality' in de Wit, J. & Hartup, W. W. (eds), *Determinants and Origins of Aggressive Behaviour*, The Hague: Mouton, 1974.

Hutchings, B. & Mednick, S. A. 'Registered criminality in the adoptive and biological parents of registered male criminal adoptees' in Fieve, L. et al (eds), *Genetic Research in Psychiatry*, Baltimore: Johns Hopkin, 1975.

Knight, L. 'Is there justice for children?', *Community Care*, Feb. 1, 1978.

Kohlberg, L. 'Stage and sequence: the cognitive developmental approach to socialisation' in Goslin, D. A. (ed.), *Handbook of Socialisation Theory and Research*, Chicago: Rand McNally, 1969.

Lepine, A. 'Tattooing in approved schools and remand homes', *Health Trends*, 1, 11–13, 1969.

Lerman, P. *Community Treatment and Social Control*, Chicago: University of Chicago Press, 1975.

Logan, R. 'State of Montana Jail Survey, Helena, Governor's Crime Control Commission', 1972, quoted in Sarri, R. *Under Lock & Key: Juveniles in Jails and Detention*, Ann Arbor: National Assessment of Juvenile Corrections, 1974.

McClintock, F. H. & Avison, N. H. *Crime in England and Wales*, London: Heinemann, 1968.

Maccoby, E. & Jacklin, C. N. *The Psychology of Sex Differences*, Stanford: Stanford University Press, 1974.

Mayhew, P., Clarke, R. V. G., Sturman, A. & Hough, J. M. *Crime as Opportunity*, London: HMSO, 1976.

Measey, L. G. 'The psychiatric and social relevance of tattoos in Royal Navy detainees', *Brit. J. Criminol.*, vol. 12, 2, 182–6, 1972.

Mercer, J. R. 'Psychological assessment and the rights of children' in Hobbs, N. (ed.), *Issues in the Classification of Children*, San Francisco: Jossey-Bass, 1975.

MIND. *Assessment of Children and Their Families*, London: National Association for Mental Health, 1975.

REFERENCES

Mischel, W. *Personality and Assessment*, London: John Wiley, 1968.
Morris, T. *The Criminal Area – a study in social ecology*. London: Routledge & Kegan Paul, 1957.
Morris, N. & Hawkins, G. *The Honest Politician's Guide to Crime Control*, Chicago: Chicago University Press, 1969.
Morrison, A. & McIntyre, D. *Teachers and Teaching*, Harmondsworth: Penguin Books, 1969.
Morrison, A. & McIntyre, D. *Social Psychology of Teaching*, Harmondsworth: Penguin Books, 1972.
Newman, O. *Defensible Space: Crime Prevention Through Urban Design*, New York: Macmillan, 1972.
Newson, J. & E. *Four Year Old in an Urban Community*, Harmondsworth: Penguin Books, 1970.
Ohlin, L. E., Miller, A. D. & Coates, R. B. *Juvenile Correctional Reform in Massachusetts*, Washington: U.S. Government Printing Office, 1977.
Personal Social Services Council. *A Future for Intermediate Treatment*, London: PSSC, 1977.
Phillips, L., Draguns, J. & Bartlett, D. 'Classification of behaviour disorders' in Hobbs, N. (ed.), *Issues in the Classification of Children*, San Francisco: Jossey-Bass, 1975.
Piliavin, I. M. & Briar, S. 'Police encounters with Juveniles', *Am. J. Sociol.*, 70, 206–14, 1964.
Polsky, H. W. *Cottage Six: The social system of delinquent boys in residential treatment*, New York: Russell Sage Foundation.
Power, M., Benn, R. T. & Morris, J. N. 'Neighbourhood, school and juveniles before the courts', *Brit. J. Criminol.*, 12, 111–32, 1972.
Priestley, P., Fears, D. & Fuller, R. *Justice for Juveniles*, London: Routledge & Kegan Paul, 1977.
Pringle, M. K. *The Needs of Children*, London: Hutchison, 1975.
Prugh, D. G., Engel, M. & Morse, W. C. 'Emotional disturbance in children' in Hobbs, N. (ed.), *Issues in Classification of Children*, San Francisco: Jossey-Bass, 1975.
Quay, H. C. 'Personality patterns in preadolescent delinquent boys', *Educational and Psychological Measurement*, vol. 26, 99–110, 1966.
Quay, H. C. 'Classification in the treatment of delinquency and antisocial behaviour' in Hobbs, N. (ed.), *Issues in the Classification of Children*, San Francisco: Jossey-Bass, 1975.
Rains, P. M., Kitsuse, J. I., Duster, T. & Freidson, T. 'The labeling approach to deviance' in Hobbs, N. (ed.), *Issues in the Classification of Children*, San Francisco: Jossey-Bass, 1975.
Rea Price, J. 'Justice for the Young', *New Society*, 5 Jan., 1978.
Redl, F. 'The concept of therapeutic milieu' in *When We Deal with Children*, New York: The Free Press, 1969.

Redl, F. & Wineman, D. *The Aggressive Child*, New York: The Free Press, 1957.

Reinach, E., Lovelock, R. & Roberts, G. *First Year at Fairfield Lodge*, Portsmouth: Hampshire Social Services Department, 1976.

Robinson, W. P. *Language and Social Behaviour*, Harmondsworth: Penguin Books, 1972.

Rose, S. *Treating Children in Groups*, San Francisco: Jossey-Bass, 1972.

Rosenheim, M. (ed.). *Pursuing Justice for the Child*, Chicago: University of Chicago Press, 1976.

Rutter, M. 'Parent-child separation: Psychological effects on children', *Journal of Child Psychology and Psychiatry*, vol. 12, 233–60, 1971, reprinted in Clarke & Clarke (1976).

Rutter, M. *Maternal Deprivation Reassessed*, Harmondsworth: Penguin Books, 1972.

Rutter, M. *Helping Troubled Children*, Harmondsworth: Penguin Books, 1975.

Rutter, M., Birch, H. G., Thomas, A. & Chess, S. 'Temperamental characteristics in infancy and the later development of behavioural disorders', *British Journal of Psychiatry*, vol. 110, pp. 651–61, 1964.

Rutter, M., Tizard, J. & Whitmore, K. *Education, Health & Behaviour*, London: Longman, 1970.

Ryall, R. *Boys in Approved School: A study of impact of residential treatment on delinquent adolescents*, unpublished Ph.D. thesis, University of Cambridge, 1971.

Ryall, R. 'Delinquency: the problem for treatment', *Social Work Today*, vol. 5, 4, 98–103, 1974.

Ryall, R. 'Social Services Departments and the treatment of delinquent children', 1977, in Hoghughi, M. S. (ed.), *Aycliffe at 35: Retrospect and Prospect*, Aycliffe: Aycliffe monographs (in Press).

Sarri, R. *Under Lock and Key: Juveniles in Jails and Detention*, Ann Arbor: National Assessment of Juvenile Corrections, 1974.

Secord, P. F. & Backman, C. W. *Social Psychology*, New York: McGraw-Hill, 1964.

Shah, S. A. & Roth, L. H. 'Biological and psychophysiological factors in criminality' in Glaser, D. (ed.), *Handbook of Criminology*, Chicago: Rand McNally, 1974.

Shepherd, M., Oppenheim, B. & Mitchell, S. *Childhood Behaviour & Mental Health*, London: University of London Press, 1971.

Solberg, D. *Especially Difficult Boys*, Aycliffe: Aycliffe Studies of Problem Children, 1975.

Stott, D. H. 'Children in the womb: the effects of stress', *New Society*, May 19, 1977.

Street, D., Vinter, R. D. & Perrow, C. *Organisation for Treatment*, New York: The Free Press, 1966.

Stumphauzer, J. S. (ed.). *Behaviour Therapy with Delinquents*, Springfield: Charles C. Thomas, 1973.

Taylor, I., Walton, P. & Young, J. *The New Criminology: for a social theory of deviance*, London: Routledge & Kegan Paul, 1973.

Trilling, L. *The Liberal Imagination*, New York: Scribners, 1950.

Turnbull, W. & Hoghughi, M. S. *The Aycliffe Special Unit – A feasibility study*, Middlesbrough: Johnson Turnbull Partnership, 1974.

Turner, B. (ed.). *Truancy*, London: Ward Lock, 1974.

Tutt, N. *Care or Custody*, London: Darton, Longman & Todd, 1974.

Tutt, N. 'The philosophy of observation and assessment' in *Use and Development of Observation and Assessment Centres for Children*, DHSS, 1977.

Tyreman, M. J. *Truancy*, London: University of London Press, 1968.

Viney, L. L. 'The concept of crisis: a tool for clinical psychologists', *Bull. Br. Psychol. Soc.*, 29, 387–95, 1976.

Vorrath, H. H. & Brendtro, L. K. *Positive Peer Culture*, Chicago: Aldine Press, 1976.

Walker, N. D. *Crime and Punishment in Britain*, Edinburgh: Edinburgh University Press, 1965.

Weaver, S. M., Broome, A. K. & Kat, B. J. B. *Some Patterns of Behaviour in a Closed Ward Environment*, St. George's Hospital, Morpeth, Northumberland, Mimeo, 1977.

West, D. J. *The Young Offender*, Harmondsworth: Penguin Books, 1967.

West, D. J. *Present Conduct & Future Delinquency*, London: Heinemann, 1969.

West, D. J. & Farrington, D. P. *Who Becomes Delinquent?*, London: Heinemann, 1973.

West, D. J. & Farrington, D. P. *The Delinquent Way of Life*, London: Heinemann, 1977.

Wilkins, L. T. 'Survey of the field from the standpoint of facts and figures' in *The Effectiveness of Punishment and Other Measures of Treatment*, Strasbourg: Council of Europe, 1967.

Wootton, B. *Social Science and Social Pathology*, London: Allen & Unwin, 1959.

Zeeman, E. C., Hall, C. S., Harrison, P. J., Marriage, G. H. & Shapland, P. H. 'A model for prison disturbances', *Brit. J. Criminol.*, vol. 17, 3, 251–63, 1977.

L

Index

absconding 25-6, 35-6, 45-6, 77, 113-14, 123, 130, 136, 163, 233-4, 238-9, 249, 261

admission, provenance of 34-5, 37-8

adolescents, approaches to 21, 38; problems of 110; psychiatry and 61, 102, 213-14; research of 175

Advancement of Psychiatry, Group for 225

agression, incidence of 26, 40, 52, 58, 73, 97-8, 113-15, 174, 226, 238

Andry, R. 38

arson, incidence of 49, 242

assessment (*see also* under disordered children) abuses of 205-8; corporate 213; dynamics of 203; expectations from 203-4; function of 202; philosophy of 206-7; psychiatric 209-13; uses of 204-5

assessment centres 23, 126, 181, 207-208, 229, 256; classification by 201-2

assessment facilities 204, 206

assessment meetings 120, 127, 131, 198, 256

assessment reports 28, 30-1, 68-9, 94, 106, 117, 181, 205

assessment settings 85, 202

autonomy, educational facilities and 192; group living and 144, 149, 197

Avison, N. H. 49

Aycliffe School (*see also* Royston House) 9, 10, 19, 21, 23ff, 201-2; perimeter security of 27; Training School 23

backgrounds, family 39, 40, 110-12 174-80; parental 38-41, 43-5, 110-112; scholastic 109

Backman, C. W. 153

Bandura, A. 85, 92, 167

Barker, R. C. 134

behaviour, constancy in 206-7; environment and 134, 177-8, 217; reports on 102, 105

behavioural boundaries 177-80, 233; enforcement of 179, 181-2; school and 171-2

behavioural observations 68-9, 72-4, 76-8, 89, 92-105, 106ff, 200, 206-7, 220

Belson, W. A. 50

Benneche, G. 256

Bittner, E. 253

Bloch, D. A. 43

Borstals 127, 130, 228, 231, 240

Bowlby, J. 38

Box, S. 234

boys, aggression by 114; characteristics of 107-8, 113-15, 122; eccentricities of 101-2, 114; employment for 119; integration in group 101, 113; popularity of 101-2; relationships with staff 101; study data of 29-30, 34-7, 39-40, 45ff, 100-5, 107ff, 159ff, 241; treatment of 25, 36, 52, 105, 119, 130

Brendtro, L. K. 135

Briar, S. 75

British Association of Social Workers 253

secure residential (*see also* security) 15, 18–20, 21ff, 52, 67ff, 83–4, 88–9, 96–8, 100, 124, 131, 140, 147, 181, 196–7, 204–5, 228–32, 235–8, 242–250, 257, 260; specialised 134, 136, 145–6, 148–9, 181, 193, 207, 259; stress in secure 71–2, 80; visiting secure 245, 248

Farrington, D. P. 63, 177

Ferdinand, T. N. 242

Floud, J. 232

Ford, D. 240

fostering 135

frustration, effects of 73–4, 96, 98, 174, 245

functional areas 218–21, 224

functioning, levels of 54–5, 57

Gibson, R. 40

girls, characteristics of 95–100, 104, 108, 114–15, 122, 154–5, 159, 174; confrontations by 79–80, 93, 97, 158–9; mood swings of 72, 96–99, 114–15, 162, 174; popularity of 96, 98–9; reaction to boundaries 88, 96–8, 100, 131; relations with staff 86–7, 91, 93, 96–8, 100, 104; retardation of 109–10; self destructive acts of 35–6, 60, 115, 162–4, 194; social training for 122; study data on 29, 30, 34–7, 39–40, 44ff, 95–100, 107ff, 159ff, 241; treatment of 25–6, 29–30, 36, 93, 120–2, 124–5, 130, 154–5; violence by 97, 114–15, 160, 162, 174

Glasser, P. 135

Greer, S. 40

group living (*see also* staff) 67–8, 105; admission procedure 70–1; boy/girl differences 70, 72–4, 77–82, 84–86, 93, 103–4, 122, 159–60, 162–3; changes in 67–8, 146; conflict in 78–80, 93, 99, 108, 152, 160; extreme children and 71–2, 74–5, 78, 88, 90, 93, 95–7, 135–70, 196–7; frustration tolerance in 73, 96, 98, 100; group dependence 76–7; group relations 78, 96–7, 122;

leadership in 76–7; settling in 71; state on admission 70–1, 98, 101–2; stress in 71–2, 78, 115, 138–9, 146–7, 149, 154

Hare, R. D. 78

Hargreaves, D. H. 110

Hartshorne, H. 207

Hawkins, G. 232

Hazel, N. 135

Heptinstall, J. 50, 239

Hobbs, N. 201, 215

Hoghughi, M. S. 24, 31, 32, 50, 68, 91, 134, 177, 202, 217, 239, 243

Home Office 240

hospitals 127–8, 130; special 229

Howard League for Penal Reform 46, 228, 231, 244

Hurst, L. A. 174

Hutchings, B. 174

ideologies, professional 190, 192, 195, 205

illegitimacy 47

information (*see also* data) interpretation of 31, 55, 202; lack of 16–18, 54, 68, 208, 230; sources of 30–1, 54

innovations, social 17, 18, 106

intelligence quotients 54, 150

International Classification of Diseases 225

intervention 15, 19, 20 49–51, 109–10, 164–6, 168, 175–99, 207, 251–5; bases of 253–4, 259; crisis 33, 164–170, 189, 192–4, 199, 220; failures of 195–9, 254; inadequate 17,18, 179, 191, 255, 262; justification for 182–3, 189–92, 253–4; medical 64; psychiatric 35, 58–61, 124, 181, 193–4, 209, 212–15; resources in 191–2; society's reaction to 190–1

Jacklin, C. N. 175

Kingswood School 23

Knight, L. 253

Kohlberg, L. 207